THE DEAD SEA SCROLLS IN ENGLISH

Geza Vermes was born in Hungary in 1924. He attended the University of Budapest and subsequently studied at Louvain, where he obtained a degree in oriental history and philology and a doctorate in theology. For some years afterwards he was employed as a research worker in Paris by the Centre National de la Recherche Scientifique. He came to England in 1957, was appointed to a University lectureship in biblical history and literature in Newcastle upon Tyne, and in 1965 was elected to the Readership in Jewish Studies at the University of Oxford. He is a Professorial Fellow of Wolfson College. In 1975 he became first president of the newly founded British Association for Jewish Studies.

Dr Vermes is one of the pioneers of Qumran research. His first book, *Les manuscrits du désert de Juda*, appeared in 1953, and was later issued in English under the title *Discovery in the Judean Desert*, in New York. He is also the author of *Scripture and Tradition in Judaism*, first published in 1961 in Leiden and reprinted in 1973. His study, *Jesus the Jew – A Historian's Reading of the Gospels*, also appeared in 1973. He has now completed, in association with the Oxford Roman Historian, Fergus Millar, the thorough revision and modernization of the first volume of Emil Schürer's classic work, *The History of the Jewish People in the Age of Jesus Christ: 175 B.C.–A.D. 135* (1973). He has contributed to various scholarly periodicals on the Scrolls and other Jewish subjects, and since 1971 has been the Editor of the *Journal of Jewish Studies*. He is married, and pursues his writing in close collaboration with his wife, who acts also as Literary Editor for the Schürer project.

THE
DEAD SEA SCROLLS
IN ENGLISH

G. VERMES

SECOND EDITION

PENGUIN BOOKS

Penguin Books Ltd, Harmondsworth, Middlesex, England
Penguin Books Inc., 7110 Ambassador Road, Baltimore, Maryland 21207, U.S.A.
Penguin Books Australia Ltd, Ringwood, Victoria, Australia
Penguin Books Canada Ltd, 41 Steelcase Road West, Markham, Ontario, Canada
Penguin Books (N.Z.) Ltd, 182–190 Wairau Road, Auckland 10, New Zealand

—

First published 1962
Reprinted (with revisions) 1965
Reprinted 1966
Reprinted (with revisions) 1968
Reprinted 1970, 1972, 1973, 1974
Second edition 1975
Reprinted 1976

—

Copyright © G. Vermes, 1962, 1965, 1968, 1975

—

Made and printed in Great Britain
by C. Nicholls & Company Ltd
Set in Monotype Baskerville

For Pam

THE FRUITS OF OUR
COMMON LABOUR

CONTENTS

7

Abbreviations

CHab: Commentary on Habakkuk
CHos: Commentary on Hosea
CHah: Commentary on Nahum
CPs 37: Commentary on Psalm 37
CR: Community Rule
DJD: Discoveries in the Judaean Desert
DR: Damascus Rule
DR A: Damascus Rule, first manuscript
DR B: Damascus Rule, second manuscript
H: Hymns
MA: Messianic Anthology
MR: Messianic Rule
WR: War Rule

PREFACE TO THE SECOND EDITION

WHEN *The Dead Sea Scrolls in English* first appeared in 1962, it offered the reader a complete collection of the then available religious writings attributable to the Qumran community. During the thirteen years which have elapsed since then, however, a considerable amount of additional material has been published in the series *Discoveries in the Judaean Desert*, volumes III (1962), IV (1965) and V (1968), and in preliminary editions of other manuscripts. A substantial part of these texts are too mutilated to permit a meaningful English rendering, and for this reason have not been introduced into the present volume. Others, such as the Aramaic paraphrase of Job (J.P.M. van der Ploeg, A.S. van der Woude, *Le Targum de Job de la grotte 11 de Qumrân*, Leiden, 1971; see also M. Sokoloff, *The Targum to Job from Qumran Cave XI*, Ramat Gan, 1974), several non-canonical Psalms appearing in the Psalms scroll from Cave XI (J. A. Sanders, *Discoveries in the Judaean Desert*, vol. IV, Oxford, 1965), and sundry passages from the Enoch literature (see J. T. Milik's forthcoming work, *The Books of Enoch: Aramaic Fragments from Qumran Cave 4*), are unlikely to have been composed by the Qumran sectaries, and consequently remain outside the scope of this translation.

Those supplementary documents which have been chosen for inclusion mainly represent familiar themes, such as sectarian regulations, poems and Bible exegesis, but some of them, e.g. the brief extracts from the *Temple Scroll* and the Melkizedek fragments, afford important new insights into the Qumran ideology, and beyond it, into inter-Testamental Judaism in general. There are, in addition, a few entirely new departures, prominent among them the horoscopes.

As in the original collection, each individual composition will be preceded by a special introductory note, and bibliographical information regarding the published sources (*editio princeps* or preliminary edition) of the documents. A revised list of books recommended for further reading is printed on pp. 274-5.

The Oriental Institute,
University of Oxford   G.V.

INTRODUCTION

O N the western shore of the Dead Sea, about eight miles south of Jericho, is Khirbet Qumran. It lies in one of the lowest parts of the earth, on the fringe of the hot and arid wastes of the Wilderness of Judaea, and is today silent, empty, and in ruins. But from that place, members of an ancient Jewish sect whose centre it was, hurried out one day and in haste and secrecy climbed the nearby cliffs in order to hide away in caves their precious writings. And there they remained for some two thousand years.

This, briefly, is the story of their discovery.

The first lot of documents, consisting of several biblical and non-biblical scrolls, was found accidentally by an Arab shepherd in the spring of 1947. In 1949, the place was identified and explored by archaeologists, and the authenticity and antiquity of the find were established. Then, between February 1952 and January 1956, ten more caves were located. For two of them (III and V), the archaeologists were responsible; workmen on the site discovered four others (VII, VIII, IX and X); and the indefatigable Ta'amireh tribesmen, who most of the time succeeded in outwitting their professional rivals, were able to uncover four more (II, IV, VI and XI), two of them (IV and XI) containing extremely rich manuscript deposits.

Also, between 1951 and 1956, the archaeologists, after an initial blunder when they failed to recognize the connexion between the scrolls and the nearby ruins, were occupied with the excavation of the Qumran community settlement itself and, in 1958, with its dependence at Ain Feshkha, two miles or so farther south. The significance of their findings is discussed in Chapter 3.

Altogether, the ten complete Dead Sea Scrolls and the thousands of fragments belonging originally to almost six hundred manuscripts, amount to a substantial body of literature covering the Hebrew Bible, other religious compositions, and works proper to a particular Jewish sect.

The books and articles written on the subject would fill a large library, but in the main they have been highly technical and therefore accessible only to the specialist. The present work gives the actual text of the non-biblical religious writings, so to a large extent the reader will now be able to judge them for himself. It may nevertheless be useful if I first do what I can to dispel confusion by defining the nature of their contribution to scholarship and to a fuller appreciation of Judaism and Christianity.

The Qumran biblical documents cover the whole Hebrew Bible, with the exception of the book of Esther, and are about a thousand years older than the ancient codices previously extant. With this newly discovered material at their disposal, experts concerned with the study of the text and transmission of the Scriptures are now able to achieve far greater accuracy in their deductions and can trace the process by which the text of the Bible attained its final shape. Moreover, they are in a position to prove that it has remained virtually unchanged for the last two thousand years.

The Qumran fragments of the Pseudepigrapha (non-biblical religious compositions) and Apocrypha (considered non-biblical by Jews and some Christian bodies, but accepted as secondarily or fully canonical by other Churches) have also been of vast benefit to learning. Preserved by the early Church, these books had been handed down in translation – in Greek, Latin, Syriac, Ethiopian, etc. – but had inevitably suffered some degree of interference at the hands of interpreters and copyists. Now that several of them are available in their original language, it is for the first time possible to assess the fidelity of the translated texts.

It goes without saying, however, that beside the profit to

specialists in textual criticism, palaeography, linguistics, and so on, the major gain has fallen to the student of the history and religion of Palestinian Judaism in the inter-Testamental period (150 B.C. to A.D. 70). For him, the sectarian writings, which form the bulk of the Dead Sea literature and were formerly quite unknown, have opened new avenues of exploration into the shadowy era of the preparation and institution of Christianity and of the establishment of Judaism. Previously, very little of it was known. First- and second-century Rabbinic teachers had not permitted religious writings of that epoch to go down to Jewish posterity unless they fully conformed to orthodoxy, and although, as I have said, some of them were preserved by the Church, the fact that they had been used as a vehicle for Christian apologetics caused their textual reliability to be suspect. But the Scrolls are unaffected by either Christian or Rabbinic censorship, and once their evidence is complete – a great deal remains to be published – the historian will be thoroughly acquainted, not with just another aspect of Jewish beliefs or customs, but with the whole organization, teaching, and aspirations of an inter-Testamental religious community.

In the following pages I have nowhere applied the title 'Essene' to this community and have made little reference to the independent accounts of Essenism appearing in ancient literature; it has been my intention to allow the Scrolls to speak for themselves. But as A. Dupont-Sommer was the first to insist, and as most scholars including myself have come to agree, the Essenes and the sect responsible for the Scrolls were in all probability identical. The first-century Jewish philosopher Philo of Alexandria, the historian Flavius Josephus, and the geographer and naturalist Pliny the Elder have all discoursed on this sect of ascetics whose common life and severe discipline they seem greatly to have admired, and any profound study of the Community as a religious group demands careful scrutiny, not only of its own compositions, but also of these classical reports.

The foregoing remarks will, I hope, give some idea of the reason why the Scrolls have awakened such intense interest in the academic world. But why have they appealed so strongly to the imagination of the non-specialist? After all, other manuscripts of biblical significance have been discovered in recent years, such as the Coptic documents from Chenoboskion, including the *Gospel according to Thomas*; yet these have raised comparatively little stir.

The outstanding characteristic of our age appears to be a desire to reach back to the greatest attainable purity, to the basic truth. Affecting the whole of our outlook, it has necessarily included the domain of religious thought and behaviour, and with it the whole subject of Judeo-Christian culture and spirituality. A search is being made for the original meaning of issues with which we have become almost too familiar and which with the passing of the centuries have tended to become choked with inessentials, and it has led not only to a renewed preoccupation with the primitive but fully developed expression of these issues in the Scriptures, but also to a desire for knowledge and understanding of their prehistory.

The Rules, Hymns, biblical Commentaries, and other liturgical works of the Qumran Community respond to this need in that they add substance and depth to the historical period in which Christianity and Rabbinic Judaism originated. They reveal one facet of the spiritual ferment at work among the various parties of Palestinian Judaism at that time, a ferment which culminated in a thorough examination and reinterpretation of the fundamentals of the Jewish faith. By dwelling in such detail on the intimate organization of their society, on their interpretation of Scripture and history, on the role attributed to their Teacher, and on their ultimate hopes and expectations, the sect of the Scrolls has exposed its own resulting doctrinal synthesis. This in its turn has thrown into relief and added a new dimension to its dissenting contemporaries. Thus, compared with the ultra-conservatism and rigidity of the

Essene Rule, orthodox Judaism appears progressive and flexible, and beside Essenism and Rabbinic orthodoxy the Christian revolution stands out invested with inspired actuality. Yet at the same time, the common ground from which they all sprang, and their affinities and borrowings, emerge more clearly than ever before. The faith of each of these three religious movements was, in fact, a separate and distinct commentary on the one body of traditional Jewish teaching and – this is a point which is slowly being realized – neither of them can properly be understood independently of the others.

Essenism is dead. The brittle structure of its stiff and exclusive organization was unable to withstand the national catastrophe which struck Palestinian Judaism in A.D. 70. Animated by the loftiest ideals and devoted to the observance of 'perfect holiness', it yet lacked the pliant strength which enabled orthodox Judaism to survive. And although its Teacher of Righteousness clearly sensed the deeper obligations implicit in the Mosaic Law, he was without the genius of Jesus who laid bare the inner core of spiritual truth and exposed the essence of religion as an existential relationship between man and man, and between man and God.

· I ·

THE COMMUNITY

THE sect of the Scrolls, the followers of the still unidentified Teacher of Righteousness, flourished in Palestine about two thousand years ago. Its communities were distributed throughout the towns and villages of the land as well as in desert places such as Qumran, but their precise location is as yet unknown.

These religious schismatics withdrew from the Judaism of their time, which they considered wicked and corrupt, and vowed themselves to absolute obedience to the particular interpretation of the Law of Moses taught within the sect and to the search for perfection. In their own eyes they constituted the one true Israel, the Church of God's elect. The revelation of all truth had been granted to their Teacher, finally and definitively, and they themselves were the minority chosen by God to inherit the Covenant, the Promise, and ultimate Salvation. They were not only the faithful 'remnant', but also the last in the great line of God's chosen ones, for they believed that they would, during their lifetime, participate in the great battles of Light against Darkness, and that they would see and share with the triumphant Messiah the fruits of his victory.

The common life of those who retired to the desert settlements, 'the assemblies of the camps' as they are called in the Damascus Rule, appears to have been highly organized and self-sufficient. Archaeologists working at Qumran have discovered the remains of a scriptorium where manuscripts were copied, a pottery with its kiln, a kitchen and pantry, various water installations, and at a short distance from the site, a farm, as well as community halls proper, such as a large meeting hall which served also as a refectory, and a council chamber. But the sectaries did not actually live in these buildings; some of them occupied neighbouring caves and others doubtless lived in huts or tents in the vicinity.

The 'assemblies of the towns' (DR), i.e. those members who lived an urban life, were subject to other rules and were separated somewhat less rigorously from their fellow Jews, but their hopes and ideals were identical with those of their desert brethren. With them, they were convinced that their beliefs and way of life conformed fully to the will of God and qualified them to claim the honour of being the only true Israel.

This concept was reflected in the way the sect modelled its organization on that of the historical Israel. Its members were distinguished as belonging either to the House of Aaron or to the House of Israel. They were divided, that is to say, into clergy and laity; the Priests and Levites had specific rights and duties which I will discuss presently, and the rest were elders and simple Israelites. The Damascus Rule (XIV)* mentions a third group of strangers or proselytes, but this reference is purely incidental. We are told nothing about them, but in biblical and post-biblical Judaism a 'stranger', *ger*, was a person of non-Jewish descent who adopted some of the Jewish religious laws and customs.

The sect was further divided symbolically into twelve tribes and into the smaller Israelite units of Thousands, Hundreds, Fifties, and Tens. As in the New Testament,

* Except for the Hymns, texts from the Dead Sea literature are indicated in the following pages by the title of the Scroll in which each passage appears, together with its column number: e.g. Community Rule VI, Commentary on Habakkuk VII, etc. The Hymns are counted differently. Hymn 10, for instance, is the tenth of a collection of twenty-five poems.

Readers may be puzzled to find that many of the scriptural quotations given in this volume do not agree with the texts with which they are familiar. The discrepancy is partly due to variants in the Scrolls themselves, but mainly to my attempt to render the Bible in accordance with the sense ascribed to it by the Qumran writers. Had I not done this, it might often have been impossible to perceive any coherence between a text and its interpretation.

where the twelve apostles are the new tribal chiefs and the Letter of James is addressed to the 'twelve tribes of the dispersion', so among the Community the tribal system corresponded to an ideal. Thus the supreme Council in the pre-Messianic age appears to have been formed by twelve laymen and three Priests, the latter no doubt representative of the three clans of the tribe of Levi. Again, some of the documents apply the title 'House of Judah' to the sect (symbolizing the tribes of Judah and Benjamin and, of course, the faithful Levites), whereas Jews remaining outside are called the 'House of Joseph' (symbolizing the tribes of Ephraim and Manasseh and the north in general which abandoned Jerusalem and the Temple after the death of Solomon). As regards the lesser units (Thousands, Hundreds, etc.), they all play a part in the tactics of the great battles described in the War Rule, but otherwise only the Tens seem to have been of effective importance, this being the quorum of an autonomous congregation. Here, the sect followed the general Jewish custom with regard to public worship.

AUTHORITY AND ADMINISTRATION

Final authority lay in the hands of the Priests. The phrase 'according to the decision of the multitude of the men of their Covenant' occurs wherever there is reference in the Scrolls to the acceptance of new members or to the expulsion and punishment of offenders; but it is always coupled with, and preceded by, the obviously more important decision of the 'sons of Zadok'. In the fields of doctrine, justice, and common ownership, it was they who held the reins; newcomers were to 'unite, with respect to the Law and possessions, under the authority of the sons of Zadok' (CR v) and, with even more emphasis, 'The sons of Aaron alone' were to 'command in matters of justice and property, and every rule concerning the men of the Community' was to be 'determined according to their word' (CR IX). There is no indication that the Levites were to be distinguished from the Priests, so it is reasonable to suppose that both clerical classes are envisaged in these general statements. But to see how such principles were put into practice it may be useful to examine first of all the part played by authority in the smaller groups, and then turn to the direction of the sect as a whole.

As has been said, the Community Rule (VI) and the Damascus Rule (XIII) give the quorum of a group – a 'camp' according to the latter document – as ten men. In each of these autonomous communities both Rules appear to require the presence of two superiors, one of them a Priest. He was to be 'learned in the Book of Meditation' (the Bible) and all his brethren were to be 'ruled by him' (DR XIII). He was to fulfil all the priestly duties within the Community such as pronouncing the blessing over the meals (CR VI), preside over the assemblies, and perform those legal functions specifically reserved to the priesthood (DR XIII). Nothing more than this appears in any of the manuscripts about the part he was expected to play. In particular, no teaching duties are assigned to him, or anything to do with the administration of the communities.

These tasks were the responsibility of a person called the *Mebakker* (or *Pakid*) in the same two Rules and described in the Community Rule (VI) (as I hope to show later) as the *Doresh ha-Torah*, one who was to 'study the Law continually, day and night, concerning the right conduct of a man with his companion'. In my translation of the text I have rendered *Mebakker* as 'Guardian'. Literally it means 'overseer', someone who looks after the welfare and spiritual direction of the people in his care. The Greek synonym is *episkopos*, and its English equivalent, 'bishop'; but 'bishop' in the context of a Jewish sect seems inapt, and 'overseer' smacks more of a gang of labourers than of a religious community. Hence 'Guardian'.

The chief duty assigned to the Guardian by the Community Rule and the Damascus Rule lay in the field of instruction. He was to interview all who sought admission to the sect and teach the Rule of the Community to the people he judged worthy to enter. But he was not only to be a sort of novice-master; for the 'professed' also he was to act as final arbiter in all matters concerned with orthodoxy and right conduct. In the words of the Damascus Rule (xiii), he was to 'instruct the congregation in the works of God'. He was to 'love them as a father loves his children and carry them in all their distress like a shepherd his sheep'. He was to 'examine every man entering his congregation with regard to his deeds, understanding, strength, ability, and possessions, and inscribe him in his place according to his rank'; no member of the camp was allowed to admit anyone to the congregation 'against the decision of the Guardian of the camp'.

Between them, therefore, the Priest and the Guardian held control in all matters concerned with ritual and instruction; but of course there were other necessary tasks to be performed in the communities. Since they were self-supporting, there had to be someone to cope with the practical administration of their activities and revenue, to take charge of the finances of the Community and provide for its material interests and needs. This person was the *Mebakker 'al melekheth ha-rabbim*: literally, 'overseer of the work of the congregation'. In the text I have named him (a little freely) 'Bursar of the Congregation'.

Passing now to the organization of the sect as a whole, we find a situation exactly parallel to that existing in the smaller groups. In a passage dealing with the 'assembly of all the camps', the Damascus Rule (xiv) describes the superior as 'the Priest who enrols the Congregation', a man aged 'from thirty to sixty years, learned in the Book of Meditation and in all the judgements of the Law'. As for the 'Guardian of all the camps', he must be 'from thirty to fifty years old, one who has mastered all the secrets of men and the languages of all their clans. Whoever enters the Congregation shall do so according to his word, each in his rank. And whoever has anything to say with regard to any suit or judgement, let him say it to the Guardian.'

It is difficult to assess the limits and extent of the personal authority wielded by these two figures, but in the administration of justice and in the admission and expulsion of members they enjoyed the collaboration of various bodies such as the college of ten judges appointed to the city communities, and the Community Council. These tribunals were required to ratify by a show of hands the decisions made by the 'sons of Zadok', but whether it was in their power to refuse to confirm the judgements of their superiors we do not know.

It might seem from this brief summary of the roles of Priest, Guardian, and Bursar that there can be little room for obscurity in such an apparently simple administrative structure. But this is not so. To begin with, it is not clear whether the Bursar was distinct from the Guardian, or whether one man dealt with both tasks. For example, the Damascus Rule (XIII) states that it was for the Guardian to decide whether members of his congregation could enter into a business association. It also mentions him (together with the Judges) in connexion with the charitable funds distributed to the poor (XIV). On the other hand, in the Community Rule (VI) the offices seem to be separate. Those who prefer to identify the one with the other point out that in the primitive Church the bishop was entrusted with both the material and the spiritual well-being of his flock. For myself, I would suggest that in the smaller communities one man could very well have performed both functions, but the larger ones may have needed two men for these different duties.

The next problem concerns the Priest and the Guardian. Were these two individuals? Scholars are divided in their views. Those who use the Community Rule as a basis for their argument incline to identify the two roles, and it is true that this Scroll tends to blur the distinction between them. But the Damascus Rule differentiates quite clearly between the Priest and the Guardian of the camp, going so far as to describe their offices in two separate sections. Similarly, there is no ambiguity at all in the case of 'all the camps'. The Priest-Superior and the Guardian of all the camps are separate individuals and, as we have seen, do not even belong to the same age-group.

On the strength of the same straightforward statements in the Damascus Rule it is possible at the same time to place the *Doresh ha-Torah*, the Interpreter of the Law, described in the Community Rule (vi) as officiating in the small communities in conjunction with the Priest. Since, in this particular passage of the Community Rule, there is no mention whatever of the Guardian, it is not unreasonable to suppose that the Guardian and the Interpreter of the Law were one and the same person.

Finally, we arrive at a difficulty unmentioned as yet: what are the implications of *Maskil*, a word recurring throughout the Scrolls? Once more, it has not been easy to find the correct equivalent in English. Literally, it could mean 'man of understanding', 'man of insight', or 'instructor'. In this translation, however, I have rendered it as a title, 'Master', because I believe that the evidence goes to show that it corresponds to a particular office in the Community.

This office is defined in a long passage under the heading 'These are the precepts in which the Master shall walk in his commerce with all the living . . .', where the Community Rule (ix) observes that he was to select, instruct, and guide the members of his community. 'He shall separate and weigh the sons of righteousness according to their spirit . . . He shall admit (each man) in accordance with the cleanness of his hands and advance him in accordance with his understanding . . . He shall impart true knowledge and righteous judgement to those who have chosen the Way. He shall guide them . . .'

But these were the duties of the Guardian, as we have seen. Furthermore, turning to the Damascus Rule (xiii) a philological link makes its appearance. It is said of the Guardian that 'he shall instruct', *yaskil*, 'the Congregation': now *yaskil* and *maskil* derive from the same Hebrew root.

Despite the fact that this word *maskil* plays such an important part in the Scrolls – many of the documents are addressed to him – insufficient attention has been paid to its significance. Most writers are content to leave it vague. Some believe that the phrase 'For the *maskil*' is a sign that the document or section is intended for initiates only. Others think that the term applies to the wise and intelligent man in general. In these pages I would suggest another interpretation.

In the Bible,* and in the Book of Daniel in particular, a *maskil* is one who is both endowed with the gift of insight into divine wisdom and a teacher of that wisdom. 'The *maskilim* (plural of *maskil*) of the people shall give understanding to the multitude' (Dan. xi, 33). 'The *maskilim* shall be as bright as the brightness of the firmament, and those who bring righteousness to the multitude, like the stars for ever and ever' (xii, 3).

The verb *haskil* and its derivatives (to understand, to teach) also occurs several times in the work of the Chronicler (Chronicles, Ezra, Nehemiah). For example, we read in Ezra (viii, 18): 'And by the good hand of our God upon us they brought us *ish sekhel*, a man of discretion, of the sons of Mahli the son of Levi.' In Nehemiah (viii, 7–8) we find: 'The Levites helped the people to understand the Law ... And they read from the Book, from the Law of God, clearly; *som sekhel*, they gave the sense, so that the people understood the reading'; and in 2 Chronicles (xxx, 32): 'And Hezekiah encouraged all the Levites *ha-maskilim*, who taught *sekhel tob*, the good knowledge, of the Lord.'

The important point to notice in these quotations is the association of *haskil*, *sekhel*, and *maskil* with the Levites, an association which receives unexpected confirmation in the

* A note on the Bible translation used in this book is given on page 17.

Psalms, where *maskil* appears in twelve titles, and in the text of Psalm 47, 7. Although the exact meaning of *maskil* in the Psalms has never been established, there is little doubt that it describes a certain type of poem. But the remarkable feature is that eight of the thirteen psalms in which it figures are ascribed to Levitical authors: the sons of Korah (42, 44, 45, 47, 88), Asaph (74, 78), Heman (joint-author with the sons of Korah of Ps. 88), and Ethan (89).

The reader may be wondering, justifiably, where all this is leading to. The answer is that as a first step it leads to a correct understanding of the role of the Levites in post-exilic Judaism. According to the Chronicler (1 Chron. vi, 49), the priestly duties consisted in the offering of sacrifice, the care of the most holy things, and atonement. All the other religious services were assigned to the Levites (vi, 48), in particular, choir duties and everything connected with liturgical music (vi, 31), and the instruction of the people (2 Chron. vii, 7–9). This latter fact emerges clearly from the account given in the Book of Nehemiah (viii, 1–8) of the promulgation of the Law of Moses. The ceremony opens with a blessing pronounced by the Priest Ezra; but then the Levites take over. 'The Levites gave the meaning of the Law to the people. . . . They read aloud clearly from the Book, the Law of God; they gave the sense and the people understood the reading' (Neh. viii, 7–8). Whereas Ezra, the president of the Congregation, merely performs his priestly task of offering blessings to God, the Levites act as the teachers of the people; in fact, in the following verse they are specifically described as such, as the 'instructors of the people'.

Returning once more to the Scrolls and to the significance there of *maskil*, is there any evidence linking the bearers of this title with the Levites? Study will show that the latter are mentioned many times in conjunction with the Priests, but it is noteworthy that no definite tasks are openly allotted to them except in two passages, one from the Messianic Rule and the other from the Damascus Rule.

According to the first, the Levites were to be attached to the various groups of Israelites 'to cause all the congregation to go and come, each man in his rank, under the direction of the heads of family of the Congregation'(MR I). The second passage (DR XIII) ordains that every camp containing at least ten men must be presided over by a Priest 'learned in the Book of Meditation', and then continues: 'should he not be experienced in these matters (the Law), whereas one of the Levites is experienced in them, then it shall be determined that all the members of the camp shall go and come according to the latter's word. But should there be a case of applying the law of leprosy to a man, then the Priest shall come and shall remain in the camp, and the Guardian shall instruct him in the exact interpretation of the Law.'

This causing the people 'to go and come' obviously alludes to the spiritual guidance of the members of the Community. Furthermore, on reading this passage from the Damascus Rule it is difficult to avoid the conclusion that the Levite and the Guardian were one and the same person. Since the sect expressly intended to model its organization as a microcosmic Israel it followed that, as in Judaism generally, the prime religious duties of worship and instruction were divided between Priest and Levite.

The solution to this highly involved problem is therefore, I think, the following. (1) At the head of the whole sect, and at the head of each dependent community, stood two distinct figures, the Priest and the Guardian. (2) The Guardian was a Levite. (3) As the teacher of his congregation, this Levite-Guardian was also known by the title *Maskil*, Master.

COVENANT AND COUNCIL

Despite much research and reflection, there is still a great deal of uncertainty concerning the exact nature and significance of the various phases through which the sectaries passed in their community life.

The first step towards full initiation was entry into the

Covenant, the New Covenant. Candidates for admission to the sect were required to be native Israelites and were obliged to undergo a preliminary scrutiny by the Guardian so that he might assess their mental and moral capacities. If they passed muster, they were then permitted to enter the Covenant of God in the presence of the whole Community, freely pledging themselves 'by a binding oath' to return with all their heart and soul 'to every commandment of the Law of Moses in accordance with all that has been revealed to the sons of Zadok, the Keepers of the Covenant and Seekers of His will' (CR I, V, VI; DR XV, XVI; MR I).

Many writers imagine that this adherence to the Covenant constituted a temporary phase, a probationary period during which 'postulants' were put to the test; they think that if they failed to reach the necessary standard of moral discipline during this time they were not allowed to continue but ceased altogether to belong to the Community. In my view, there is little justification for this theory. With his 'binding oath' a man took on himself, once and for all, the sacred obligation to accept the teachings of the sons of Zadok and to abide by their Rule. Having done this, he then submitted himself to the Guardian for further instruction so that he might be 'converted to the truth and depart from all falsehood'.

Advancement in the Community was quite another matter. Although every member was party to the Covenant and remained so for the rest of his life, he could either move up the sect's hierarchical ladder, with more training and a fresh initiation, or else, for want of ambition or talent, he could remain a simple 'man of the Covenant'. Those who were able to follow the first course eventually moved on to the stricter discipline of the Council of the Community.

There is also a measure of disagreement concerning this Council of the Community. Some experts consider it to be just another of the sect's titles, though they are obliged to admit from the evidence of the texts that within this Council there must have existed another smaller body, also called 'council'. The confusion is dispelled, I think, once it is accepted that the Council of the Community was formed by a group of sectaries who had undergone the training and initiation necessary to qualify them for the highest rank in the sect's hierarchy.

Once more, initiation demanded a preliminary examination to ascertain the candidate's worthiness and ability, and if the Council found them adequate he had to take instruction for another two years, submitting himself to further public scrutiny at the end of each one. During the first year he took no part in the more sacred activities of the Council, such as its solemn Meals and its *tohorah*, 'purity', by which I understand its daily meals prepared in accordance with special ritual purity. He also retained his money and belongings. In the second year, provided he had satisfied his examiners, he handed over all his possession to the Bursar who put them aside until his training was complete. He was admitted to the refectory, but was still not allowed to participate in the Meals reserved to the fully initiated. He was probably able to attend those study meetings at which no secret matters were discussed, but without taking any active share in them. If, at the end of all this, he was judged worthy by the Council, he was then solemnly admitted to full membership. 'He shall be inscribed among his brethren in the order of his rank', we read in the Community Rule (VI), and 'his property shall be merged and he shall offer his counsel and judgement to the Community'. From this time on he was 'set apart as holy' and was entitled to share in all the sect's secret doctrine. It was his duty and privilege to separate himself 'from the habitation of ungodly men' and to 'prepare the way' of the Lord through study and contemplation of the Scriptures (CR VIII).

No 'man of the Covenant' who had committed any deliberate sin against the commandments was allowed to join this Council of Holiness. Furthermore, if any member of the Council transgressed the Law of Moses, either deliberately or through negligence, he was expelled forthwith and none of his former brethren were permitted to have any contact with him. 'He shall be expelled from the Council of the Community and shall return no more: no man of holiness shall be associated with his property or counsel in any matter at all' (CR VIII). Minor offences against the Community Rule were punished with a penance lasting from ten days to two years (CR VI–VII), and even sins of inadvertence against the Law of Moses entailed two years of probation during which the culprit was cut off from participation in the common life. But if a member of the Council lost courage, going so far as to leave it of his own accord, he was regarded as having committed a most serious offence. Junior members of less than ten years' standing were treated with some consideration in that if they repented they could be re-admitted on condition that they underwent their two years' training all over again, but the senior members of ten years' standing and more were sentenced to irrevocable expulsion. 'He shall return no more to the Council of the Community. Moreover, if any member of the Community share with him his food or property ... his sentence shall be the same; he shall be expelled' (CR VII).

It would appear that status within the Community was invested with particular importance. We meet constantly in the Scrolls the phrase, 'each man according to his rank', as well as the injunction that every member of lesser rank should show deference and obedience towards his senior. But as far as the actual superiors are concerned, we are unfortunately told nothing of how they obtained their office. On the other hand, it is made clear that Priests, Guardians, and Judges etc. were obliged to relinquish their posts at the age of sixty. We read in the Damascus Rule (quoting Jubilees xxxiii, 11): 'No man over the age of sixty shall hold office as Judge of the Congregation, for "because man sinned his days have been shortened, and in the heat of His anger against the inhabitants of the earth God has ordained that their understanding should depart even before

their days are completed"' (DR X). By imposing an obli-
gatory retiring age on its dignitaries the sect saved the
machinery of its government from an encumbrance of aged
men and allowed for healthy renewal. In fact, despite the
rigidity of its framework, there was in no sense stasis within
the Community, but periodic movement both up and down
the hierarchical ladder.

PROPERTY AND MARRIAGE

From the point of view of the Community's hierarchical
structure it has been established that the 'men of the
Covenant' were distinct from the men of the 'Council of the
Community'.

The 'men of the Covenant' appear to have lived not very
differently from their fellow Jews, except that they were
bound by the stricter religious duties peculiar to the sect.
They settled in towns and villages, and also in 'camps'; but
even here, although their separation from the rest of Jewry
was more complete than in the towns, they were still not subject to the rule of common ownership of property. Each
member retained his private money and belongings, but
they were to be used in a holy manner and not to be mixed with
the 'wealth of wickedness'. The Damascus Rule (XIII; cf.
CR V) lays it down that 'no member of the Covenant of
God shall give or receive anything from the sons of the Pit
except for payment'. That is to say, all transactions between
the sectaries and the outside world had to be on a commer-
cial footing, with none of the amicable give and take which
might prevail in any ordinary society. Within limits, they
were even able to trade with the Gentiles (see DR XII).

This freedom to provide for themselves did not, however,
absolve them from the responsibility of supporting their
own poor. They had to hand over to the Guardians and
the Judges the revenue of two days out of every month, and
from this fund aid was given to the widows and orphans,
the sick and aged, etc., in their midst.

By contrast, the property and income of the members of

the Council was communally owned; everything was placed in the hands of the Bursar and it was his duty to administer this common property for the benefit of his companions. An economic system such as this distinguished them markedly from their Jewish contemporaries, among whom religious 'communism' was unknown, but it bears a close resemblance to the custom adopted by the primitive Church of Jerusalem, where the faithful were encouraged to convey all their possessions to the apostles (cf. Acts ii, 44–5; iv, 32–v, 2). It may be remembered too that in the Fourth Gospel it is said explicitly that the community formed by Jesus and the apostles lived out of a common purse entrusted to the care of Judas (John xii, 6; xiii, 29).

There has been much speculation as to whether the sectaries were married or celibate. On the face of it, it would seem that marriage was the general custom since the Damascus Rule, the Messianic Rule, and the War Rule make open reference to married members and none of the Qumran writings allude to celibacy as such. In addition, archaeologists working in the large cemetery at Qumran (about eleven hundred tombs) have uncovered on the fringes of the graveyard a few female and child skeletons.

The difficulty arises from the fact that most scholars have now come to accept that this religious body belonged to the Essene sect, and that on the evidence of Josephus, Philo, and Pliny the Elder, the Essenes were noted throughout the ancient world for their practice of celibacy, a state most unusual in Judaism. But Josephus adds that *some* Essenes married and produced children, and this, I think, describes the true situation. Most of the sectaries – the 'men of the Covenant' – married, but the few who devoted themselves to the search for higher perfection and ritual purity found celibacy more appropriate to their ends. Although argument *e silentio* demands delicate handling, the fact that in the Community Rule there is no mention at all of women and marriage suggests that the seekers of perfect holiness, like the followers of Jesus, found it more fitting to be without family ties, without 'wife or brothers or parents or children' (Luke xiv, 26; xviii, 29).

ASSEMBLIES

Whether or not its members were linked by bonds of kinship, for the Community to function as a group it was necessary that there should be some kind of social apparatus to hold it together. This took the form of periodic assemblies.

It is not as yet possible to define in detail how often the members of the Covenant were convened among themselves, but it appears from the Community Rule (II) and the Damascus Rule (xv) that the whole sect was required to attend a general assembly at least once a year, on the Feast of the Renewal of the Covenant, celebrated, as I will show later, on the Feast of Weeks, the Feast of Pentecost. This was the occasion when new arrivals demanding entry into the sect solemnly pledged themselves by the oath of the Covenant, and it was also the time when the status of all the members was re-assessed. The ritual for the festival is described at the beginning of the Community Rule, but since its importance resides chiefly in the context of the sect's religious teaching, I will at this point do no more than quote the concluding paragraph. 'Thus shall they do, year by year, for as long as the dominion of Satan endures. The Priests shall enter first, ranked one after another according to the perfection of their spirit; then the Levites; and thirdly, all the people one after another ... that every Israelite may know his place in the Community of God according to the everlasting design' (CR II; cf. DR XIV).

We are better informed about the meetings of the Council of the Community. The Community Rule (VI) orders its members to assemble nightly under the supervision of the Priest for the purpose of Bible reading, study, and prayer. They were to sit before him in the order of their rank, taking care to speak only when questioned, and were never to interrupt each other. Non-members attended these meetings also, but were forbidden to play any active part unless they had first obtained the consent of the Guardian and of the members of the Council.

Some of the assemblies, and perhaps all of them, were followed by a solemn Meal. The Community Rule (VI) writes of it as follows: 'When the table has been prepared for eating, and the new wine for drinking, the Priest shall be the first to stretch out his hand to bless the first-fruits of the bread and new wine.' Mention of the first-fruits of bread and wine seems to indicate that the Meal was originally a Pentecostal supper reserved to Priests and Levites (Exod. xxiii, 16; Deut. xvi, 11; xviii, 4) where the first-fruits were holy offerings set aside for the clergy. But in the Community they were eaten by the 'men of holiness', by the sons of Zadok and the members of their Council. In short, they lost their exclusive connexion with the Feast of Pentecost in exactly the same way that the Christian Eucharist has lost its exclusive connexion with Easter.

The remaining type of Council meeting, and one that played a vital part in the control and direction of the sect, was the 'Community *midrash*', which I have called the 'Community Court of Inquiry'. One of the functions of this body was to examine the conduct of candidates and decide whether or not they should be promoted. The other duty was to try and pass sentence on members reported for offending against the Rule or the Law of Moses. Again, we are not told what circumstances governed the summoning of the Court of Inquiry, but the Community Rule (VI–VII) dwells at some length on how it should proceed, and gives a list of offences with their corresponding sentences. These vary according to the gravity of the fault. A slight transgression, such as the interruption of a companion in his speech, entails a penance of ten days, but a deliberate sin against the Law of Moses results in unequivocal expulsion from the Community. The Damascus Rule makes no mention of the Court of Inquiry but refers to a group of ten Judges, four of them Priests and Levites, and six of them Israelites, a judicial assembly no doubt concerned with the 'men of the Covenant' (x). The same Rule (ix–x) also defines the part to be played by witnesses and its list of sentences includes even the death penalty.

This inquiry into the hierarchical, economic, and social structure of the sect has so far done no more than piece together the skeleton of the Community of the sons of Zadok. To give it substance and life we need to understand the spiritual ideals and convictions which animated them and which induced them to seek truth and holiness apart from the mainstream of Judaism.

· 2 ·

RELIGIOUS BELIEF AND PRACTICE

IT is, I hope, no distortion of Old Testament religion to say that it rests on three fundamental ideas, the concepts of election, covenant, and salvation. God chose Israel. Faithful to His promise to Abraham, He singled out the patriarch's descendants to be His own people, His elect. On Mount Sinai He revealed to them the Way, the Law of Moses, and ratified His unique relationship with them by means of a Covenant. The essence of biblical religion is adherence to that Covenant – to both the spirit and the letter of the Law – firm trust in God, and the confident expectation that ultimately He will reign triumphantly over the whole world.

It is also an integral part of Jewish faith that the Covenant is an eternal one. The sins of the great mass of the people will never affect it because God, not permitting His promise to be thwarted, provides that in every age at least a handful of just Israelites, a 'remnant', hold fast to their faith and heed the divine message; the Covenant remains valid for their sake. They are a 'remnant' in another sense too, in that by their fidelity they escape the manifestations of divine anger visited on the wicked of the world.

At the time of the Qumran sect, in the period known as 'inter-Testamental' (roughly between 150 B.C. and A.D. 70), these basic concepts gave rise to a great deal of controversy among the various parties of Palestinian Judaism. The Pharisees, Sadducees, the Community of the Scrolls, etc., all engaged in a process of doctrinal interpretation, and although the emerging syntheses never departed from their biblical foundations, each showed a distinct individuality. Of the first two, no detailed contemporary evidence has been

34

handed down; Sadducee teaching is mainly known through its critics, the Pharisees, and for Pharisaic doctrine we are mainly dependent on documents compiled after A.D. 200. By contrast, in the Qumran library we are confronted with the beliefs of a sect recorded by its living members, and we are in consequence indebted to them not only for information about their own views and aspirations, but also, indirectly, for a fuller appreciation of the stand taken by those who dissented from their teaching, namely, the parties already mentioned and the Judeo-Christians of the primitive Church.

THE NEW COVENANT

It was, as I have said, the profound conviction of the Community of the Scrolls that they were the faithful 'remnant' of their time, and indeed the final 'remnant' of all time. It governed their whole religious outlook. God had chosen to reveal knowledge and understanding of His purpose and will to their Teacher of Righteousness and to those of the Teacher's followers who trod the path laid down by him, the Way of Holiness. Only the Teacher was able to decipher the mysteries concealed in the Scriptures; consequently, only those who accepted his interpretation of the written word of God could be sure of living in conformity with His desire.

From this consciousness of having been chosen by God it followed that the Community regarded themselves as true heirs to the eternal Covenant between God and Israel; the first obligation of those entering the sect was to commit themselves to it anew. As in the New Testament, the phrase 'New Covenant' even became part of the idiom of the sect, 'men of the Community' and 'men of the New Covenant' being employed in their writings as synonyms.

The obligations imposed by the New Covenant were materially the same as those implicit in the Old; namely, perfect obedience to the teachings of Moses and the Prophets. The members of the Community pledged themselves to 'seek God with a whole heart and soul, and do what is good and right before Him as He commanded by the hand of Moses and all His servants the Prophets' (CR I). But to this they added the, for them, necessary stipulation that the 'return to the Law of Moses' required of those entering the sect must be 'in accordance with all that has been revealed of it to the sons of Zadok' (CR v).

As far as the Law itself was concerned, the revelations granted to these sons of Zadok, the sect's priestly hierarchy, added fresh severity and rigour to a legal code already strict in itself. Their marriage laws are an example. Whereas it is written in Leviticus xviii, 13, 'You shall not approach your mother's sister, she is your near kin', in the Damascus Rule (v) this precept is extended to include a man and his niece within the degrees of forbidden kinship, with the comment: 'Although the laws against incest are written for men, they also apply to women', i.e., if a nephew is forbidden to marry his aunt, so is a niece prohibited from marrying her uncle. No doubt those Jews who did not subscribe to the Community's teaching argued against this that if Moses had wished to forbid the uncle-niece relationship in marriage he would have said so.

Similarly, according to the Damascus Rule (IV–V), those who live in polygamy fail to understand the true teaching of Moses and in 'taking a second wife while the first is alive' commit the sin of fornication. The principle laid down by God since the time of the creation is one of monogamy: 'Male and female created He them' (Gen. i, 27). This principle was observed by those who were saved at the time of the Flood; according to Genesis vii, 9, Noah and his sons had only one wife each and entered the ark 'two by two'. Moreover, Moses forbade even the king to 'multiply wives to himself' (Deut. xvii, 17). For the ignorant this might seem to imply that the king must not imitate Solomon whose harem amounted to seven hundred wives and three hundred concubines (1 Kings xi, 3) but must restrict the number of his wives to a more modest figure (eighteen according to the

Mishnah). In the Community, however, to 'multiply wives' meant to be married to more than one wife, and if the king was to be bound by such a law, so must every commoner. In parenthesis, it may be of interest to note that the same text, 'Male and female created He them', is introduced into the New Testament as an argument for the prohibition of divorce followed by remarriage (Matt. xix, 4; Mark x, 6) and may underlie the early Christian dislike for the re-marriage of widows and widowers (cf. 1 Tim. iii, 2, 12; v, 9; Titus i, 6).

In addition to its increased severity, the Community's interpretation of the Law was distinguished by its claim to infallibility. Whereas traditional Judaism allowed for some elasticity within orthodoxy itself (Rabbi X declaring lawful an action forbidden by Rabbi Y), no such latitude was apparent in the sect. The true meaning of the Law had been revealed to them by God, and since there is only one God and one truth, there can only be one interpretation of that truth.

Besides the Law, the Community also interpreted the Books of the Prophets in such a way as to bring them into harmony with their own convictions. They believed every-thing foretold there, but held that the words of the Prophets were concealed in a mystery to which only their Teacher had been granted the key. It was the Teacher of Righteous-ness 'to whom God made known all the mysteries of His servants the Prophets' (cHab VII) and who discovered that the end of time was at hand, and that all the prophecies alluding to the final age referred to the Community of the Covenant and either had been, or were about to be, fulfilled. Their attitude may perhaps best be seen in a passage in the Commentary on Habakkuk (ii, 14). 'The righteous shall live by his faith' is interpreted to refer to 'all those who observe the Law in the House of Judah (the Community), whom God will deliver from the House of Judgement because of their suffering and because of their faith in the Teacher of Righteousness' (cHab VIII).

In short, this Chosen People of the New Covenant, with its claims to infallible truth, believed that it was to be a 'refuge' for seekers of righteousness during the age of final wickedness. It was to be a 'sure House', a 'House of truth', 'that tried wall, that *precious corner-stone*, whose foundations shall neither rock nor sway in their place' (CR VIII). The same metaphor appears in the Hymns, where the psalmist writes of a House of God built on rock against which the powers of evil would never prevail.

> But I shall be as one who enters a fortified city,
>   as one who seeks refuge behind a high wall
>   until deliverance comes;
> I will lean on Thy truth, O my God.
> For Thou wilt set the foundation on rock
>   and the framework by the measuring-cord of justice;
> and the tried stones Thou wilt lay
>   by the plumb-line of truth,
> to build a mighty wall which shall not sway;
>   and no man entering there shall stagger.
>
> For no enemy shall ever invade it
>   since its doors shall be doors of protection
>   through which no man shall pass;
> and its bars shall be firm
>   and no man shall break them.

(Hymn 10)

THE HOLY LIFE

For every Jew, consciousness of belonging to a chosen people is the cause of wonder and thankfulness; but for the members of the Community it meant something special. Israel's election is that of a nation. The divine promise of blessing given to Abraham concerns all his posterity, the Covenant made on Sinai affects the whole Jewish race. On the eighth day after his birth, every male Israelite enters the Covenant through the rite of circumcision, shedding his own blood as the blood of a covenantal sacrifice. But he shares the exalted destiny of his people as a birthright; even though he may remain pious and faithful till death, he does not and cannot experience the personal commitment to God which was, perhaps, the distinctive hallmark of the Community's spirituality.

For the sectary, election was not an accident of birth, an inherited privilege. Every individual, even those born into the Community, was required to take the oath of the Covenant of his own free will because he had, as a person, been chosen by God from all eternity to become one of His elect.

In preference to thousands of his fellow Jews, he had been loved by God from before creation. Whereas the man outside the sect had been destined to walk in the ways of darkness and to be ruled by the spirit of falsehood, he, God's elect, had been destined by Him to walk in the ways of light under the guidance of the spirit of truth.

'From the God of Knowledge comes all that is and shall be' we read in the Community Rule (III). 'Before ever they existed He established their whole design, and when, as ordained for them, they come into being, it is in accord with His glorious design that they accomplish their task ... He has created man to govern the world and has appointed for him two spirits in which to walk until the time of His visitation: the spirits of truth and falsehood ... All the children of righteousness are ruled by the Prince of Light and walk in the ways of light; but all the children of falsehood are ruled by the Angel of Darkness and walk in the ways of darkness' (CR III).

A deep realization of God's personal benevolence towards every member of the Community, and of the all-pervading reality of His grace, was accompanied by an equally profound awareness of human frailty, unworthiness, and nothingness. No note of self-righteousness sounds in the Qumran writings; on the contrary, the sectary is amazed by the blessings showered on him and expresses himself in the Hymns in tones of self-abasement.

Behold, I was taken from dust
   and fashioned out of clay
as a source of uncleanness,
   and a shameful nakedness,
a heap of dust,
   and a kneading with water . . .
   a creature of clay returning to dust.
(Hymn 19)

On the other hand, he knew that he had been saved from human misery and sinfulness, and that his final destiny was to be one with that of the heavenly spirits who stand in the presence of God for ever.

For the sake of Thy glory
   Thou hast purified man of sin
that he may be made holy for Thee
   with no abominable uncleanness
   and no guilty wickedness;
that he may be one with the children of Thy truth
   and partake of the lot of Thy Holy Ones;
that bodies gnawed by worms may be raised from dust
   to the counsel of Thy truth,
and that the perverse spirit (may be lifted)
   to the understanding which comes from Thee;
that he may stand before Thee
   with the everlasting host
   and with Thy Spirits of Holiness,
to be renewed together with all the living
   and to rejoice together with them that know.
(Hymn 17)

With this awareness of blessing and salvation, and balancing any tendency towards arrogance, comes the constant reminder that all goodness and truth proceed from God and that no act of virtue can be accomplished without His help.

As for me,
   I belong to wicked mankind,
      to the company of ungodly flesh . . .
For mankind has no way
   and man is unable to establish his steps

since justification is with God
    and perfection of way is out of His hand ...
He will draw me near by His grace,
    and by His mercy will He bring my justification.

(CR XI)

Any strictly organized religious society where the boundaries between right and wrong are rigidly defined exposes its members to the danger of feeling pleased with themselves for having conformed to the rules, of presuming themselves justified by their 'works', and to have acquired merit thereby in the sight of God. Providing for this pitfall, the sect taught that even the correct observance of the Rule was an act of divine grace. Besides, since the Rule itself was known only through the gift of revelation granted to the Community, its members were doubly beholden for their salvation; they were indebted to God for their knowledge, the infinitely valuable gift of *gnosis*, and also for the divine succour which permits a man with an inborn tendency to evil to cling faithfully and unceasingly to truth and justice. This is emphasized in the final hymn of the Community Rule.

From the source of His righteousness
    is my justification,
and from His marvellous mysteries
    is the light in my heart.
My eyes have gazed
    on that which is eternal,
on wisdom concealed from men,
    on knowledge and wise design
    (hidden) from the sons of men ...
God has given them to His chosen ones
    as an eternal possession,
and has caused them to inherit
    the lot of the Holy Ones.
He has joined their assembly
    to the Sons of Heaven
to be a Council of the Community,
a foundation of the Building of Holiness,
an everlasting Plant throughout all ages to come.

(CR XI)

41

Grace and knowledge were the twin foundations of the sect's spirituality. Knowledge, it taught, proceeding from the God of knowledge through the mediation of the spirits of 'truth' and 'light', directs a man into the Way he must follow and illuminates the mysteries of God's purpose for mankind; it penetrates the secrets of the heavenly world and divines the nature and ministry of the spirits. Even the abode of the Creator Himself was thought to have been manifested in visions such as that of the Divine Throne-Chariot. By means of knowledge and grace the aim of the Rule was realized. Its rigorous separation from the world of the wicked and its call for meticulous personal holiness enabled the Community to withstand the ravages of the devil and his allies, and so to be part, even in this life, of the fellowship of the Sons of Heaven.

WORSHIP

According to the Bible, the first duty of the heavenly beings – the Seraphim of Isaiah, the Cherubim of Ezekiel, and the angels of Psalm 148 – is the praise and worship of God; and so it was for the followers of the Teacher of Righteousness. They were to join their voices to those of the Angels of the Presence raised in prayer and blessing in the celestial Temple.

Broadly speaking, the sectaries' whole life was one of uninterrupted adoration. More precisely, however, their Rule required them to worship God in the correct manner and at set times, these set times conforming to the eternal and unchanging laws affecting the rhythm of time itself (the rhythm of day and night, the seasons, the years, etc.). The moments fixed for daily prayer – 'at the beginning of the dominion of light' and 'at the beginning of the dominion of darkness' (G R x) – coincided with the daily sacrifice at dusk and dawn of the burnt offerings in the Temple (Exod. xxix, 39; Num. xxviii, 4). But the other 'appointed times' are more complex and affect the whole question of the liturgical calendar.

In Judaism, the reckoning of months and years was

governed by the moon, but because of the absence of correlation between the lunar year (354 days) and the solar seasons of solstice and equinox, the orthodox calendar effected a compromise between the two; after every three-yearly period of thirty-six lunar months it inserted one supplementary month.

To the Community this was an abomination of the Gentiles and directly counter to the 'certain law from the mouth of God' (H 19). It had itself inherited, probably from priestly circles, a solar calendar based on 'the laws of the Great Light of heaven' (H 19) in which the year was divided into fifty-two weeks exactly: into, that is to say, four seasons of thirteen weeks. Each season consisted of three months thirty days long, and a day was added to every season as a link between one season and the next. This solar calendar, which figures also in the Book of Jubilees and in the First Book of Enoch, recommended itself to the sect because of its belief in the unchanging order of God in the universe. As a French scholar, Mlle Annie Jaubert, has pointed out, its strict periodic regularity ensured that the year always began on a Wednesday, the fourth day of the Jewish week, and thus remained in perfect conformity with the work of God who created the sun on the fourth day. Furthermore, not only did the year begin on a Wednesday, but so also did every season of thirteen weeks. In fact, any date during the year fell on exactly the same day of the week in every other year. For instance, Passover, the fifteenth day of the first month, fell always on a Wednesday, and the Day of Atonement, the tenth day of the seventh month, always on a Friday, etc. Of course, this method of reckoning presents difficulties also, the astronomical year consisting of $365\frac{1}{4}$ days, not 364; but we are not told how, if at all, the Community dealt with them.

The practical result of the adoption of this calendar was that the Community feast days were celebrated differently from the rest of Judaism. It is for this reason that the Damascus Rule (VI), for example, orders that 'the feasts and the

Day of Fasting' must be kept 'according to the finding of the members of the New Covenant'. It also explains how the Wicked Priest was able to disturb the celebration by the Teacher of Righteousness and his disciples of the Day of Atonement (CHab IX); for him it was not a holy day.

It is not as yet possible to write in any detail about the peculiarities of the Qumran liturgical calendar because material from cave IV giving a list of the sect's feasts and of its priestly families is still unpublished. I can only repeat the scanty information divulged by J. T. Milik, the person responsible for editing these texts, namely, that the yearly cycle included seven principal feasts, each following the other at intervals of seven weeks.

The most important of their festivals was the Feast of Weeks, the Feast of the Renewal of the Covenant. Its ritual is described at the beginning of the Community Rule and in an unpublished section of the Damascus Rule. Opening the ceremony, the Priests and Levites offer blessings to God and those entering the Covenant with them reply 'Amen, Amen'. The Priests go on to recall the past favours of God and the Levites follow them with a recital of Israel's transgressions. This culminates in a public confession, 'We have strayed! We have disobeyed!' etc., after which the penitents are blessed by the Priests. Then the Levites pronounce a long curse on the 'lot of Satan', and with the Priests they solemnly adjure all those whose repentance is incomplete not to enter the Covenant. 'Cursed be the man', they say, 'who enters this Covenant while walking among the idols of his heart ... He shall be cut off from the midst of the Sons of Light and ... his lot shall be among them that are cursed for ever' (CR I–II).

Besides public prayer, Jewish worship included other rites and ceremonies such as circumcision, purification, and the cult of offerings and sacrifice with, sometimes, a subsequent sacrificial meal. Studying the Community's attitude towards these liturgical customs, it seems strange to find no mention of circumcision in the Scrolls, although it appears more than once in its figurative sense with respect to circumcision of the tongue and lips. Doubtless this fundamental Jewish rite commanded by the Law of Moses was taken for granted.

Ritual bathing was practised in the Community. The Damascus Rule (XI) devotes a section to purification by water, and the War Rule (XIV) foresees that the victorious Sons of Light will so cleanse themselves after battle before attending the final ceremony of thanksgiving. The Community Rule (III, v) refers also to a purificatory rite in connexion with entry into the Covenant. This seems to have been a peculiar and solemn act similar to Christian baptism, and to have symbolized purification by the 'spirit of holiness'. 'For it is through the spirit of true counsel concerning the ways of man that all his sins shall be expiated that he may contemplate the light of life. He shall be cleansed from all his sins by the spirit of holiness ... And when his flesh is sprinkled with purifying water and sanctified by cleansing water, it shall be made clean by the humble submission of his soul to all the precepts of God' (CR III).

From the same Rule it may be deduced that this 'baptism' was to take place in 'seas and rivers' (III), like the baptism of John and Jesus, and that true conversion was the absolute condition for the efficacy of the sacrament (v). It may be of interest to note that the nearest Jewish parallel to this rite was the baptism administered to proselytes; in the case of women it was the only ceremony of entry into the Covenant of Israel.

As regards the offering of sacrifice, Jewish law held that this essential form of worship was valid only in the Temple of Jerusalem. But the Scrolls demonstrate that the Community regarded the Priests officiating in the sanctuary as wicked, the Temple itself profaned by uncleanness, and the orthodox liturgical calendar unlawful. The sect was consequently faced with a dilemma which they appear to have solved in the following way: (1) Sacrificial worship as such was not to be condemned despite the abuses of the wicked priesthood, but the Community's Priests and Levites must

in no circumstances actively participate in Temple services
(DR VI). The sectaries were nevertheless able to send their
offerings to Jerusalem provided they were carried there by
a person in a state of ritual purity, and that they were not
placed on the altar on the Sabbath day (DR XI). (2) As soon
as the Community conquered Jerusalem, Temple worship
would be reorganized in conformity with the divine statutes
relating to it. This event was expected to take place in the
seventh year of the final forty years' war of the Sons of Light
against the Sons of Darkness (WR II). (3) In the meantime,
the Council of the Community represented and fulfilled the
role of sanctuary. Atonement was to be made by means of
prayer, through the 'offering of the lips', 'perfection of way',
and acceptance of suffering (CR VIII–IX; Midrash on the
Last Days I).

Perhaps the most remarkable aspect of this transforma-
tion of sacrificial worship into an inward spirituality was the
way the Community attributed a sacrificial value to the
exercise of virtue and to suffering. The pre-exilic Prophets
had emphasized the emptiness of sacrifice without right
moral behaviour, but the sect went further. It taught that,
even without the performance of sacrificial rites, a holy life
was endowed with expiatory and sanctifying value. For
them, 'perfection of way' was the true remedy against the
disease of sin and guilt, and mortification (poverty, purity,
and self-abnegation) the vehicle of healing and life. They
would, in fact, have found no quarrel with the words of St
Paul appealing to the Christians of Rome to offer spiritual
worship by presenting their bodies 'as a living sacrifice, holy
and acceptable to God' (Rom. xii, I).

The last phenomenon to be discussed in this section on
worship is the sacred Meal. Its holiness is reflected in the
high degree of purity and perfection demanded of the participants who, as I have said, seem to have been restricted
to members of the Council of the Community. We are told
that the Meal followed the Council meeting, but there is no
indication as to how often it was celebrated: Josephus,

writing of the Essenes, refers to a daily repast, whereas Philo relates of the Therapeutae, or contemplative Essenes, that they gathered for their supper only on Sabbaths and great festivals.

The most detailed account of the common Meal, together with an allusion to its doctrinal significance, appears in the Messianic Rule (ii). Following a description of a Council meeting to be attended by the Priest-Messiah and the King-Messiah, we read:

> And when they shall gather for the common table, to eat and to drink new wine, when the common table shall be set for eating and the new wine poured for drinking, let no man extend his hand over the first-fruits of bread and wine before the Priest; for it is he who shall bless the first-fruits of bread and wine, and shall be the first to extend his hand over the bread. Thereafter, the Messiah of Israel shall extend his hand over the bread, and all the congregation of the Community shall utter a blessing, each man in the order of his dignity.
>
> It is according to this statute that they shall proceed at every meal at which at least ten men are gathered together.

It may be assumed from the similarity between the Meal and the Messianic Banquet that the former was believed to be a ritual anticipation of the latter. This being so, the Meal was a liturgical drama expressing the participants' ardent hope of sharing in the great Communion Supper of the Messianic triumph. Such a banquet is foretold in the Book of Isaiah (xxv, 6) and is alluded to in the New Testament when, during the Last Supper, Jesus tells the apostles that he will not drink wine again 'until the day when I drink it new with you in my Father's house' (Matt. xxvi, 29).

MESSIANIC EXPECTATION

It was the belief in ancient Judaism, as it is in the New Testament concerning the glorious return of Christ, that the coming of the Messiah would be preceded by an age of tribulation and war during which Satan would do his utmost to lead astray the chosen of God. It was also traditional from biblical times to represent final salvation as a new exodus. The sect inherited both these common Jewish teachings and fabricated out of them a highly original and somewhat complex Messianic synthesis.

According to the Damascus Rule (B II), the Community expected the Messianic age to begin forty years after the death of the Teacher of Righteousness. At first, this figure must have been accepted as a real one, but with the passage of time it doubtless came merely to symbolize the forty years of wandering in the wilderness before Israel entered the Promised Land. It is apparent in the Messianic Rule (I) that the sectaries envisaged a large-scale conversion to the Community on the eve of this new age, but after that moment there would be 'no more joining the House of Judah', to quote the Damascus Rule (IV). All the elect would be safely within the fold under the command of the Prince of Light, and the rest of sinful mankind, Jews as well as Gentiles, would be irrevocably committed to the party of the Sons of Darkness under the rule of the Angel of Darkness. For another forty years a bloody and terrible struggle would be fought between them, but finally all wickedness would be wiped from the face of the earth and, with the help of the mighty hand of God, goodness and truth would triumph for ever. The world would be renewed; the elect would inherit the 'glory of Adam', 'every blessing and eternal joy in life without end, a crown of glory and a garment of majesty in unending light' (CR IV).

All this is quite straightforward and clear; but the same cannot be said of the various Messianic characters themselves. The Community Rule, in a passage already quoted, expects them to be three in number: the Prophet, the Messiah of Aaron, and the Messiah of Israel (CR IX). The Prophet is mentioned nowhere else in the Qumran writings (except, perhaps, indirectly in the Messianic Anthology), but the two Messiahs, one a Priest and the other a King, appear in many other Dead Sea texts. The Messianic Rule introduces the Priest and the Messiah of Israel. The Book of

Blessings writes of two individuals blessed by the Master, one of them the Prince of the Congregation, described as the final ruler. Because of lacunae in the manuscript the identity of the other cannot be determined with absolute certainty, but he seems to be the priestly companion of the King-Messiah. The latter is referred to in the Midrash on the Last Days as the 'Branch of David' whose coming is to coincide with the appearance of the Interpreter of the Law.

It is the Damascus Rule that introduces confusion into the issue. In several passages it alludes to *one* Messiah, the Messiah of Aaron and Israel, and it seems that this singular is no accident since it appears in the still unpublished fragments of the Damascus Rule found in cave IV. However, the same Damascus Rule (VII) writes of the Interpreter of the Law, and of the Sceptre, the 'Prince of all the Congregation'. In short, despite a variance in terminology, this document too presents the sect's general Messianic belief that the final leadership of the chosen of God would rest in the hands of the Priest and the Layman. The King-Messiah was to be the Prince of the Congregation, and the Priestly Anointed, the Messiah of Aaron and Israel, was to be the Interpreter of the Law, and probably also the character described as 'he ... who shall teach righteousness at the end of days'(DR VI).

The respective tasks of the two Messiahs can be determined with relative ease. The Davidic Prince was to lead the people to triumph, to defeat the Gentiles, and bring into being the Kingdom of God. In matters of doctrine he was to obey the Priests; the first Commentary on Isaiah states expressly that 'as they teach him, so shall he judge'. At the Banquet, also, he was to follow after the Priest.

The Messiah of Aaron, on the other hand, is represented as the High Priest of the Kingdom. He was to conduct the liturgy during the battle against the ultimate foe, and as the final Interpreter of the Law he was to reveal the significance of the Scriptures and their relevance to events of the Messianic age and to the endless time of eternal bliss.

It is not so simple to define the role of the mysterious

Prophet since he is named only once and his duties are not given. But if I have understood it correctly, the functions ascribed to the person alluded to in the Community Rule (IV) as *geber*, 'Man', correspond to those of the expected Prophet: *geber* was to 'instruct the upright in the knowledge of the Most High' at the end of time, and 'to teach the wisdom of the Sons of Heaven to the perfect of way'. *Geber*, however, seems to have been identified with the Teacher of Righteousness. In the Commentary on Psalm 37, the verse 'The steps of *geber* are confirmed by the Lord' is interpreted: 'This concerns the Priest, the Teacher of Righteousness, whom He established to build for Himself the congregation of . . .'

Are we justified in concluding that the Prophet, *geber*, and the Teacher of Righteousness are all one and the same person? If so, it would seem to lead to the hypothesis that after a certain moment in its history all mention of the expected Prophet, or *geber*, vanished from the sect's writings because it had come to believe that he had already appeared in the person of the Teacher of Righteousness.

Although the Messianic beliefs of the sect may at first sight appear foreign to both Judaism and Christianity, closer examination reveals that this is not entirely so. The figure of the Prophet probably evolved from two biblical sources, the first being Deuteronomy xviii, 18–19, where Moses announces the coming of a Prophet similar to himself (this text is included in the Messianic Anthology from cave IV), and the second being Malachi iv, 5, where it is prophesied that Elijah will return before the coming of the day of the Lord. From these texts, and more precisely from the latter, Judaism derived the doctrine of the return of Elijah as the forerunner of the Messiah – a doctrine absorbed into the New Testament where Elijah *redivivus* is identified with John the Baptist, the forerunner of Jesus: 'He is Elijah who is to come' (Matt. xi, 14).

As regards the Messiah himself, both Judaism and Christianity invest one person with all the Messianic attributes. Rabbinic sources may refer to the Messiah of the House of Joseph, but *the* Messiah is to be a son of David. Similarly, in Christianity Jesus combines in his person the role of royal, prophetic, and priestly Messiah. Nevertheless, it can be said that even here the doctrine peculiar to the Community was constructed with traditional Jewish material. In an ancient text very little affected by doctrinal changes (the Palestinian Targum on Exodus xii, 42) we read that on the day of final salvation, at the Feast of Passover, the King-Messiah will appear in the company of Moses: 'On the fourth night the world shall reach its end to be delivered. The bonds of wickedness shall be destroyed and the iron yokes broken. Moses shall come out from the wilderness and the King-Messiah from Rome.' This seems to be an exact parallel to the expectation of the coming of the 'Branch of David' in the company of the Interpreter of the Law. Incidentally, the same tradition underlies the association of Jesus with Moses and Elijah in the New Testament account of the Transfiguration (Matt. xvii, 3; Mark ix, 4; Luke ix, 30).

The doctrine of resurrection does not seem to have been a major preoccupation in the Community. It may be reflected in a few passages such as the following:

> Hoist a banner,
> O you who lie in the dust!
> O bodies gnawed by worms
> raise up an ensign ...
> (*Hymn 10*)

But it is not impossible that the phraseology is metaphorical. On the other hand, considering the beliefs and expectations of the sect as a whole, it is difficult to conceive that the members would have denied their dead brethren and the saints of the past a full share in the eternal joys of the Messianic Kingdom.

Viewed in the perspective of its hopes and ideals, the common life of the sect takes on significance and value. Bearing in mind the history of religion in general and the customary gulf between belief and conduct, it is not impossible that their convictions gave rise to rigidity, bigotry, and hatred. But by intention they were a company of poor and humble men constantly attentive to the word of God and grateful for His favours. The severity of their judgement of the wicked was more dogmatic than practical, as appears from their insistence that vengeance is for God alone. As in all religious bodies which embrace the doctrine of eternal predestination, their minds were absorbed by the election of the holy rather than by the rejection and damnation of the unjust. Besides, those who refused to join the Community were personally responsible for their failure to repent. The apparent contradiction between predestination and free will was never directly envisaged; in their eyes it was a divine mystery of which no man has the right to demand an explanation.

It remains now to search for clues to the history of these 'men of holiness'. The Qumran literature is not lacking in innuendoes concerning persons and events connected with the Community's origins and ordeals, but as will be seen, they have to be deciphered.

· 3 ·
PERSONS AND EVENTS

FOLLOWING the pattern set by the book of Daniel composed shortly before 160 B.C., writers living in the inter-Testamental period, and convinced that they were seeing the 'last days', never alluded directly to persons and events. As in Daniel xi, where the various Ptolemaic and Seleucid rulers of the Hellenistic kingdoms are called simply 'the king of the north', 'the king of the south', etc., and the Romans are named 'Kittim', so in the Scrolls the term 'Kittim' is applied to the final foe and the identity of personalities connected with the history of the sect is concealed under such pseudonyms as 'Teacher of Righteousness', 'Wicked Priest', and 'Chief of the Kings of Greece'.

To present-day scholars this deliberate avoidance of precision and clarity is a great handicap, particularly as there are no chronicles or annals to help them, not even a letter bearing directly on contemporary events. In all that mass of manuscripts and fragments representing several hundred works, not a single document is dated. Fortunately, archaeological discovery has to some extent remedied this lack of literary evidence, and has allowed the historian to narrow his field of research before setting out to interpret the cryptic material contained in the Qumran writings.

ARCHAEOLOGICAL DATA

Archaeological findings at Qumran have made it possible to set the activities of the Community within a chronological framework; to ascertain, that is to say, the duration of their stay there and the approximate date of the abandonment of the site. The following brief survey, largely dependent on the preliminary reports issued by R. de Vaux, director of the French School of Archaeology in Jerusalem, presents these data in simple outline.

The Qumran settlement was built some time during the second half of the second century B.C. on the deserted ruins of a town belonging to the ancient kings of Judah – perhaps the 'City of Salt' mentioned in the book of Joshua (xv, 62). Its occupation covered two main periods. During the earlier part of period I, the place seems to have been only sparsely inhabited. But later, as testified by, among other things, three Seleucid silver coins dating from 132–129 B.C., a coin from the time of John Hyrcanus (134–104 B.C.), another of Judas Aristobulus (104–103 B.C.), and, especially, the discovery of 143 coins minted during the reign of Alexander Jannaeus (103–76 B.C.), it grew into a full-scale religious establishment and reached what must have been its golden age. This came to an end as the result of an earthquake which brought down the buildings and disrupted community life: Josephus reports that a catastrophe of this nature occurred in the area in 31 B.C. Subsequently, the monastery lay deserted for some years. But this theory of de Vaux is to be accepted with caution, particularly since ten coins of the reign of Herod the Great (37–4 B.C.) have also been found.

Period II began in the final years of the pre-Christian era during the reign of Archelaus (4 B.C. to A.D. 6). The community buildings were restored and from then on they were fully occupied until the third year of the Jewish War which broke out in A.D. 66. R. de Vaux reports the discovery of eighty-three coins minted by the Jewish rebels in the second year of the war, but only five coins have been found dating from the third year. The remains of ashes and signs of conflagration show that the place was destroyed by fire, probably in A.D. 68, and probably also as the result of an attack by the Romans, some of whose arrowheads have been recovered.

For the next few years, Qumran served as quarters for the Roman soldiery, and then in the second century A.D.

the followers of Bar Kokhba took refuge there and left behind them as evidence of their stay six coins from the time of the second Jewish revolt (A.D. 132–5). Since then, Qumran has never been permanently occupied.

The first conclusion to be drawn from these findings is that, as the monastery was abandoned in A.D. 68, all the events referred to in the Scrolls, which were stowed away in the neighbouring caves immediately prior to the Community's flight, must have happened before that date. This time limit might be stretched slightly, were there any strong evidence to justify doing so, but although it has been suggested that the inhabitants of Qumran were Judeo-Christian Ebionites or members of the warlike party of Zealots, both these theories are in themselves far too unlikely to outweigh the archaeological evidence measured against them. No properly Judeo-Christian characteristic emerges from the Scrolls, and unless we are much mistaken, the Zealots were scarcely a company of ascetics. For the events reported in the Qumran literature it therefore seems reasonable to turn to the historical period prior to A.D. 66–70, and more precisely – for various reasons which will appear later – to the epoch beginning with the accession of Antiochus Epiphanes (175 B.C.) and ending with fall of Hyrcanus II (40 B.C.).

The chronological table of the inter-Testamental history of Palestine given below may help the reader to follow the argument more closely.

B.C.

197	Judaea became a province of the Seleucid Empire ruled by the Syrian successors of ALEXANDER THE GREAT.
187–175	SELEUCUS IV. Beginning of Hellenistic infiltration, resisted by the Zadokite High Priest ONIAS III.
175–164	ANTIOCHUS IV (EPIPHANES). ONIAS deposed and replaced by his Hellenophile brother JASON.
172	JASON expelled from office in favour of MENELAUS, Hellenizing High Priest from 172–162 B.C.
171	ONIAS III murdered at the instigation of MENELAUS. Forced Hellenization.

169	ANTIOCHUS led by MENELAUS profaned and plundered the Temple of Jerusalem.
168	ANTIOCHUS thwarted by the Romans in his second campaign against Egypt.
167	Persecution of those Jews who opposed the unification of the Seleucid Empire on the basis of Greek culture and religion. Official abolition of Jewish religion and practice under threat of death. The Temple transformed into a sanctuary of Olympian Zeus.
166	Rising of the Maccabees supported by all the traditional parties under the leadership of JUDAS MACCABEE.
164	Truce. Cleansing of the Temple, still held by MENELAUS.
162–150	DEMETRIUS I. MENELAUS executed by the Syrians. ALCIMUS appointed High Priest by the king.
160	JUDAS killed in battle. JONATHAN assumed leadership of the rebels (160–152 B.C.).
159	ALCIMUS, the last Hellenizing High Priest, died of a stroke. End of Syrian military intervention.
152–145	ALEXANDER BALAS usurped the Seleucid throne and appointed JONATHAN High Priest (152–143 B.C.).
145–142	ANTIOCHUS VI, son of ALEXANDER, raised to the throne by TRYPHON, his father's general. JONATHAN named governor of Syria. SIMON, his brother, made military governor of the Palestinian littoral.
143	JONATHAN arrested by TRYPHON.
143–134	SIMON High Priest and ethnarch.
142	JONATHAN executed in prison.
140	SIMON's titles confirmed as hereditary. Foundation of the Maccabean, or Hasmonean, dynasty.
134	SIMON murdered by his son-in-law.
134–104	JOHN HYRCANUS I High Priest and ethnarch. Opposed by the Pharisees.
104–103	ARISTOBULUS I High Priest and king.
103–76	ALEXANDER JANNAEUS High Priest, king, and conqueror. Resisted by the Pharisees.
76–67	ALEXANDRA, widow of JANNAEUS, queen. Friend of the Pharisees. HYRCANUS II High Priest.

67	HYRCANUS II king and High Priest. Deposed by his brother ARISTOBULUS.
67–63	ARISTOBULUS II king and High Priest. Taken prisoner by POMPEY in 63 B.C. after the fall of Jerusalem. Judaea became a Roman province.
63–40	HYRCANUS II reinstated as High Priest without the royal title.
40–37	ANTIGONUS, son of ARISTOBULUS II, occupied the throne and pontificate with Parthian support. HYRCANUS maimed and exiled.
37–4	HEROD THE GREAT. End of Hasmonean dynasty. HYRCANUS executed in 30 B.C.
27–A.D. 14	AUGUSTUS emperor.
6 B.C. (?)	Birth of JESUS OF NAZARETH.
4 B.C.–A.D. 6	ARCHELAUS ethnarch of Judaea and Samaria.

A.D.

14–37	TIBERIUS emperor.
26–36	PONTIUS PILATE prefect of Judaea.
27–30 (?)	Ministry and crucifixion of JESUS.
66–70	First Jewish War ending with the capture of Jerusalem and the destruction of the Temple by TITUS.

These then are the persons, events, and dates which the experts have had to bear in mind when assessing the origins of the sect and, more particularly, the time of the ministry of the Teacher of Righteousness. In the main, they have tended to advance three theories. The first, supported by H. H. Rowley, I. Rabinowitz, H. Bardtke, M. Black, and others, recognizes that the occurrences alluded to in the Scrolls took place in the era of the Hellenistic crisis, i.e., during the reigns of Antiochus Epiphanes and Demetrius I (c. 175–160 B.C.). The second is the Maccabean theory proposed by the present writer and adopted with certain modifications by J. T. Milik, F. M. Cross, P. Winter, E. F. Sutcliffe, R. de Vaux, G. Jeremias, etc.; this identifies the Wicked Priest with Jonathan and/or Simon. The third theory inclines to the period of the later Hasmoneans (134–40 B.C.), with marked preference for the reign of either Alexander Jannaeus (M. Delcor, H. M. Segal,

J. M. Allegro, F. F. Bruce, and others) or Hyrcanus II (A. Dupont-Sommer, K. Elliger).

Whichever of these three periods is adopted, and each holds some degree of probability, the life and ministry of the Teacher of Righteousness will fall between the years 175 and 63 B.C. Doubtless, the fact that the few personalities mentioned by name in two of the Scroll fragments lived during the same period brings added support to this general conclusion. Antiochus (most likely Epiphanes) and Demetrius (probably Demetrius III, contemporary of Alexander Jannaeus) figure in the Commentary on Nahum, and we are informed that in an as yet unpublished religious calendar occasional reference is made to historical persons, among them Queen Alexandra, Hyrcanus (I or II), and Aemilius (Scaurus, Pompey's general).

If our only purpose were to place the sect and its doctrine within the larger frame of the historical evolution of Palestinian institutions and Jewish religious thought, the most prudent move would be to rest content with the wider limits of the century and a quarter covered by all three of the theories just mentioned. Like this there would be little danger of grave miscalculation. But the subject is of such interest and importance that it urges the student to attempt the risky task of placing events and personalities more exactly. This is bound to lead some distance into the realm of conjecture, and in presenting my own interpretation I must make it plain that it in no way pretends to be infallible, but is only, as it seems to me, the least unsatisfactory explanation among many others.

HISTORICAL ALLUSIONS

The concealed references to the Teacher of Righteousness and the history of his followers are scattered throughout the first section of the Damascus Rule and the biblical Commentaries. As a first move it is important to collect them into a coherent whole.

Damascus Rule. The founder members of the Community

were chosen by God in the 'age of wrath', 390 years after the destruction of the Temple by Nebuchadnezzar. They repented, and for twenty years went 'groping for the way'. God then raised up for them the Teacher of Righteousness 'to guide them in the way of His heart' (I). The Teacher and his disciples encountered opposition and hostility. Their adversaries, called seekers of 'smooth things' (I), 'removers of the bound' (v), and 'builders of the wall' (IV, VIII), were led astray by the 'Scoffer' (I), the 'Spouter of Lies' (VIII), the 'Liar' (B I), and embraced false doctrine concerning the laws of purity and impurity, justice and ungodliness, and the Temple ritual (v); they were lovers of wealth (VIII) and stirred up civil strife (I). The despised and persecuted Priests and Levites of the Community abandoned the Temple of Jerusalem together with the faithful Israelites (IV, VI; B II) and entered a 'New Covenant' in 'the land of Damascus' (VI). They were forbidden to rejoin the Jewish people, who continued to be governed and misled by the new masters of Jerusalem and its sanctuary even after the death of the Teacher of Righteousness (B II). Although God's anger was kindled against them (I) and the 'Chief of the Kings of Greece' came 'to wreak vengeance upon them' (VIII), they persisted in their evil ways. Their rule would be brought to an end by the 'Sceptre', the 'Prince of the whole Congregation', i.e., by the King-Messiah (VII).

The somewhat vague image emerging from this analysis of the Damascus Rule is brought into sharper focus when set beside the information provided by the Habakkuk Commentary. This work is not concerned with the earliest stages of the sect's history, but with the struggle of the Teacher of Righteousness against his principal opponent and with the future destiny of the sect's enemies.

Commentary on Habakkuk. Once again, the villain is described as the 'Liar', the 'Spouter of Lies', but chiefly as the 'Wicked Priest'. He was 'called by the name of truth' when he first appeared, but on becoming Israel's ruler he betrayed God for the sake of riches and defiled himself with wealth amassed by robbing the 'men of violence who rebelled against God' and the 'peoples' (VIII). He led many astray in order to 'build his city of vanity with blood and raise a congregation on deceit' (X). He defiled Jerusalem and the Temple (XII). He 'plotted to destroy the Poor (the Community)' (XII), sinned against the Teacher of Righteousness and his disciples (IX), chastised him whilst the 'House of Absalom' was silent (V), 'pursued the Teacher of Righteousness to the house of his exile', and appeared before the Community on their Day of Atonement 'to confuse them, and to cause them to stumble' (XI); and he 'robbed the Poor of their possessions' (XII). But God punished him by delivering him 'into the hand of his enemies' so that he should be humbled by a 'destroying scourge, in bitterness of soul'; and they 'took vengeance upon his body of flesh' (IX). His successors, 'the last Priests of Jerusalem', continued to 'amass money and wealth', but finally all their possessions would be seized by the Kittim, the 'remnant of the peoples' (IX). At the time of Judgement, the Wicked Priest would have to drink 'the cup of the wrath of God' (XI) and would suffer punishment 'with fire of brimstone' (X).

Commentary on Psalm 37. Again, it is said that the Wicked Priest sought to lay hands on the Teacher. In chastisement for this deed God delivered him 'into the hands of the violent of the nations' (I).

Messianic Anthology. A new and rather important detail may be deduced from the extract of the Psalms of Joshua, quoted at the end of the Messianic Anthology, mentioning the misdeeds of 'two instruments of violence', clearly two brothers, who rebuilt and fortified Jerusalem, committed abominations, spilt blood, and destroyed their neighbours. That this text follows a series of Messianic passages from the Bible indicates that the two men were thought to have played a part of major significance as the chief enemies of the Community from which the Messiahs were to arise.

Commentary of Nahum. Although it makes no allusion to the Teacher, this Commentary contributes a point of great historical interest in identifying the 'lion's den' with Jerusalem, into which 'Demetrius king of Greece' tried to enter 'on the counsel of those who seek smooth things'. He failed: the kings of Greece were unable to take the city 'from the time of Antiochus until the coming of the rulers of the Kittim'. The sovereign of Jerusalem, 'the furious young lion', then took revenge on 'the seekers of smooth things' and crucified them, thereby adopting a form of execution unknown to the Jewish Law.

War Rule. It appears from this work that the sect expected to remain in 'exile' until the Messianic war, and then to reoccupy Jerusalem and conquer the world by defeating all the Gentiles, including the king of the Kittim, the lords of the universe.

DECIPHERMENT

The next step is to establish some measure of correlation between the enigmatic story told in the Scrolls and Jewish history itself.

It is my belief that the ministry of the Teacher of Righteousness took place during the historical period dominated by the two Maccabee brothers, Jonathan and Simon, and that the person described as the sect's principal opponent was the younger brother, Jonathan. Projected against this background, the various innuendoes in the Scrolls seem to acquire a greater significance and intelligibility than when placed within any other historical setting. To illustrate the point, I will first examine the oblique references to events which, in addition to their importance to the Community, were of interest to the Jewish nation as a whole. I refer to the 'age of wrath' 390 years after Nebuchadnezzar, and to the career of the Wicked Priest who ruled Israel.

390 years. In the Damascus Rule, as will be recalled, the 'age of wrath' 390 years after the overthrow of Jerusalem by the Babylonians (587 B.C.) is given as the period in which the sect was founded. Scholars agree almost unanimously that the date thus obtained (197 B.C.) should not be taken literally. Some of them – with no cogent reason – maintain that the figure is purely symbolical; others argue with greater probability that it may be approximately right, and that the author of the Damascus Rule had in mind an eventful epoch during the first half of the second century B.C. Their caution is due to the fact that no ancient Jewish historian was correctly informed of the duration of the Persian period. For example, Demetrius, a Jew living in Alexandria at the end of the third century B.C., reckoned 338 years and three months from the deportation of the Jews by Nebuchadnezzar (587 B.C.) to the accession of Ptolemy IV (221 B.C.), whereas the actual lapse of time was 366 years. Allowing for a similar misreckoning of from twenty to thirty years in the Damascus Rule, '390 years' would point to the time of the accession of Antiochus Epiphanes (175 B.C.) and the Hellenistic crisis, an age well suited to be dubbed an 'age of wrath'. As a matter of fact, even some of those scholars who ascribe only a figurative value to '390 years' have come to date the foundation of the Community in the same period, on the ground that in all historical probability the founders of the sect were drawn from the religious group called Hasidim or Pious Ones which, according to I Maccabees ii, was formed during the reign of Antiochus Epiphanes.

These Hasidim, representing conservative Judaism, strongly opposed the infiltration of Greek culture. When Hellenization became official policy under the pressure of Jason and Menelaus, and especially after the edict of Antiochus forbidding the observance of the Jewish religion, many of them, 'zealous for righteousness and the Law', flocked into the desert to escape defilement (I Macc. ii, 29–30). At first, their rigid adherence to the Law caused them even to refuse to defend their lives on the Sabbath day when attacked by the pro-Greek faction, but later they joined forces with the Maccabees. Nevertheless, their participation in the rebellion (I Macc. ii, 42) resulted from necessity rather than from whole-hearted approval of the conduct and views of the leaders of the insurrection, and in fact the Hasidim parted company from the Maccabees as soon as Alcimus was promoted High Priest in 162 B.C. after the execution of Menelaus. They were ready to recognize this son of Aaron as pontiff, but for reasons of which we are unaware, their trust was deceived and he put sixty of them to death (1 Macc. vii, 13–16). Compromised with the Maccabees and betrayed by Alcimus, they no doubt returned to the desert to grope their way there 'like blind men' until the appearance of the priestly Teacher of Righteousness.

In short, the '390 years' lead to the opening decades of the second century B.C., when the Hellenistic crisis came to a head and gave rise, in an 'age of wrath', to the foundation of the religious party of the Hasidim. From their known history it is safe to assume that they constituted the nucleus of the Teacher's first disciples and, as appears from the Scrolls, they must have included a strong priestly element firmly attached to the Zadokite pontifical dynasty which held supreme power in the Temple of Jerusalem from the time of Solomon to that of Antiochus Epiphanes.

The Wicked Priest. The Teacher of Righteousness made his appearance twenty years after the sect was founded: that is, if our chronology is acceptable, in about 155 B.C. By that time the war against the Seleucids had ended. The pontifical throne had been unoccupied since the death of Alcimus in 159 B.C. and the nation was governed by Jonathan, who continued to cleanse the country of all traces of Hellenism. But in 152 B.C. he was promoted High Priest by Alexander Balas, the usurper of the Seleucid throne, and accepted this appointment despite the fact that he was neither of pontifical descent nor took any real interest in matters of religion. He was by nature more suited to be a soldier or a political organizer than a High Priest.

To the Teacher of Righteousness and his followers Jonathan's claims were worthless and his behaviour objectionable. He was the Wicked Priest who was 'called by the name of truth' (cHab VIII), i.e., who was a true disciple of Moses, before he assumed the offices of High Priest and ruler; but when he came to power he betrayed God for the sake of the riches amassed by plundering both Hellenophile Jews – the 'men of violence who rebelled against God' (CHAB VIII) – and the neighbouring Gentiles (cf. 1 Macc. xii, 24–34). With Simon, the other 'instrument of violence' (MA), he took it on himself to fortify Jerusalem and build strongholds throughout Judaea (cf. 1 Macc. xii, 35–8).

The Teacher's opposition was resented, and eventually eliminated. He went to live in 'the house of his exile' (CHAB XI), perhaps at Qumran, and there the Wicked Priest visited him, though it is impossible to tell with certainty what happened on that famous occasion. The author of the Commentary on Habakkuk (v) reproaches the 'House of Absalom', a family which played an important part during the rule of Jonathan and Simon (cf. 1 Macc. xi, 70; xiii, 11), for not having intervened on the Teacher's behalf. On the other hand, we are told that the Wicked Priest was punished by his foreign enemies who took 'vengeance upon his body of flesh' (CHAB IX; cf. CPS 37). If my interpretation is correct, the person who carried out this act of revenge was the 'Chief of the Kings of Greece' (DR VIII).

These allusions refer to Jonathan's arrest by Tryphon, a general of Alexander Balas and Antiochus VI, who finally proclaimed himself king and dominated the Seleucid scene for about ten years. 1 Maccabees xii, 39–48 relates how Tryphon trapped Jonathan in Ptolemais in 143 B.C. after massacring his escort of one thousand men. In the following year, Jonathan was put to death by his captor (1 Macc. xiii, 23).

The 'last Priests of Jerusalem' and the 'young lion'. The death of the Wicked Priest did not mark the end of the domination of Israel by other Priests who continued to lead the nation astray. They – the 'last Priests of Jerusalem' (CHAB IX; CNah) – incurred the same guilt as the Wicked Priest. They are said to have amassed 'money and wealth by plundering the peoples', and accusations of having taught false doctrine (DR) and of having adopted the Gentile calendar (CHos) no doubt refer to them, as well as the reproach for cruelty (CNah); but they are never mentioned in connexion with the Community. Their punishment was to be executed on them by the Kittim (CHab, IX; CNah).

In effect, from John Hyrcanus to Aristobulus II, the policy of Simon's successors, the Hasmonean rulers, was one of conquest and plunder at the expense of the neighbouring countries of Transjordan, Samaria, Idumea, Iturea, etc. Aristobulus II was even accused of piracy on the seas. One of these 'last Priests of Jerusalem', Alexander Jannaeus, is no doubt the villain of the Commentary on Nahum, the 'furious young lion' who crucified as an act of revenge the 'seekers of smooth things' who had called in 'Demetrius king of Greece'. The historian Josephus relates that in 88 B.C. the Pharisees encouraged the Seleucid king, Demetrius III, to invade Judaea. He was, however, unable to exploit his initial victory over Jannaeus, and when he had returned to Syria Jannaeus ordered eight hundred Pharisees to be executed.*

The 'Kittim'. The rule of the 'last Priests of Jerusalem' will end, according to the Commentary on Habakkuk, with the triumph of the invincible Kittim. These 'quick and valiant' warriors who came from distant shores and inspired 'all the nations with fear and dread', whose 'commanders' (not kings) laid waste the earth, and who sacrificed 'to their standards' (*signa*), were the Roman legions. Under the leadership of Licinius Lucullus and Pompey, they conquered between 69 and 63 B.C. the powerful states of Pontus, Armenia, the Seleucid Empire, and finally the Jewish kingdom. In 63 B.C., Pompey himself entered Jerusalem and deprived the Hasmonean dynasty of its royal title.

*

The texts at present available do not allow us to probe any further into the history of the Community. It is clear that

* It may be inferred from CNah II-IV that at this stage of the sect's history the 'seekers of smooth things' and 'Ephraim' were, in fact, the Pharisees, and that 'Manasseh' was a nickname for the Sadducees.

the sectaries' interest in political events was limited to the formative period of their society, and the absence in their literature of all reference to later happenings obliges us to rely for their subsequent history on archaeological evidence. We know from this that the Qumran centre continued to flourish, with possibly an interruption of about thirty years, until the first Jewish revolt against Rome. And from the accounts of the Essenes and Therapeutae written by Josephus and Philo we learn that the sect became a widespread and highly respected religious movement, not only in Palestine but also in Syria and Egypt. However, the great crisis of the war against Rome, in which some of its members may have actively participated, dealt a fatal blow to the Community. Its settlements must have been ruined, and its occupants dispersed. The survivors either rejoined the remnant of Palestinian Jewry, or were assimilated into Judeo-Christian sects, or entered the great Church proper.

In this reconstruction of the history of the sect, a modified version of the theory which I launched several years ago, most of the allusions contained in the Scrolls have been given concrete meaning. The founder members of the group have been identified with the Hasidim, the Wicked Priest with Jonathan, the two 'instruments of violence' with Jonathan and Simon, the enemy of the Wicked Priest with Tryphon, the 'last Priests of Jerusalem' with the later Hasmonean rulers, the 'young lion' with Alexander Jannaeus, and the 'Kittim' with the Romans. Yet there are still two important lacunae in this synthesis: the significance of the 'Damascus' exile, and above all the identity of the Teacher of Righteousness.

The 'land of Damascus'. Three theories have so far been advanced: (1) The 'land of Damascus' is to be understood in its proper geographical sense, i.e., some early members of the sect migrated from Judaea to the north. (2) 'Damascus' is a symbolical name for Qumran. (3) The Community settled at Qumran, but the area was under the domination of the Nabatean kings who also ruled over Damascus, i.e.,

Qumran was in the 'land of Damascus'. It is impossible to solve this dilemma. Nevertheless, we may assume that if, as in the first hypothesis, there were settlements in the Damascus area (or northern Transjordan?), they must have maintained contact with the Qumran centre since early copies of the Damascus Rule were kept in the Qumran library.

The Teacher of Righteousness. Turning to the identity of the Teacher, we are confronted with a mystery. Several suggestions have, of course, been proposed, and the Teacher has been identified with various historical characters of the second and first centuries B.C.: the High Priest Onias III, for example, murdered in 171 B.C.; the Priest Jose ben Joezer, said to have been executed in 162 B.C.; Eleazar the Pharisee, an opponent of John Hyrcanus; the Essene Judas mentioned by Josephus as a diviner during the reign of Aristobulus I; Onias the Just, a wonder-worker stoned to death in 65 B.C., etc. Yet none of these suggestions is entirely satisfactory. The dearth of concrete detail in the Scrolls in connexion with the Teacher's life, and the complete lack of information about the opposition to the Maccabees in accounts written by their sympathizers, makes it at present impossible to identify the great prophet of the Community. We know only that he was a Priest, that he began his ministry in about 155 B.C., that he openly opposed the Wicked Priest and was scorned, persecuted, and exiled. Several scholars assert that he was killed during the course of a persecution commanded by the Wicked Priest, but none of the texts justify anything so categorical. Indeed, from the expressions used in the Damascus Rule and the Commentaries on Habakkuk and Psalm 37, it might be inferred that the Teacher escaped a violent end. For the moment the question of both the manner and the date of his death must be left open.

Though several experts see in him the author of certain of the Scrolls, the Community Rule for instance, and some of the Hymns, this theory is not supported by any definite evidence. As a person the Teacher remains anonymous and appears only through the writings inspired by him, and through the role which his followers attributed to him as builder of the Community, guide to truth and knowledge, and discoverer of the mysteries of God. We know him through the faith of his disciples whose attitude to him may perhaps best be expressed by quoting the Scrolls:

'All those ... who have listened to the voice of the Teacher of Righteousness and have not despised the precepts of righteousness when they heard them, they shall rejoice and their hearts shall be strong ... God will forgive them and they shall see His salvation because they took refuge in His holy Name' (DR B II).

'*The righteous shall live by his faith.* Interpreted, this concerns all those who observe the Law in the House of Judah, whom God will deliver from the House of Judgement because of their suffering and because of their faith in the Teacher of Righteousness' (CHab VIII).

NOTE ON THE TEXTS

TRANSLATORS of the Scrolls are tempted to render them either with extreme freedom at the expense of fidelity, or else literally, word for word and line for line. I have tried to avoid both these pitfalls by providing an interpretation in simple English which is at the same time faithful and intelligible.

Lacunae impossible to complete with any measure of confidence are indicated by dots.

Hypothetical but likely reconstructions are placed between [   ] and glosses necessary for fluency between (   ).

Biblical quotations appearing in the text are printed in italics, as well as the titles and headings which figure in the manuscripts.

Each scroll is divided into columns. The beginning of each of these columns is indicated in the translation by bold Roman numerals: **I, II, III** etc.

I have included only those fragments which are large enough to convey some meaning and have similarly omitted from the Scrolls any passage too mutilated to reconstruct.

· 4 ·

THE COMMUNITY RULE

DISCOVERED in cave I, the eleven relatively well preserved columns of this manuscript were first published in 1951 by M. Burrows under the title, *The Manual of Discipline* (The Dead Sea Scrolls of St Mark's Monastery II, New Haven). Important fragments of eleven other manuscripts of the Rule containing a certain number of variant readings were also found in caves IV and V. A list of these has been drawn up by J. T. Milik (*Revue Biblique*, 1960, pp. 412–15) and some of them have been adopted in the present translation.

The principal manuscript bears the stamp of editorial modification. For instance, in column X the original 'I will *conceal* knowledge with discretion' is corrected to 'I will *impart* knowledge with discretion'. The section covered by columns VIII–IX was particularly subject to alteration and is considerably abridged in one of the fragmentary manuscripts.

The Community Rule is probably one of the oldest documents of the sect; its original composition may date from the latter part of the second century B.C. It seems to have been intended for the Community's teachers, for its Masters or Guardians, and contains extracts from liturgical ceremonies, an outline of a model sermon on the spirits of truth and falsehood, statutes concerned with initiation into the sect and with its common life, organization and discipline, a penal code, and finally a poetic dissertation on the fundamental religious duties of the Master and his disciples, and on the sacred seasons proper to the Community.

There are, to my knowledge, no writings in ancient Jewish sources parallel to the Community Rule, but a similar type of literature flourished among Christians between the second and fourth centuries, the so-called 'Church Orders' represented by the Didache, the Didascalia, the Apostolic Constitution, etc.

The contents may be divided into three main sections, but further sub-headings appear in the text itself:

71

1. Entry into the Covenant, followed by an instruction on the two spirits (I–IV).

2. Statutes relating to the Council of the Community (V–IX).

3. Directives addressed to the Master, and the Master's Hymn (IX–XI).

I [The Master shall teach the sai]nts to live [according to] the Book of the Community Rule, that they may seek God with a whole heart and soul, and do what is good and right before Him as He commanded by the hand of Moses and all His servants the Prophets; that they may love all that He has chosen and hate all that He has rejected; that they may abstain from all evil and hold fast to all good; that they may practise truth, righteousness, and justice upon earth and no longer stubbornly follow a sinful heart and lustful eyes committing all manner of evil. He shall admit into the Covenant of Grace all those who have freely devoted themselves to the observance of God's precepts, that they may be joined to the counsel of God and may live perfectly before Him in accordance with all that has been revealed concerning their appointed times, and that they may love all the sons of light, each according to his lot in God's design, and hate all the sons of darkness, each according to his guilt in God's vengeance.

All those who freely devote themselves to His truth shall bring all their knowledge, powers, and possessions into the Community of God, that they may purify their knowledge in the truth of God's precepts and order their powers according to His ways of perfection and all their possessions according to His righteous counsel. They shall not depart from any command of God concerning their times; they shall be neither early nor late for any of their appointed times, they shall stray neither to right nor to left of any of His true precepts. All those who embrace the Community Rule shall enter into the Covenant before God to obey all His commandments so that they may not abandon Him during the dominion of Satan because of fear or terror or affliction.

On entering the Covenant, the Priests and Levites shall

bless the God of salvation and all His faithfulness, and all those entering the Covenant shall say after them, 'Amen, Amen!'

Then the Priests shall recite the favours of God manifested in His mighty deeds and shall declare all His merciful grace to Israel, and the Levites shall recite the iniquities of the children of Israel, all their guilty rebellions and sins during the dominion of Satan. And after them, all those entering the Covenant shall confess and say: 'We have strayed! We have [disobeyed!] We and our fathers before us have sinned and done wickedly in walking [counter to the precepts] of truth and righteousness. [And God has] judged us and our fathers also; **II** but He has bestowed His bountiful mercy on us from everlasting to everlasting.' And the Priests shall bless all the men of the lot of God who walk perfectly in all His ways, saying: 'May He bless you with all good and preserve you from all evil! May He lighten your heart with life-giving wisdom and grant you eternal knowledge! May He raise His merciful face towards you for everlasting bliss!'

And the Levites shall curse all the men of the lot of Satan, saying: 'Be cursed because of all your guilty wickedness! May He deliver you up for torture at the hands of the vengeful Avengers! May He visit you with destruction by the hand of all the Wreakers of Revenge! Be cursed without mercy because of the darkness of your deeds! Be damned in the shadowy place of everlasting fire! May God not heed when you call on Him, nor pardon you by blotting out your sin! May He raise His angry face towards you for vengeance! May there be no "Peace" for you in the mouth of those who hold fast to the Fathers!' And after the blessing and the cursing, all those entering the Covenant shall say, 'Amen, Amen!'

And the Priests and Levites shall continue, saying: 'Cursed be the man who enters this Covenant while walking among the idols of his heart, who sets up before himself his stumbling-block of sin so that he may backslide! Hearing

73

the words of this Covenant, he blesses himself in his heart and says, "Peace be with me, even though I walk in the stubbornness of my heart" (Deut. xxix, 18–19), whereas his spirit, parched (for lack of truth) and watered (with lies), shall be destroyed without pardon. God's wrath and His zeal for His precepts shall consume him in everlasting destruction. All the curses of the Covenant shall cling to him and God will set him apart for evil. He shall be cut off from the midst of all the sons of light, and because he has turned aside from God on account of his idols and his stumbling-block of sin, his lot shall be among those who are cursed for ever.' And after them, all those entering the Covenant shall answer and say, 'Amen, Amen!'

Thus shall they do, year by year, for as long as the dominion of Satan endures. The Priests shall enter first, ranked one after another according to the perfection of their spirit; then the Levites; and thirdly, all the people one after another, in their Thousands, Hundreds, Fifties, and Tens, that every Israelite may know his place in the Community of God according to the everlasting design. No man shall move down from his place nor move up from his allotted position. For according to the holy design, they shall all of them be in a Community of truth and virtuous humility, of loving kindness and good intent one towards the other, and (they shall all of them be) sons of the everlasting Company.

No man [shall be in the] Community of His truth who refuses to enter [the Covenant of] God so that he may walk in the stubborness of his heart, for **III** his soul detests the wise teaching of just laws. He shall not be counted among the upright for he has not persisted in the conversion of his life. His knowledge, powers, and possessions shall not enter the Council of the Community, for whoever ploughs the mud of wickedness returns defiled(?). He shall not be justified by that which his stubborn heart declares lawful, for seeking the ways of light he looks towards darkness. He shall not be reckoned among the perfect; he shall neither be purified by atonement, nor cleansed by purifying waters, nor sanctified by seas and rivers, nor washed clean with any ablution. Unclean, unclean shall he be. For as long as he despises the precepts of God he shall receive no instruction in the Community of His counsel.

For it is through the spirit of true counsel concerning the ways of man that all his sins shall be expiated that he may contemplate the light of life. He shall be cleansed from all his sins by the spirit of holiness uniting him to His truth, and his iniquity shall be expiated by the spirit of uprightness and humility. And when his flesh is sprinkled with purifying water and sanctified by cleansing water, it shall be made clean by the humble submission of his soul to all the precepts of God. Let him then order his steps to walk perfectly in all the ways commanded by God concerning the times appointed for him, straying neither to right nor to left and transgressing none of His words, and he shall be accepted by virtue of pleasing atonement before God and it shall be to him a Covenant of the everlasting Community.

The Master shall instruct all the sons of light and shall teach them the nature of all the children of men according to the kind of spirit which they possess, the signs identifying their works during their lifetime, their visitation for chastisement, and the time of their reward.

From the God of Knowledge comes all that is and shall be. Before ever they existed He established their whole design, and when, as ordained for them, they come into being, it is in accord with His glorious design that they accomplish their task without change. The laws of all things are in His hand and He provides them with all their needs.

He has created man to govern the world, and has appointed for him two spirits in which to walk until the time of His visitation: the spirits of truth and falsehood. Those born of truth spring from a fountain of light, but those born of falsehood spring from a source of darkness. All the children of righteousness are ruled by the Prince of Light and walk in the ways of light, but all the children of falsehood are ruled by the Angel of Darkness and walk in the ways of darkness.

The Angel of Darkness leads all the children of righteousness astray, and until his end, all their sin, iniquities, wickedness, and all their unlawful deeds are caused by his dominion in accordance with the mysteries of God. Every one of their chastisements, and every one of the seasons of their distress, shall be brought about by the rule of his persecution; for all his allotted spirits seek the overthrow of the sons of light.

But the God of Israel and His Angel of Truth will succour all the sons of light. For it is He who created the spirits of Light and Darkness and founded every action upon them and established every deed [upon] their [ways]. And He loves the one **IV** everlastingly and delights in its works for ever; but the counsel of the other He loathes and for ever hates its ways.

These are their ways in the world for the enlightenment of the heart of man, and that all the paths of true righteousness may be made straight before him, and that fear of the laws of God may be instilled in his heart: a spirit of humility, patience, abundant charity, unending goodness, understanding, and intelligence; (a spirit of) mighty wisdom which trusts in all the deeds of God and leans on His great lovingkindness; a spirit of discernment in every purpose, of zeal for just laws, of holy intent with steadfastness of heart, of great charity towards all the sons of truth, of admirable purity which detests all unclean idols, of humble conduct sprung from an understanding of all things, and of faithful concealment of the mysteries of truth. These are the counsels of the spirit to the sons of truth in this world.

And as for the visitation of all who walk in this spirit, it shall be healing, great peace in a long life, and fruitfulness, together with every everlasting blessing and eternal joy in life without end, a crown of glory and a garment of majesty in unending light.

But the ways of the spirit of falsehood are these: greed, and slackness in the search for righteousness, wickedness and lies, haughtiness and pride, falseness and deceit, cruelty and abundant evil-ill-temper and much folly and brazen insolence, abominable deeds (committed) in a spirit of lust, and ways of lewdness in the service of uncleanness, a blaspheming tongue, blindness of eye and dullness of ear, stiffness of neck and heaviness of heart, so that man walks in all the ways of darkness and guile.

And the visitation of all who walk in this spirit shall be a multitude of plagues by the hand of all the destroying angels, everlasting damnation by the avenging wrath of the fury of God, eternal torment and endless disgrace together with shameful extinction in the fire of the dark regions. The times of all their generations shall be spent in sorrowful mourning and in bitter misery and in calamities of darkness until they are destroyed without remnant or survivor.

The nature of all the children of men is ruled by these (two spirits), and during their life all the hosts of men have a portion in their divisions and walk in (both) their ways. And the whole reward for their deeds shall be, for everlasting ages, according to whether each man's portion in their two divisions is great or small. For God has established the spirits in equal measure until the final age, and has set everlasting hatred between their divisions. Truth abhors the works of falsehood, and falsehood hates all the ways of truth. And their struggle is fierce in all their arguments for they do not walk together.

But in the mysteries of His understanding, and in His glorious wisdom, God has ordained an end for falsehood, and at the time of the visitation He will destroy it for ever. Then truth, which has wallowed in the ways of wickedness during the dominion of falsehood until the appointed time of judgement, shall arise in the world for ever. God will then purify every deed of Man with his truth; He will refine for Himself the human frame by rooting out all spirit of falsehood from the bounds of his flesh. He will cleanse him of all wicked deeds with the spirit of holiness; like purifying waters He will shed upon him the spirit of truth (to cleanse him) of all abomination and falsehood. And he shall be plunged into the spirit of purification that he may instruct the upright in the knowledge of the Most High and teach the wisdom of the sons of heaven to the perfect of way. For God has chosen them for an everlasting Covenant and all the glory of Adam shall be theirs. There shall be no more lies and all the works of falsehood shall be put to shame.

Until now the spirits of truth and falsehood struggle in the hearts of men and they walk in both wisdom and folly. According to his portion of truth so does a man hate falsehood, and according to his inheritance in the realm of falsehood so is he wicked and so hates truth. For God has established the two spirits in equal measure until the determined end, and until the Renewal, and He knows the reward of their deeds from all eternity. He has allotted them to the children of men that they may know good [and evil, and] that the destiny of all the living may be according to the spirit within [them at the time] of the visitation.

V *And this is the Rule for the men of the Community who have freely pledged themselves to be converted from all evil and to cling to all His commandments according to His will*

They shall separate from the congregation of the men of falsehood and shall unite, with respect to the Law and possessions, under the authority of the sons of Zadok, the Priests who keep the Covenant, and of the multitude of the men of the Community who hold fast to the Covenant. Every decision concerning doctrine, property, and justice shall be determined by them.

They shall practise truth and humility in common, and justice and uprightness and charity and modesty in all their ways. No man shall walk in the stubbornness of his heart so that he strays after his heart and eyes and evil inclination, but he shall circumcise in the Community the foreskin of evil inclination and of stiffness of neck that they may lay a foundation of truth for Israel, for the Community of the everlasting Covenant. They shall atone for all those in Aaron who have freely pledged themselves to holiness, and for those in Israel who have freely pledged themselves to the House of Truth, and for those who join them to live in community and to take part in the trial and judgement and condemnation of all those who transgress the precepts.

On joining the Community, this shall be their code of behaviour with respect to all these precepts.

Whoever approaches the Council of the Community shall enter the Covenant of God in the presence of all who have freely pledged themselves. He shall undertake by a binding oath to return with all his heart and soul to every commandment of the Law of Moses in accordance with all that has been revealed of it to the sons of Zadok, the Keepers of the Covenant and Seekers of His will, and to the multitude of the men of their Covenant who together have freely pledged themselves to His truth and to walking in the way of His delight. And he shall undertake by the Covenant to separate from all the men of falsehood who walk in the way of wickedness.

For they are not reckoned in His Covenant. They have neither inquired nor sought after Him concerning His laws that they might know the hidden things in which they have sinfully erred; and matters revealed they have treated with insolence. Therefore Wrath shall rise up to condemn, and Vengeance shall be executed by the curses of the Covenant, and great chastisements of eternal destruction shall be visited on them, leaving no remnant. They shall not enter the water to partake of the pure Meal of the saints, for they shall not be cleansed unless they turn from their wickedness: for all who transgress His word are unclean. Likewise, no man shall consort with him with regard to his work or property lest he be burdened with the guilt of his sin. He shall indeed keep away from him in all things; as it is written, *Keep away from all that is false* (Exod. xxiii, 7). No member of the Community shall follow them in matters of doctrine and justice, or eat or drink anything of theirs, or take anything from them except for a price; as it is written, *Keep away from the man in whose nostrils is breath, for wherein is he counted?* (Isa, ii, 22). For all those not reckoned in His Covenant are to be set apart, together with all that is theirs. None of the saints shall lean upon works of vanity: for they are all vanity who know not His Covenant, and He will blot from the earth all them that despise His word. All their deeds are defilement before Him, and all their possessions unclean.

But when a man enters the Covenant to walk according to all these precepts that he may join the holy congregation, they shall examine his spirit in community with respect to his understanding and practice of the Law, under the authority of the sons of Aaron who have freely pledged themselves in the Community to restore His Covenant and to heed all the precepts commanded by Him, and of the multitude of Israel who have freely pledged themselves in the Community to return to His Covenant. They shall inscribe them in the order, one after another, according to their understanding and their deeds, that every one may obey his companion, the man of lesser rank obeying his superior. And they shall examine their spirit and deeds yearly, so that each man may be advanced in accordance with his understanding and perfection of way, or moved down in accordance with the offences committed by him.

They shall rebuke one another in truth, humility, and charity. Let no man address his companion with anger, or ill-temper, or obduracy, or with envy prompted by the spirit of wickedness. Let him not hate him [because of his uncircumcised] heart, but let him rebuke him on the very same day lest **VI** he incur guilt because of him. And furthermore, let no man accuse his companion before the Congregation without having first admonished him in the presence of witnesses.

These are the ways in which all of them shall walk, each man with his companion, wherever they dwell.

The man of lesser rank shall obey the greater in matters of work and money. .

They shall eat in common and pray in common and deliberate in common.

Wherever there are ten men of the Council of the Community there shall not lack a Priest among them. And they shall all sit before him according to their rank and shall be asked their counsel in all things in that order. And when the table has been prepared for eating, and the new wine for drinking, the Priest shall be the first to stretch out his hand to bless the first-fruits of the bread and new wine.

And where the ten are, there shall never lack a man among them who shall study the Law continually, day and night, concerning the right conduct of a man with his companion. And the Congregation shall watch in community for a third of every night of the year, to read the Book and to study Law and to pray together.

This is the Rule for an Assembly of the Congregation

Each man shall sit in his place: the Priests shall sit first, and the elders second, and all the rest of the people according to their rank. And thus shall they be questioned concerning the Law, and concerning any counsel or matter coming before the Congregation, each man bringing his knowledge to the Council of the Community.

No man shall interrupt a companion before his speech has ended, nor speak before a man of higher rank; each man shall speak in his turn. And in an Assembly of the Congregation no man shall speak without the consent of the Congregation, nor indeed of the Guardian of the Congregation. Should any man wish to speak to the Congregation, yet not be in a position to question the Council of the Community, let him rise to his feet and say: 'I have something to say to the Congregation.' If they command him to speak, he shall speak.

Every man, born of Israel, who freely pledges himself to join the Council of the Community, shall be examined by the Guardian at the head of the Congregation concerning his understanding and his deeds. If he is fitted to the discipline, he shall admit him into the Covenant that he may be converted to the truth and depart from all falsehood; and he shall instruct him in all the rules of the Community. And later, when he comes to stand before the Congregation, they shall all deliberate his case, and according to the decision of the Council of the Congregation he shall either enter or depart. After he has entered the Council of the Community he shall not touch the pure Meal of the Congregation until one full year is completed, and until he has been examined concerning his spirit and deeds; nor shall he have any share of the property of the Congregation. Then when he has completed one year within the Community, the Congregation shall deliberate his case with regard to his understanding and observance of the Law. And if it be his destiny, according to the judgement of the Priests and the multitude of the men of their Covenant, to enter the company of the Community, his property and earnings shall be handed over to the Bursar of the Congregation who shall register it to his account and shall not spend it for the Congregation. He shall not touch the Drink of the Congregation until he has completed a second year among the men of the Community. But when the second year has passed, he shall be examined, and if it be his destiny, according to the judgement of the Congregation, to enter the Community, then he shall be inscribed among his brethren in the order of his rank for the Law, and for justice, and for the pure Meal; his property shall be merged and he shall offer his counsel and judgement to the Community.

These are the Rules by which they shall judge at a Community (Court of) Inquiry according to the cases

If one of them has lied deliberately in matters of property, he shall be excluded from the pure Meal of the Congregation for one year and shall do penance with respect to one quarter of his food.

Whoever has answered his companion with obstinacy, or has addressed him impatiently, going so far as to take no account of the dignity of his fellow by disobeying the order of a brother inscribed before him, he has taken the law into his own hand; therefore he shall do penance for one year [and shall be excluded].

If any man has uttered the [Most] Venerable Name **VII** even though frivolously, or as a result of shock or for any other reason whatever, while reading the Book or praying, he shall be dismissed and shall return to the Council of the Community no more.

If he has spoken in anger against one of the Priests inscribed in the Book, he shall do penance for one year and shall be excluded for his soul's sake from the pure Meal of the Congregation. But if he has spoken unwittingly, he shall do penance for six months.

Whoever has deliberately lied shall do penance for six months.

Whoever has deliberately insulted his companion unjustly shall do penance for one year and shall be excluded.

Whoever has deliberately deceived his companion by word or by deed shall do penance for six months.

If he has failed to care for his companion, he shall do penance for three months. But if he has failed to care for the property of the Community, thereby causing its loss, he shall restore it in full. And if he be unable to restore it, he shall do penance for sixty days.

Whoever has borne malice against his companion unjustly shall do penance for six months/one year; and likewise, whoever has taken revenge in any matter whatever.

Whoever has spoken foolishly: three months.

Whoever has interrupted his companion whilst speaking: ten days.

Whoever has lain down to sleep during an Assembly of the Congregation: thirty days. And likewise, whoever has left, without reason, an Assembly of the Congregation as many as three times during one Assembly, shall do penance for ten days. But if he has departed whilst they were standing he shall do penance for thirty days.

Whoever has gone naked before his companion, without having been obliged to do so, he shall do penance for six months.

Whoever has spat in an Assembly of the Congregation shall do penance for thirty days.

Whoever has been so poorly dressed that when drawing his hand from beneath his garment his nakedness has been seen, he shall do penance for thirty days.

Whoever has guffawed foolishly shall do penance for thirty days.

Whoever has drawn out his left hand to gesticulate with it shall do penance for ten days.

Whoever has gone about slandering his companion shall be excluded from the pure Meal of the Congregation for one year and shall do penance. But whoever has slandered the Congregation shall be expelled from among them and shall return no more.

Whoever has murmured against the authority of the Community shall be expelled and shall not return. But if he has murmured against his companion unjustly, he shall do penance for six months.

Should a man return whose spirit has so trembled before the authority of the Community that he has betrayed the truth and walked in the stubbornness of his heart, he shall do penance for two years. During the first year he shall not touch the pure Meal of the Congregation, and during the second year he shall not touch the Drink of the Congregation and shall sit below all the men of the Community. Then when his two years are completed, the Congregation shall consider his case, and if he is admitted he shall be inscribed in his rank and may then question concerning the Law.

If, after being in the Council of the Community for ten full years, the spirit of any man has failed so that he has betrayed the Community and departed from the Congregation to walk in the stubbornness of his heart, he shall return no more to the Council of the Community. Moreover, if any member of the Community has shared with him his food or property which ... of the Congregation, his sentence shall be the same; he shall be ex[pelled].

VIII In the Council of the Community there shall be twelve men and three Priests, perfectly versed in all that is revealed of the Law, whose works shall be truth, righteousness, justice, lovingkindness, and humility. They shall preserve the faith in the Land with steadfastness and meekness and shall atone for sin by the practice of justice and by suffering the sorrows of affliction. They shall walk with all men according to the standard of truth and the rule of the time.

When these are in Israel, the Council of the Community shall be established in truth. It shall be an Everlasting Plantation, a House of Holiness for Israel, an Assembly of Supreme Holiness for Aaron. They shall be witnesses to the truth at the Judgement, and shall be the elect of Goodwill who shall atone for the Land and pay to the wicked their reward. It shall be that tried wall, that *precious corner-stone*, whose foundations shall neither rock nor sway in their place (Isa. xxviii, 16). It shall be a Most Holy Dwelling for Aaron, with everlasting knowledge of the Covenant of justice, and shall offer up sweet fragrance. It shall be a House of Perfection and Truth in Israel that they may establish a Covenant according to the everlasting precepts. And they shall be an agreeable offering, atoning for the Land and determining the judgement of wickedness, and there shall be no more iniquity. When they have been confirmed for two years in perfection of way by the authority of the Community, they shall be set apart as holy within the Council of the men of the Community. And the Interpreter shall not conceal from them, out of fear of the spirit of apostasy, any of those things hidden from Israel which have been discovered by him.

And when these become members of the Community in Israel according to all these rules, they shall separate from the habitation of ungodly men and shall go into the wilderness to prepare the way of Him; as it is written, *Prepare in the wilderness the way of . . . make straight in the desert a path for our God* (Isa. xl, 3). This (path) is the study of the Law which He commanded by the hand of Moses, that they may do according to all that has been revealed from age to age, and as the Prophets have revealed by His Holy Spirit.

And no man among the members of the Covenant of the Community who deliberately, on any point whatever, turns aside from all that is commanded, shall touch the pure Meal of the men of holiness or know anything of their counsel until his deeds are purified from all falsehood and he walks in perfection of way. And then, according to the judgement of the Congregation, he shall be admitted to the Council and shall be inscribed in his rank. This rule shall apply to whoever enters the Community.

And these are the rules which the men of perfect holiness shall follow in their commerce with one another

Every man who enters the Council of Holiness, (the Council of those) who walk in the way of perfection as commanded by God, and who deliberately or through negligence transgresses one word of the Law of Moses, on any point whatever, shall be expelled from the Council of the Community and shall return no more: no man of holiness shall be associated in his property or counsel in any matter at all. But if he has acted inadvertently, he shall be excluded from the pure Meal and the Council and they shall interpret the rule (as follows). For two years he shall take no part in judgement or ask for counsel; but if, during that time, his way becomes perfect, then he shall return to the (Court of) Inquiry and the Council, in accordance with the judgement of the Congregation, provided that he commit no further inadvertent sin during two full years. **IX** For one sin of inadvertence (alone) he shall do penance for two years. But as for him who has sinned deliberately, he shall never return; only the man who has sinned inadvertently shall be tried for two years that his way and counsel may be made perfect according to the judgement of the Congregation. And afterwards, he shall be inscribed in his rank in the Community of Holiness.

When these become members of the Community in Israel according to all these rules, they shall establish the spirit of holiness according to everlasting truth. They shall atone for guilty rebellion and for sins of unfaithfulness that they may obtain lovingkindness for the Land without the flesh of holocausts and the fat of sacrifice. And prayer rightly offered shall be as an acceptable fragrance of righteousness, and perfection of way as a delectable free-will offering. At that time, the men of the Community shall set apart a House of Holiness in order that it may be united to the most holy things and a House of Community for Israel, for those who walk in perfection. The sons of Aaron alone shall command in matters of justice and property, and every rule concerning the men of the Community shall be determined according to their word.

As for the property of the men of holiness who walk in perfection, it shall not be merged with that of the men of falsehood who have not purified their life by separating themselves from iniquity and walking in the way of perfection. They shall depart from none of the counsels of the Law to walk in the stubbornness of their hearts, but shall be ruled by the primitive precepts in which the men of the Community were first instructed until there shall come the Prophet and the Messiahs of Aaron and Israel.

These are the precepts in which the Master shall walk in his commerce with all the living, according to the rule proper to every season and according to the worth of every man

He shall do the will of God according to all that has been revealed from age to age.

He shall measure out all knowledge discovered throughout the ages, together with the Precept of the age.

He shall separate and weigh the sons of righteousness according to their spirit.

He shall hold firmly to the elect of the time according to His will, as He has commanded.

He shall judge every man according to his spirit. He shall admit him in accordance with the cleanness of his hands and advance him in accordance with his understanding. And he shall love and hate likewise.

He shall not rebuke the men of the Pit nor dispute with them.

He shall conceal the teaching of the Law from men of falsehood, but shall impart true knowledge and righteous judgement to those who have chosen the Way. He shall guide them all in knowledge according to the spirit of each and according to the rule of the age, and shall thus instruct them in the mysteries of marvellous truth that in the midst of the men of the Community they may walk perfectly together in all that has been revealed to them. This is the time for the preparation of the way into the wilderness, and he shall teach them to do all that is required at that time and to separate from all those who have not turned aside from all ungodliness.

These are the rules of conduct for the Master in those times with respect to his loving and hating.

Everlasting hatred in a spirit of secrecy for the men of perdition! He shall leave to them wealth and earnings like a slave to his lord and like a poor man to his master.

He shall be a man zealous for the Precept whose time is for the Day of Revenge. He shall perform the will of God in all his deeds, and in all his dominion as He has commanded. He shall freely delight in all that befalls him and nothing shall please him save God's will. He shall delight in all the words of His mouth and shall desire nothing except His command. He shall watch always [for] the judgement of God, and shall bless his Maker [for all His goodness] and declare [His mercies] in all that befalls.

He shall bless Him [with the offering] of the lips   **X**   at

the times ordained by Him: at the beginning of the dominion of light, and at its end when it retires to its appointed
place; at the beginning of the watches of darkness when He
unlocks their storehouse and spreads them out, and also at
their end when they retire before the light; when the
heavenly lights shine out from the dwelling-place of Holiness, and also when they retire to the place of Glory; at the
entry of the (monthly) seasons on the days of new moon, and
also at their end when they succeed to one another. Their
renewal is a great day for the Holy of Holies, and a sign for
the unlocking of everlasting mercies at the beginning of
seasons in all times to come.

At the beginning of the months of the (yearly) seasons
    and on the holy days appointed for remembrance,
in their seasons I will bless Him
    with the offering of the lips
    according to the Precept engraved for ever:
at the beginning of the years
    and at the end of their seasons
    when their appointed law is fulfilled,
on the day decreed by Him
    that they should pass from one to the other –
the season of early harvest to the summer time,
the season of sowing to the season of grass,
the seasons of years to their weeks (of years) –
and at the beginning of their weeks
    for the season of Jubilee.
All my life the engraved Precept shall be on my tongue
    as the fruit of praise
    and the portion of my lips.

I will sing with knowledge and all my music
    shall be for the glory of God.
(My) lyre (and) my harp shall sound
    for His holy order
and I will tune the pipe of my lips
    to His right measure.

With the coming of day and night
   I will enter the Covenant of God,
and when evening and morning depart
   I will recite His decrees.
I will place in them my bounds without return.

I will declare His judgement concerning my sins,
   and my transgressions shall be before my eyes
   as an engraved Precept.
I will say to God, 'My Righteousness'
   and 'Author of my Goodness' to the Most High,
'Fountain of Knowledge' and 'Source of Holiness',
   'Summit of Glory' and 'Almighty Eternal Majesty'.
I will choose that which He teaches me
   and will delight in His judgement of me.

Before I move my hands and feet
   I will bless His Name.
I will praise Him before I go out or enter,
   or sit or rise,
   and whilst I lie on the couch of my bed.
I will bless Him with the offering
   of that which proceeds from my lips
   from the midst of the ranks of men,
and before I lift my hands to eat
   of the pleasant fruits of the earth.
I will bless Him for His exceeding wonderful deeds
   at the beginning of fear and dread
   and in the abode of distress and desolation.
I will meditate on His power
   and will lean on His mercies all day long.
I know that judgement of all the living
   is in His hand,
   and that all His deeds are truth.
I will praise Him when distress is unleashed
   and will magnify Him also because of His salvation.

I will pay to no man the reward of evil;

I will pursue him with goodness.
For judgement of all the living is with God
    and it is He who will render to man his reward.
I will not envy in a spirit of wickedness,
    my soul shall not desire the riches of violence.
I will not grapple with the men of perdition
    until the Day of Revenge,
but my wrath shall not turn from the men of falsehood
    and I will not rejoice until judgement is made.
I will bear no rancour
    against them that turn from transgression,
but will have no pity
    on all who depart from the Way.
I will offer no comfort to the smitten
    until their way becomes perfect.

I will not keep Satan within my heart,
and in my mouth shall be heard
    no folly or sinful deceit,
    no cunning or lies shall be found on my lips.
The fruit of holiness shall be on my tongue
    and no abominations shall be found upon it.
I will open my mouth
    in songs of thanksgiving,
and my tongue shall always proclaim
    the goodness of God and the sin of men
    until their transgression ends.
I will cause vanities
    to cease from my lips,
uncleanness and crookedness
    from the knowledge of my heart.

I will impart/conceal knowledge with discretion
    and will prudently hedge it within a firm bound
to preserve faith and strong judgement
    in accordance with the justice of God.
I will distribute the Precept

    by the measuring-cord of the times,
and ... righteousness
    and lovingkindness towards the oppressed,
encouragement to the troubled heart
    XI   and discernment to the erring spirit,
teaching understanding to them that murmur
    that they may answer meekly
    before the haughty of spirit
and humbly before men of injustice
    who point the finger and speak of iniquity
    and who are zealous for wealth.

As for me,
    my justification is with God.
In His hand are the perfection of my way
    and the uprightness of my heart.
He will wipe out my transgression
    through His righteousness.

For my light has sprung
    from the source of His knowledge;
my eyes have beheld His marvellous deeds,
    and the light of my heart, the mystery to come.
He that is everlasting
    is the support of my right hand;
the way of my steps is over stout rock
    which nothing shall shake;
for the rock of my steps is the truth of God
    and His might is the support of my right hand.

From the source of His righteousness
    is my justification,
and from His marvellous mysteries
    is the light in my heart.
My eyes have gazed
    on that which is eternal,
on wisdom concealed from men,
    on knowledge and wise design
    (hidden) from the sons of men;

on a fountain of righteousness
  and on a storehouse of power,
on a spring of glory
  (hidden) from the assembly of flesh.
God has given them to His chosen ones
  as an everlasting possession,
and has caused them to inherit
  the lot of the Holy Ones.
He has joined their assembly
  to the Sons of Heaven
to be a Council of the Community,
a foundation of the Building of Holiness,
an eternal Plantation throughout all ages to come.

As for me,
  I belong to wicked mankind,
  to the company of ungodly flesh.
My iniquities, rebellions, and sins,
  together with the perversity of my heart,
belong to the company of worms
  and to those who walk in darkness.
For mankind has no way,
  and man is unable to establish his steps
since justification is with God
  and perfection of way is out of His hand.
All things come to pass by His knowledge;
He establishes all things by His design
  and without Him nothing is done.

As for me,
  if I stumble, the mercies of God
  shall be my eternal salvation.
If I stagger because of the sin of flesh,
  my justification shall be
  by the righteousness of God which endures for ever.
When my distress is unleashed
  He will deliver my soul from the Pit
  and will direct my steps to the way.

He will draw me near by His grace,
  and by His mercy will He bring my justification.
He will judge me in the righteousness of His truth
  and in the greatness of His goodness
  He will pardon all my sins.
Through His righteousness He will cleanse me
  of the uncleanness of man
  and of the sins of the children of men,
that I may confess to God His righteousness,
  and His majesty to the Most High.

Blessed art Thou, my God,
  who openest the heart of Thy servant to knowledge!
Establish all his deeds in righteousness,
and as it pleases Thee to do for the elect of mankind,
  grant that the son of Thy handmaid
  may stand before Thee for ever.

For without Thee no way is perfect,
  and without Thy will nothing is done.
It is Thou who has taught all knowledge
  and all things come to pass by Thy will.
There is none beside Thee to dispute Thy counsel
  or to understand all Thy holy design,
or to contemplate the depth of Thy mysteries
  and the power of Thy might.

Who can endure Thy glory,
  and what is the son of man
  in the midst of Thy wonderful deeds?
What shall one born of woman
  be accounted before Thee?
Kneaded from the dust,
  his abode is the nourishment of worms.
He is but a shape, but moulded clay,
  and inclines towards dust.
What shall hand-moulded clay reply?
  What counsel shall it understand?

· 5 ·

THE DAMASCUS RULE

EXTENSIVE fragments of the Damascus Rule have been recovered from three of the Qumran caves, but two incomplete medieval copies of this document had been found already many years earlier, in 1896-7, amongst a mass of discarded manuscripts in a store-room (*geniza*) of an old Cairo synagogue. Published in 1910 by S. Schechter (*Fragments of a Zadokite Work*, Cambridge), they were re-edited by Chaim Rabin in 1954 under the title, *The Zadokite Documents* (Oxford).

Dating from the tenth and twelfth centuries respectively, the manuscripts found in Cairo – Manuscript A and Manuscript B – raise a certain number of textual problems in that they present two different versions of the original composition. I have settled the difficulty as satisfactorily as I can by following Manuscript A, to which the unpublished Qumran fragments correspond, and by inserting the Manuscript B variants in brackets or footnotes. At a certain point, as the reader will see, Manuscript A comes to an end and we then have to rely entirely on Manuscript B. Furthermore, following the suggestion made by J. T. Milik in *Ten Years of Discovery in the Wilderness of Judaea* (London, 1959, pp. 151-2), I have rearranged the order of the pages and placed pages xv and xvi before page ix.

The title 'Damascus Rule' derives from the references in the Exhortation to the 'New Covenant' made 'in the land of Damascus'. The significance of this phrase is discussed in Chapter 3 (p. 53) together with the chronological data included in the manuscript. They suggest that the document was written in about 100 B.C. and this hypothesis is indirectly supported by the absence of any mention in the historical passages of the Kittim (Romans) whose invasion of the Orient did not take place until after 70 B.C.

The work is divided into an Exhortation and a list of Statutes. In the Exhortation, the preacher – probably a Guardian of the Community – addresses his 'sons' on the themes of the sect's

95

teaching, many of which appear also in the Community Rule. His aim is to encourage the sectaries to remain faithful, and with this end in view he sets out to demonstrate from the history of Israel and the Community that fidelity is always rewarded and apostasy chastised.

During the course of his argument, the author of the Damascus Rule frequently interprets biblical passages in a most unexpected way. I have mentioned two of these commentaries on the marriage laws in Chapter 2 (p. 34), but there is another involved exposition of Amos v, 26–7 on page VII which may not be easy to understand.

In the Bible these verses convey a divine threat: the Israelites were to take themselves and their idols into exile. 'You shall take up Sakkuth your king and Kaiwan your star-god, your images which you made for yourselves, for I will take you into exile beyond Damascus.' But the Damascus Rule transforms this threat into a promise of salvation; by changing certain words in the biblical text and omitting others its version reads: 'I will exile the tabernacle of your king and the bases of your statues from my tent to Damascus.'

In this new text, the three key phrases are interpreted symbolically as follows: 'tabernacle' = 'Books of the Law'; 'king' = 'congregation'; 'bases of statues' = 'Books of the Prophets'. Thus: 'The Books of the Law are the *tabernacle* of the king; as God said, *I will raise up the tabernacle of David which is fallen* (Amos ix, 11). The *king* is the congregation; and the *bases of the statues* are the Books of the Prophets whose sayings Israel despised.'

The omission of any reference to the 'star-god' is made good by introducing a very different 'Star', the Messianic 'Interpreter of the Law' with his companion the 'Prince of the congregation'. 'The star is the Interpreter of the Law who shall come to Damascus; as it is written, *A star shall come forth out of Jacob and a sceptre shall rise out of Israel* (Num. xxiv, 17). The sceptre is the Prince of the whole congregation . . .'

The second part of the Damascus Rule, the Statutes, consists of a collection of laws which mostly reflect a sectarian reinterpretation of the biblical commandments relative to vows and oaths, tribunals, purification, the Sabbath, and the distinction between ritual purity and impurity. They are followed by rules concerned with the institutions and organization of the Community.

Whereas the Exhortation represents a literary *genre* adopted by both Jewish and Christian religious teachers (e.g. the Letter to the Hebrews), the methodical grouping of the Statutes prefigures that of the Mishnah, the oldest Jewish code extant.

The Statutes as they appear in the Qumran fragments include the form of the ritual for the Feast of the Renewal of the Covenant, so it may be assumed that the entire Damascus Rule was orginally connected with that festival.

The Exhortation

I Hear now, all you who know righteousness, and consider the works of God; for He has a dispute with all flesh and will condemn all those who despise Him.

For when they were unfaithful and forsook Him, He hid His face from Israel and His Sanctuary and delivered them up to the sword. But remembering the Covenant of the forefathers, He left a remnant to Israel and did not deliver it up to be destroyed. And in the age of wrath, three hundred and ninety years after He had given them into the hand of king Nebuchadnezzar of Babylon, He visited them, and He caused a plant root to spring from Israel and Aaron to inherit His Land and to prosper on the good things of His earth. And they perceived their iniquity and recognized that they were guilty men, yet for twenty years they were like blind men groping for the way.

And God observed their deeds, that they sought Him with a whole heart, and He raised for them a Teacher of Righteousness to guide them in the way of His heart. And he made known to the latter generations that which God had done to the latter generation, the congregation of traitors, to those who departed from the way. This was the time of which it is written, *Like a stubborn heifer thus was Israel stubborn* (Hos. iv, 16), when the Scoffer arose who shed over Israel the waters of lies. He caused them to wander in a pathless wilderness, laying low the everlasting heights, abolishing the ways of righteousness and removing the boundary with which the forefathers had marked out their inheritance, that he might call down on them the curses of His Covenant and deliver them up to the avenging sword of the Covenant. For they sought smooth things and preferred illusions (Isa. xxx, 10) and they watched for breaks (Isa. xxx, 13) and chose the fair neck; and they justified the wicked and condemned the just, and they transgressed the Covenant and violated the Precept. They banded together against the life of the righteous (Ps. xciv, 21) and loathed all who walked in perfection; they pursued them with the sword and exulted in the strife of the people. And the anger of God was kindled against **II** their congregation so that He ravaged all their multitude; and their deeds were defilement before Him.

Hear now, all you who enter the Covenant, and I will unstop your ears concerning the ways of the wicked.

God loves knowledge. Wisdom and understanding He has set before Him, and prudence and knowledge serve Him. Patience and much forgiveness are with Him towards those who turn from transgression; but power, might, and great flaming wrath by the hand of all the Angels of Destruction towards those who depart from the way and abhor the Precept. They shall have no remnant or survivor. For from the beginning God chose them not; He knew their deeds before ever they were created and He hated their generations, and He hid His face from the Land until they were consumed. For He knew the years of their coming and the length and exact duration of their times for all ages to come and throughout eternity. He knew the happenings of their times throughout all the everlasting years. And in all of them He raised for Himself men called by name, that a remnant might be left to the Land, and that the face of the earth might be filled with their seed. And He made known His Holy Spirit to them by the hand of His anointed ones, and He proclaimed the truth (to them). But those whom He hated He led astray.

Hear now, my sons, and I will uncover your eyes that you may see and understand the works of God, that you choose that which pleases Him and reject that which He hates, that you may walk perfectly in all His ways and not follow after thoughts of the guilty inclination and after eyes of lust. For through them, great men have gone astray and mighty heroes have stumbled from former times till now. Because they walked in the stubbornness of their heart the Heavenly Watchers fell; they were caught because they did not keep the commandments of God. And their sons also fell who were tall as cedar trees and whose bodies were like mountains. All flesh on dry land perished; they were as though they had never been because they did their own will and did not keep the commandment of their Maker so that His wrath was kindled against them. **III** Through it, the children of Noah went astray, together with their kin, and were cut off. Abraham did not walk in it, and he was accounted friend of God because he kept the commandments of God and did not choose his own will. And he handed them down to Isaac and Jacob, who kept them, and were recorded as friends of God and party to the Covenant for ever.

The children of Jacob strayed through them and were punished in accordance with their error. And their sons in Egypt walked in the stubbornness of their hearts, conspiring against the commandments of God and each of them doing that which seemed right in his own eyes. They ate blood, and He cut off their males in the wilderness.

And at Kadesh He said to them, *Go up and possess the land* (Deut. ix, 23). But they chose their own will and did not heed the voice of their Maker, the commands of their Teacher, but murmured in their tents; and the anger of God was kindled against their congregation. Through it their sons perished, and through it their kings were cut off; through it their mighty heroes perished and through it their land was ravaged. Through it the first members of the Covenant sinned and were delivered up to the sword, because they forsook the Covenant of God and chose their own will and walked in the stubbornness of their hearts each of them doing his own will.

But with the remnant which held fast to the commandments of God, He made His Covenant with Israel for ever, revealing to them the hidden things in which all Israel had gone astray. He unfolded before them His holy Sabbaths and His glorious feasts, the testimonies of His righteousness and the ways of His truth, and the desires of His will which a man must do in order to live. And they dug a well rich in water; and he who despises it shall not live. Yet they wallowed in the sin of man and in ways of uncleanness, and they said, 'This is our (way).' But God, in His wonderful mysteries, forgave them their sin and pardoned their wickedness; and He built them a sure house in Israel whose like has never existed from former times till now. Those who hold fast to it are destined to live for ever and all the glory of Adam shall be theirs. As God ordained for them by the hand of the Prophet Ezekiel, saying, *The Priests, the Levites, and the sons* **IV** *of Zadok who kept the charge of my sanctuary when the children of Israel strayed from me, they shall offer me fat and blood* (Ezek. xliv, 15).

The *Priests* are the converts of Israel who departed from the land of Judah, and (the *Levites* are) those who joined them. The *sons of Zadok* are the elect of Israel, the men called by name who shall stand at the end of days. Behold the exact list of their names according to their generations, and the time when they lived, and the number of their trials, and the years of their sojourn, and the exact list of their deeds . . .

(They were the first men) of holiness whom God forgave, and who justified the righteous and condemned the wicked. And until the age is completed, according to the number of those years, all who enter after them shall do according to that interpretation of the Law in which the first were instructed. According to the Covenant which God made with the forefathers, forgiving their sins, so shall He forgive their sins also. But when the age is completed, according to the number of those years, there shall be no more joining the house of Judah, but each man shall stand on his watch-tower: *The wall is built, the boundary far removed* (Mic. vii, 11).

During all those years Satan shall be unleashed against Israel, as He spoke by the hand of Isaiah, son of Amoz, saying, *Terror and the pit and the snare are upon you, O inhabitant of the land* (Isa. xxiv, 17). Interpreted, these are the three nets of Satan with which Levi son of Jacob said that he catches Israel by setting them up as three kinds of righteous-ness. The first is fornication, the second is riches, and the third is profanation of the Temple. Whoever escapes the first is caught in the second, and whoever saves himself from the second is caught in the third (Isa. xxiv, 18).

The builders of the wall (Ezek. xiii, 10) who have followed after 'Precept' – 'Precept' was a spouter of whom it is written, *They shall surely spout* (Mic. ii, 6) – shall be caught in fornication twice by taking a second wife while the first is alive, whereas the principle of creation is, *Male and female created He them* (Gen. i, 27). **V** Also, those who entered the Ark went in two by two. And concerning the prince it is written, *He shall not multiply wives to himself* (Deut. xvii, 17); but David had not read the sealed book of the Law which was in the ark (of the Covenant), for it was not open-ed in Israel from the death of Eleazar and Joshua, and the elders who worshipped Ashtoreth. It was hidden and (was not) revealed until the coming of Zadok. And the deeds of David rose up, except for the murder of Uriah, and God left them to him.

Moreover, they profane the Temple because they do not observe the distinction (between clean and unclean) in accordance with the Law, but lie with a woman who sees her bloody discharge.

And each man marries the daughter of his brother or sister, whereas Moses said, *You shall not approach your mother's sister; she is your mother's near kin* (Lev. xviii, 13). But although the laws against incest are written for men, they also apply to women. When, therefore, a brother's daughter uncovers the nakedness of her father's brother, she is (also his) near kin.

Furthermore, they defile their holy spirit and open their mouth with a blaspheming tongue against the laws of the Covenant of God saying, 'They are not sure.' They speak abominations concerning them; *they are all kindlers of fire and lighters of brands* (Isa. l, 11), *their webs are spiders' webs and their eggs are vipers' eggs* (Isa. lix, 5). No man that approaches them shall be free from guilt; the more he does so, the guiltier shall he be, unless he is pressed. For (already) in ancient times God visited their deeds and His anger was kindled against their works; *for it is a people of no discernment* (Isa. xxvii, 11), *it is a nation void of counsel inasmuch as there is no discernment in them* (Deut. xxxii, 28). For in ancient times, Moses and Aaron arose by the hand of the Prince of Lights and Satan in his cunning raised up Jannes and his brother when Israel was first delivered.

And at the time of the desolation of the Land there arose removers of the bound who led Israel astray. And the land was ravaged because they preached rebellion against the commandments of God given by the hand of Moses and **VI** of His holy anointed ones, and because they prophesied lies to turn Israel away from following God. But God remembered the Covenant with the forefathers, and He raised from Aaron men of discernment and from Israel men of wisdom, and He caused them to hear. And they dug the Well: *the well which the princes dug, which the nobles of the people delved with the stave* (Num. xxi, 18).

The *Well* is the Law, and those who dug it were the converts of Israel who went out of the land of Judah to sojourn in the land of Damascus. God called them all *princes* because they sought Him, and their renown was disputed by no man. The *Stave* is the Interpreter of the Law of whom Isaiah said, *He makes a tool for His work* (Isa. liv, 16); and the *nobles of the people* are those who come to dig the *Well* with the staves with which the *Stave* ordained that they should walk in all the age of wickedness – and without them they shall find nothing – until he comes who shall teach righteousness at the end of days.

None of those brought into the Covenant shall enter the Temple to light His altar in vain. They shall bar the door, forasmuch as God said, *Who among you will bar its door?* And, *You shall not light my altar in vain* (Mal. i, 10). They shall take care to act according to the exact interpretation of the Law during the age of wickedness. They shall separate from the sons of the Pit, and shall keep away from the unclean riches of wickedness acquired by vow or anathema or from the Temple treasure; they shall not rob the poor of His people, to make of widows their prey and of the fatherless their victim (Isa. x, 2). They shall distinguish between clean and unclean, and shall proclaim the difference between holy and profane. They shall keep the Sabbath day according to its exact interpretation, and the feasts and the Day of Fasting according to the finding of the members of the New Covenant in the land of Damascus. They shall set aside the holy things according to the exact teaching concerning them. They shall love each man his brother as himself; they shall succour the poor, the needy, and the stranger.

A man shall seek his brother's well-being **VII** and shall not sin against his near kin. They shall keep from fornication according to the statute. They shall rebuke each man his brother according to the commandment and shall bear no rancour from one day to the next. They shall keep apart from every uncleanness according to the statutes relating to each one, and no man shall defile his holy spirit since God has set them apart. For all who walk in these (precepts) in perfect holiness, according to all the teaching of God, the Covenant of God shall be an assurance that they shall live for thousands of generations (Ms. B: as it is written, *Keeping the Covenant and grace with those who love me and keep my commandments, to a thousand generations,* Deut. vii, 9).

And if they live in camps according to the rule of the Land (Ms. B: as it was from ancient times), marrying

(Ms. B: according to the custom of the Law) and begetting children, they shall walk according to the Law and according to the statute concerning binding vows, according to the rule of the Law which says, *Between a man and his wife and between a father and his son* (Num. xxx, 17). And all those who despise (Ms. B: the commandments and the statutes) shall be rewarded with the retribution of the wicked when God shall visit the Land, when the saying shall come to pass which is written* among the words of the Prophet Isaiah son of Amoz: *He will bring upon you, and upon your people, and upon your father's house, days such as have not come since the day that Ephraim departed from Judah* (Isa. vii, 17). When the two houses of Israel were divided, Ephraim departed from Judah. And all the apostates were given up to the sword, but those who held fast escaped to the land of the north; as God said, *I will exile the tabernacle of your king and the bases of your statues from my tent to Damascus* (Amos v, 26–7).

The Books of the Law are the *tabernacle* of the king; as God said, *I will raise up the tabernacle of David which is fallen* (Amos ix, 11). The *king* is the congregation; and the *bases of the statues* are the Books of the Prophets whose sayings Israel despised. The *star* is the Interpreter of the Law who shall come to Damascus; as it is written, *A star shall come forth out of Jacob and a sceptre shall rise out of Israel* (Num. xxiv, 17). The *sceptre* is the Prince of the whole congregation, and when he comes *he shall smite all the children of Seth* (Num. xxiv, 17).

At the time of the former Visitation they were saved,

---

* Ms. B continues: by the hand of the prophet Zechariah: *Awake, O Sword, against my shepherd, against my companion, says God. Strike the shepherd that the flock may be scattered and I will stretch my hand over the little ones* (Zech. xiii, 7). The humble of the flock are those who watch for Him. They shall be saved at the time of the Visitation whereas the others shall be delivered up to the sword when the Anointed of Aaron and Israel shall come, as it came to pass at the time of the former Visitation concerning which God said by the hand of Ezekiel: *They shall put a mark on the foreheads of those who sigh and groan* (Ezek. ix, 4). But the others were delivered up to the avenging sword of the Covenant.

whereas the apostates **VIII** were given up to the sword; and so shall it be for all the members of His Covenant who do not hold steadfastly to these (Ms. B: to the curse of the precepts). They shall be visited for destruction by the hand of Satan. That shall be the day when God will visit. (Ms. B: As He said,) *The princes of Judah have become* (Ms. B: *like those who remove the bound*); *wrath shall be poured upon them* (Hos. v, 10). For they shall hope for healing but He will crush them. They are all of them rebels, for they* have not turned from the way of traitors but have wallowed in the ways of whoredom and wicked wealth. They have taken revenge and borne malice, every man against his brother, and every man has hated his fellow, and every man has sinned against his near kin, and has approached for unchastity, and has acted arrogantly for the sake of riches and gain. And every man has done that which seemed right in his eyes and has chosen the stubbornness of his heart. They have not kept apart from the people (Ms. B: and their sin) and have wilfully rebelled by walking in the ways of the wicked of whom God said, *Their wine is the venom of serpents, the cruel poison* (or *head*) *of asps* (Deut. xxxii, 33).

The *serpents* are the kings of the peoples and their *wine* is their ways. And the *head of asps* is the chief of the kings of Greece who came to wreak vengeance upon them. But all these things the *builders of the wall and those who daub it with plaster* (Ezek. xiii, 10) have not understood because a follower of the wind, one who raised storms and rained down lies, had preached to them (Mic. ii, 11), against all of whose assembly the anger of God was kindled.

And as for that which Moses said, *You enter to possess these nations not because of your righteousness or the uprightness of your hearts* (Deut. ix, 5) *but because God loved your fathers and kept the oath* (Deut. vii, 8), thus shall it be with the converts of Israel who depart from the way of the people. Because God loved

* Ms. B inserts: they have entered the Covenant of repentance but they have not turned etc.

the first who* testified in His favour, so will He love those who come after them, for the Covenant of the fathers is theirs. But He hated the *builders of the wall* and His anger was kindled (Ms. B: against them and against all those who followed them); and so shall it be for all who reject the commandments of God and abandon them for the stubbornness of their hearts. This is the word which Jeremiah spoke to Baruch son of Neriah, and which Elisha spoke to his servant Gehazi.

None of the men who enter the New Covenant in the land of Damascus, (B I) and who again betray it and depart from the fountain of living waters, shall be reckoned with the Council of the people or inscribed in its Book from the day of the gathering in (B II) of the Teacher of the Community until the coming of the Messiah out of Aaron and Israel.

And thus shall it be for every man who enters the congregation of men of perfect holiness but faints in performing the duties of the upright. He is a man who has melted in the furnace (Ezek. xxii, 22); when his deeds are revealed he shall be expelled from the congregation as though his lot had never fallen among the disciples of God. The men of knowledge shall rebuke him in accordance with his sin against the time when he shall stand again before the Assembly of the men of perfect holiness. But when his deeds are revealed, according to the interpretation of the Law in which the men of perfect holiness walk, let no man defer to him with regard to money or work, for all the Holy Ones of the Most High have cursed him.

And thus shall it be for all among the first and the last who reject (the precepts), who set idols upon their hearts and walk in the stubbornness of their hearts; they shall have no share in the house of the Law. They shall be judged in the same manner as their companions were judged who deserted to the Scoffers. For they have spoken wrongly against the precepts of righteousness, and have despised the

* Ms. B adds: bore witness against the people, so will He love, etc.

Covenant and the Pact – the New Covenant – which they made in the land of Damascus. Neither they nor their kin shall have any part in the house of the Law.

From the day of the gathering in of the Teacher of the Community until the end of all the men of war who deserted to the Liar there shall pass about forty years (Deut. ii, 14). And during that age the wrath of God shall be kindled against Israel; as He said, *There shall be no king, no prince, no judge, no man to rebuke with justice* (Hos. iii, 4). But those who turn from the sin of Jacob, who keep the Covenant of God, shall then speak each man to his fellow, to justify each man his brother, that their step may take the way of God. And God will heed their words and will hear, and a book of reminder shall be written before Him of them that fear God and worship His Name, against the time when salvation and righteousness shall be revealed to them that fear God. *And then shall you distinguish once more between the just and the wicked, between one that serves God and one that serves Him not* (Mal. iii, 18); *and He will show lovingkindness to thousands, to them that love Him and watch for Him, for a thousand generations* (Exod. xx, 6).

And every member of the House of Separation who went out of the Holy City and leaned on God at the time when Israel sinned and defiled the Temple, but returned again to the way of the people in small matters, shall be judged according to his spirit in the Council of Holiness. But when the glory of God is made manifest to Israel, all those members of the Covenant who have breached the bound of the Law shall be cut off from the midst of the camp, and with them all those who condemned Judah in the days of its trials.

But all those who hold fast to these precepts, going and coming in accordance with the Law, who heed the voice of the Teacher and confess before God, (saying), 'Truly we have sinned, we and our fathers, by walking counter to the precepts of the Covenant, Thy judgements upon us are justice and truth'; who do not lift their hand against His

holy precepts or His righteous statutes or His true testimonies; who have learned from the former judgements by
which the members of the Community were judged; who
have listened to the voice of the Teacher of Righteousness
and have not despised the precepts of righteousness when
they heard them; they shall rejoice and their hearts shall be
strong, and they shall prevail over all the sons of the earth.
God will forgive them and they shall see His salvation because they took refuge in His holy Name.

The Statutes

... (He shall not) **XV** swear by (the Name), nor by
Aleph and *Lamed* (Elohim), nor by *Aleph* and *Daleth* (Adonai),
but a binding oath by the curses of the Covenant.

He shall not mention the Law of Moses for ... were he to
swear and then break (his oath) he would profane the
Name.

But if he has sworn an oath by the curses of the Covenant
before the judges and has transgressed it, then he is guilty
and shall confess and make restitution; but he shall not be
burdened with a capital sin.

And when the children of all those who have entered the
Covenant, granted to all Israel for ever, reach the age of
enrolment, they shall swear with an oath of the Covenant.

And thus shall it be during all the age of wickedness for
every man who repents of his corrupted way. On the day
that he speaks to the Guardian of the Congregation, they
shall enrol him with the oath of the Covenant which Moses
made with Israel, the Covenant to return to the Law of
Moses with a whole heart and soul, to whatever is found
should be done at that time. No man shall make known
the statutes to him until he has stood before the Guardian,
lest when examining him the Guardian be deceived by him.
But if he transgresses after swearing to return to the Law of
Moses with a whole heart and soul, then retribution shall be
exacted from him ... And all that is revealed of the Law

... the Guardian shall examine him and shall issue directions concerning him ... for a full year according to ...

No madman, or lunatic, or simpleton, or fool, no blind man, or maimed, or lame, or deaf man, and no minor, shall enter into the Community, for the Angels of Holiness are with them ...

(For God made) **XVI** a Covenant with you and all Israel; therefore a man shall bind himself by oath to return to the Law of Moses, for in it all things are strictly defined.

As for the exact determination of their times to which Israel turns a blind eye, behold it is strictly defined in the *Book of the Divisions of the Times into their Jubilees and Weeks.* And on the day that a man swears to return to the Law of Moses, the Angel of Persecution shall cease to follow him provided that he fulfils his word: for this reason Abraham circumcised himself on the day that he knew.

And concerning the saying, *You shall keep your vow by fulfilling it* (Deut. xxiii, 24), let no man, even at the price of death, annul any binding oath by which he has sworn to keep a commandment of the Law.

But even at the price of death, a man shall fulfil no vow by which he has sworn to depart from the Law.

Concerning the oath of a woman

Inasmuch as He said, *It is for her husband to cancel her oath* (Num. xxx, 9), no husband shall cancel an oath without knowing whether it should be kept or not. Should it be such as to lead to transgression of the Covenant, he shall cancel it and shall not let it be kept. The rule for her father is likewise.

Concerning the Statute for free-will offerings

No man shall vow to the altar anything unlawfully acquired. Also, no Priest shall take from Israel anything unlawfully acquired.

And no man shall consecrate the food of his house to

God, for it is as He said, *Each hunts his brother with a net* (or *votive-offering*: Mic. vii, 2).

IX Every man who vows another to destruction by the laws of the Gentiles shall himself be put to death.

And concerning the saying, *You shall not take vengeance on the children of your people, nor bear any rancour against them* (Lev. xix, 18), if any member of the Covenant accuses his companion without first rebuking him before witnesses; if he denounces him in the heat of his anger or reports him to his elders to make him look contemptible, he is one that takes vengeance and bears rancour, although it is expressly written, *He takes vengeance upon His adversaries and bears rancour against His enemies* (Nah. i, 2). If he holds his peace towards him from one day to another, and thereafter speaks of him in the heat of his anger, he testifies against himself concerning a capital matter because he has not fulfilled the commandment of God which tells him: *You shall rebuke your companion and not be burdened with sin because of him* (Lev. xix, 17.)

Concerning the oath with reference to that which He said, You shall not take the law into your own hands (1 Sam. xxv, 26)

Whoever causes another to swear in the fields instead of before the Judges, or at their decree, takes the law into his own hands. When anything is lost, and it is not known who has stolen it from the property of the camp in which it was stolen, its owner shall pronounce a curse, and any man who, on hearing (it), knows but does not tell, shall himself be guilty.

When anything is returned which is without an owner, whoever returns it shall confess to the Priest, and apart from the ram of the sin-offering, it shall be his.

And likewise, everything which is found but has no owner shall go to the Priests, for the finder is ignorant of the rule concerning it. If no owners are discovered they shall keep it.

Every sin which a man commits against the Law, and which his companion witnesses, he being alone, if it is a capital matter he shall report it to the Guardian, rebuking him in his presence, and the Guardian shall record it against him in case he should commit it again before one man and he should report it to the Guardian once more. Should he repeat it and be taken in the act before one man, his case shall be complete.

And if there are two (witnesses), each testifying to a different matter, the man shall be excluded from the pure Meal provided that they are trustworthy and that each informs the Guardian on the day that they witnessed (the offence). In matters of property, they shall accept two trustworthy witnesses and shall exclude (the culprit) from the pure Meal on the word of one witness alone.

No **X** Judge shall pass sentence of death on the testimony of a witness who has not yet attained the age of enrolment and who is not God-fearing.

No man who has wilfully transgressed any commandment shall be declared a trustworthy witness against his companion until he is purified and able to return.

And this is the Rule for the Judges of the Congregation

Ten shall be elected from the congregation for a definite time, four from the tribe of Levi and Aaron, and six from Israel. (They shall be) learned in the Book of Meditation and in the constitutions of the Covenant, and aged between twenty-five and sixty years. No man over the age of sixty shall hold office as Judge of the Congregation, for 'because man sinned his days have been shortened, and in the heat of His anger against the inhabitants of the earth God ordained that their understanding should depart even before their days are completed' (Jubilees, xxiii, 11).

Concerning purification by water

No man shall bathe in dirty water or in an amount too shallow to cover a man. He shall not purify himself with water contained in a vessel. And as for the water of every rock-pool too shallow to cover a man, if an unclean man touches it he renders its water as unclean as water contained in a vessel.

Concerning the Sabbath to observe it according to its law

No man shall work on the sixth day from the moment when the sun's orb is distant by its own fulness from the gate (wherein it sinks); for this is what He said, *Observe the Sabbath day to keep it holy* (Deut. v. 12). No man shall speak any vain or idle word on the Sabbath day. He shall make no loan to his companion. He shall make no decision in matters of money and gain. He shall say nothing about work or labour to be done on the morrow.

No man shall walk abroad to do business on the Sabbath. He shall not walk more than one thousand cubits beyond his town.

No man shall eat on the Sabbath day except that which is already prepared. He shall eat nothing lying in the fields. He shall not drink except in the camp. **XI** If he is on a journey and goes down to bathe, he shall drink where he stands, but he shall not draw water into a vessel. He shall send out no stranger on his business on the Sabbath day.

No man shall wear soiled garments, or garments brought to the store, unless they have been washed with water or rubbed with incense.

No man shall willingly mingle (with others) on the Sabbath.

No man shall walk more than two thousand cubits after a beast to pasture it outside his town. He shall not raise his hand to strike it with his fist. If it is stubborn he shall not take it out of his house.

No man shall take anything out of the house or bring anything in. And if he is in a booth, let him neither take anything out nor bring anything in. He shall not open a sealed vessel on the Sabbath.

No man shall carry perfumes on himself whilst going and

coming on the Sabbath. He shall lift neither sand nor dust in his dwelling. No foster-father shall carry a child whilst going and coming on the Sabbath.

No man shall chide his manservant or maidservant or labourer on the Sabbath.

No man shall assist a beast to give birth on the Sabbath day. And if it should fall into a cistern or pit, he shall not lift it out on the Sabbath.

No man shall spend the Sabbath in a place near to Gentiles on the Sabbath.

No man shall profane the Sabbath for the sake of riches or gain on the Sabbath day. But should any man fall into water or fire, let him be pulled out with the aid of a ladder or rope or (some such) tool.

No man on the Sabbath shall offer anything on the altar except the Sabbath burnt-offering; for it is written thus: *Except your Sabbath offerings* (Lev. xxiii, 38).

No man shall send to the altar any burnt-offering, or cereal offering, or incense, or wood, by the hand of one smitten with any uncleanness, permitting him thus to defile the altar. For it is written, *The sacrifice of the wicked is an abomination, but the prayer of the just is as an agreeable offering* (Prov. xv, 8).

No man entering the house of worship shall come unclean and in need of washing. And at the sounding of the trumpets for assembly, he shall go there before or after (the meeting), and shall not cause the whole service to stop, **XII** for it is a holy service.

No man shall lie with a woman in the city of the Sanctuary, to defile the city of the Sanctuary with their uncleanness.

Every man who preaches apostasy under the dominion of the spirits of Satan shall be judged according to the law relating to those possessed by a ghost or familiar spirit (Lev. xx, 27). But no man who strays so as to profane the Sabbath and the feasts shall be put to death; it shall fall to men to keep him in custody. And if he is healed of his error, they shall keep him in custody for seven years and he shall afterwards approach the Assembly.

No man shall stretch out his hand to shed the blood of a Gentile for the sake of riches and gain. Nor shall he carry off anything of theirs, lest they blaspheme, unless so advised by the company of Israel.

No man shall sell clean beasts or birds to the Gentiles lest they offer them in sacrifice. He shall refuse, with all his power, to sell them anything from his granary or wine-press, and he shall not sell them his manservant or maidservant inasmuch as they have been brought by him into the Covenant of Abraham.

No man shall defile himself by eating any live creature or creeping thing, from the larvae of bees to all creatures which creep in water. They shall eat no fish unless split alive and their blood poured out. And as for locusts, according to their various kinds they shall plunge them alive into fire or water, for this is what their nature requires.

All wood and stones and dust defiled by the impurity of a man shall be reckoned like men with regard to conveying defilement; whoever touches them shall be defiled by their defilement. And every nail or peg in the wall of a house in which a dead man lies shall become unclean as any working tool becomes unclean (Lev. xi, 32).

The Rule for the assembly of the towns shall be according to these precepts that they may distinguish between unclean and clean, and discriminate between the holy and the profane.

And these are the precepts in which the Master shall walk in his commerce with all the living in accordance with the statute proper to every age. And in accordance with this statute shall the seed of Israel walk and they shall not be cursed.

This is the Rule for the assembly of the camps

Those who follow these statutes in the age of wickedness

until the coming of the Messiah of Aaron **XIII** and Israel shall form groups of at least ten men, by *Thousands, Hundreds, Fifties, and Tens* (Exod. xviii, 25). And where the ten are, there shall never be lacking a Priest learned in the Book of Meditation; they shall all be ruled by him.

But should he not be experienced in these matters, whereas one of the Levites is experienced in them, then it shall be determined that all the members of the camp shall go and come according to the latter's word.

But should there be a case of applying the law of leprosy to a man, then the Priest shall come and shall stand in the camp and the Guardian shall instruct him in the exact interpretation of the Law.

Even if the Priest is a simpleton, it is he who shall lock up (the leper); for theirs is the judgement.

This is the Rule for the Guardian of the Camp

He shall instruct the Congregation in the works of God. He shall cause them to consider His mighty deeds and shall recount all the happenings of eternity to them. . . . He shall love them as a father loves his children, and shall carry them in all their distress like a shepherd his sheep. He shall loosen all the fetters which bind them that in his Congregation there may be none that are oppressed or broken.

He shall examine every man entering his Congregation with regard to his deeds, understanding, strength, ability, and possessions, and shall inscribe him in his place according to his rank in the lot of L[ight].

No member of the camp shall have authority to admit a man to the Congregation against the decision of the Guardian of the camp.

No member of the Covenant of God shall give or receive anything from the sons of the Pit except for payment.

No man shall form any association for buying and selling without informing the Guardian of the camp . . .

This is the Rule for the assembly of the camps during all [the age of wickedness, and whoever does not hold fast to] these (statutes) shall not be fit to dwell in the Land [when the Messiah of Aaron and Israel shall come at the end of days].

[And] these are the [precepts] in which the Master [shall walk in his commerce with all the living until God shall visit the earth. As He said, *There shall come upon you, and upon your people, and upon your father's house, days*] **XIV** *such as have not come since Ephraim departed from Judah* (Isa. vii, 17); but for whoever shall walk in these (precepts), the Covenant of God shall stand firm to save him from all the snares of the Pit, whereas the foolish shall be punished.

The Rule for the assembly of all the camps

They shall all be enrolled by name: first the Priests, second the Levites, third the Israelites, and fourth the proselytes. And they shall be inscribed by name, one after the other: the Priests first, the Levites second, the Israelites third, and the proselytes fourth. And thus shall they sit and thus be questioned on all matters. And the Priest who enrols the Congregation shall be from thirty to sixty years old, learned in the Book of Meditation and in all the judgements of the Law so as to pronounce them correctly.

The Guardian of all the camps shall be from thirty to fifty years old, one who has mastered all the secrets of men and the languages of all their clans. Whoever enters the Congregation shall do so according to his word, each in his rank. And whoever has anything to say with regard to any suit or judgement, let him say it to the Guardian.

This is the Rule for the Congregation by which it shall provide for all its needs

They shall place the earnings of at least two days out of every month into the hands of the Guardian and the Judges, and from it they shall give to the fatherless, and from it they shall succour the poor and the needy, the aged sick and the homeless, the captive taken by a foreign people, the virgin with no near kin, and the ma[id for] whom no man cares ...

And this is the exact statement of the assembly . . .

This is the exact statement of the statutes in which [they shall walk until the coming of the Messia]h of Aaron and Israel who will pardon their iniquity

[Whoever] deliberately lies in a matter of property . . . and shall do penance for six days . . .

[Whoever slanders his companion or bears rancour] unjustly [shall do penance for one] year . . .

· 6 ·

THE MESSIANIC RULE

THE Messianic Rule was published in 1955 by D. Barthélemy
in *Qumran Cave I* (Oxford, pp. 107–18). Originally included
in the same Scroll as the Community Rule, this short but complete work presents the translator with great difficulties owing to
its bad state of preservation and to the carelessness of the
scribe.

Barthélemy named the work 'The Rule of the Congregation',
but I have given it a new title for the following reasons: (1) it was
intended for 'all the congregation in the *last days*'; (2) it is a Rule
for a Community adapted to the requirements of the Messianic
war against the nations; (3) it refers to the presence of the Priest
and the Messiah of Israel at the Council, and at the Meal described in column II.

In the main, the precepts and doctrinal concepts of the Messianic Rule correspond to those of the War Rule, and in the absence of any direct chronological evidence it seems reasonable to
assume that they were both written during the same period, i.e.
in the final decades of the pre-Christian era or at the beginning
of the first century A.D.

I *This is the Rule for all the congregation of Israel in the last
days, when they shall join [the Community to wa]lk according to the
law of the sons of Zadok the Priests and of the men of their Covenant
who have turned aside [from the] way of the people, the men of His
Council who keep His Covenant in the midst of iniquity, offering
expiation [for the Land]*

When they come, they shall summon them all, the little
children and the women also, and they shall read into their
[ears] the precepts of the Covenant and shall expound to
them all their statutes that they may no longer stray in
their [errors].

And this is the Rule for all the hosts of the congregation, for every man born in Israel.

From [his] youth they shall instruct him in the Book of Meditation and shall teach him, according to his age, the precepts of the Covenant. He [shall be edu]cated in their statutes for ten years ...

At the age of twenty years [he shall be] enrolled, that he may enter upon his allotted duties in the midst of his family (and) be joined to the holy congregation. He shall not [approach] a woman to know her by lying with her before he is fully twenty years old, when he shall know [good] and evil. And thereafter, he shall be accepted when he calls to witness the judgements of the Law, and shall be (allowed) to assist at the hearing of judgements.

At the age of twenty-five years he may take his place among the foundations (i.e. the lower ranks) of the holy congregation to work in the service of the congregation.

At the age of thirty years he may approach to participate in lawsuits and judgements, and may take his place among the chiefs of the Thousands of Israel, the chiefs of the Hundreds, Fifties, and Tens, the Judges and the officers of their tribes, in all their families, [under the authority] of the sons of [Aar]on the Priests. And every head of family in the congregation who is chosen to hold office, [to go] and come before the congregation, shall strengthen his loins that he may perform his tasks among his brethren in accordance with his understanding and the perfection of his way. According to whether this is great or little, so shall one man be honoured more than another.

When a man is advanced in years, he shall be given a duty in the [ser]vice of the congregation in proportion to his strength.

No simpleton shall be chosen to hold office in the congregation of Israel with regard to lawsuits or judgement, nor carry any responsibility in the congregation. Nor shall he hold any office in the war destined to vanquish the nations;

his family shall merely inscribe him in the army register and he shall do his service in task-work in proportion to his capacity.

The sons of Levi shall hold office, each in his place, under the authority of the sons of Aaron. They shall cause all the congregation to go and come, each man in his rank, under the direction of the heads of family of the congregation – the leaders, Judges, and officers, according to the number of all their hosts – under the authority of the sons of Zadok the Priests, [and] (under the direction) [of all the] heads of family of the congregation. And when the whole assembly is summoned for judgement, or for a Council of the Community, or for war, they shall sanctify them for three days that every one of its members may be prepared.

These are the men who shall be called to the Council of the Community ...

All the wi[se men] of the congregation, the learned and the intelligent, men whose way is perfect and men of ability, together with the tribal chiefs and all the Judges and officers, and the chiefs of the Thousands, [Hundreds,] **II** Fifties, and Tens, and the Levites, each man in the [cla]ss of his duty; these are the men of renown, the members of the assembly summoned to the Council of the Community in Israel before the sons of Zadok the Priests.

And no man smitten with any human uncleanness shall enter the assembly of God; no man smitten with any of them shall be confirmed in his office in the congregation. No man smitten in his flesh, or paralysed in his feet or hands, or lame, or blind, or deaf, or dumb, or smitten in his flesh with a visible blemish; no old and tottery man unable to stay still in the midst of the congregation; none of these shall come to hold office among the congregation of the men of renown, for the Angels of Holiness are [with] their [congregation]. Should [one] of them have something to say to the Council of Holiness, let [him] be questioned privately; but let him not enter among [the congregation] for he is smitten.

[This shall be the ass]embly of the men of renown [called] to the meeting of the Council of the Community when [the Priest-]Messiah shall summon them

He shall come [at] the head of the whole congregation of Israel with all [his brethren, the sons] of Aaron the Priests, [those called] to the assembly, the men of renown; and they shall sit [before him, each man] in the order of his dignity. And then [the Mess]iah of Israel shall [come], and the chiefs of the [clans of Israel] shall sit before him, [each] in the order of his dignity, according to [his place] in their camps and marches. And before them shall sit all the heads of [family of the congreg]ation, and the wise men of [the holy congregation,] each in the order of his dignity.

And [when] they shall gather for the common [tab]le, to eat and [to drink] new wine, when the common table shall be set for eating and the new wine [poured] for drinking, let no man extend his hand over the first-fruits of bread and wine before the Priest; for [it is he] who shall bless the first-fruits of bread and wine, and shall be the first [to extend] his hand over the bread. Thereafter, the Messiah of Israel shall extend his hand over the bread, [and] all the Congregation of the Community [shall utter a] blessing, [each man in the order] of his dignity.

It is according to this statute that they shall proceed at every me[al at which] at least ten men are gathered together.

· 7 ·

THE WAR RULE

THE nineteen badly mutilated columns of this manuscript first appeared in 1954 in a posthumous work by E. L. Sukenik, and were re-edited in 1955, with an English introduction, under the title *The Dead Sea Scrolls of the Hebrew University* (Jerusalem).

The contents of the War Rule are as follows:

Proclamation of war against the Kittim (col. i)
Reorganization of Temple worship (col. ii)
Programme of the forty years' war (col. ii)
The trumpets (col. iii)
The standards (cols. iii–iv)
Disposition and weapons of the front formations (col. v)
Movements of the attacking infantry (col. vi)
Disposition and movements of the cavalry (col. vi)
Age of the soldiers (cols. vi–vii)
The camp (col. vii)
Duties of the Priests and Levites
    (exhortation, trumpet signals) (cols. vii–ix)
Addresses and prayers of the battle liturgy (cols. x–xii)
Prayer recited at the moment of victory (col. xiii)
Thanksgiving ceremony (col. xiv)
Battle against the Kittim (cols. xv–xix)

Since the five last columns are more or less repetitious there has been some doubt concerning the unity of the composition. Those who consider all nineteen columns to be the work of one writer find in column i an introduction, in columns ii–xiv general rules, and in columns xv–xix a 'prophetic' description of the final battle fought according to those rules. Other experts explain that columns xv–xix are a Rule annexe dependent on the principal Rule (cols. ii–xiv).

I am myself inclined to follow the theory first advanced by J. van der Ploeg (*Le Rouleau de la guerre*, Leiden, 1959, pp. 11–22). The primitive work, represented in the present composition by columns i and xv–xix, draws its inspiration from Daniel xi, 40–xii,

3, and describes the final battle against the Kittim. This account was later combined with the concept of a holy forty years' war against the entire Gentile world, and was extended by the addition of a long series of Rules concerned with the military and religious preparation and with the conduct of the fighting (cols. II–XIV). This appears to me to offer a more satisfactory explanation of the literary complexities of the manuscript than do the previous hypotheses.

The only certain pointer to the date of the compilation of the War Rule is that, since the author made use of the book of Daniel written in about 160 B.C., his own work must have been started after that time. But a more accurate dating may be attempted by studying the military strategy and tactics described in the Scroll. Scholars are divided in their opinion as to whether the sons of light modelled them on Greek or Roman custom, or whether they merely drew their ideas from the Bible. Scripture doubtless exercised a definite influence on the author of this Rule, but there is nevertheless a great deal of material completely foreign to it, and he must have possessed, in addition, at least some acquaintance with contemporary warfare.

With Y. Yadin and other archaeologists and historians, I believe that both the weapons and the tactics of the War Rule correspond to the art of war practised by the Roman legion rather than by the Greek phalanx. In particular, the square shield (*scutum*) of the foot-soldier, and the buckler of the horseman (*parma* or *clipeus*), the battle array of three lines (*acies triplex*), the openings between the units, viz. the 'gates of war' (*intervalla*), seem to be characteristically Roman. In addition, only the cavalry were to wear greaves – a custom introduced into the Roman army during the time of Julius Caesar in the middle of the first century B.C. This and similar details, as well as the general representation of the Kittim as masters of the world, lead one to conclude that the War Rule was written some time after the middle of the first century B.C., and as the reference to the 'king' of the Kittim points to the Imperial epoch (after 27 B.C.), the date of its composition should probably be placed in the last decades of the first century B.C. or at the beginning of the first century A.D.

This work should not be mistaken for a manual of military warfare pure and simple. It is a theological writing, and the war of which it treats symbolizes the eternal struggle between the spirits of Light and Darkness. The phases of its battle are fixed in advance, its plan established, and its duration predetermined. The opposing forces are equally matched and only by the intervention of 'the mighty hand of God' is the balance between them to be disturbed when He deals an 'everlasting blow' to 'Satan and all the host of his kingdom'.

I *For the M[aster. The Rule of] War on the unleashing of the attack of the sons of light against the company of the sons of darkness, the army of Satan: against the band of Edom, Moab, and the sons of Ammon, and [against the army of the sons of the East and] the Philistines, and against the bands of the Kittim of Assyria and their allies the ungodly of the Covenant*

The sons of Levi, Judah, and Benjamin, the exiles in the desert, shall battle against them in ... all their bands when the exiled sons of light return from the Desert of the Peoples to camp in the Desert of Jerusalem; and after the battle they shall go up from there (to Jerusalem?).

[The king] of the Kittim [shall enter] into Egypt, and in his time he shall set out in great wrath to wage war against the kings of the north, that his fury may destroy and cut off the horn of [the nations].

This shall be a time of salvation for the people of God, an age of dominion for all the members of His company, and of everlasting destruction for all the company of Satan. The confusion of the sons of Japheth shall be [great] and Assyria shall fall unsuccoured. The dominion of the Kittim shall come to an end and iniquity shall be vanquished, leaving no remnant; [for the sons] of darkness there shall be no escape. [The seasons of righteous]ness shall shine over all the ends of the earth; they shall go on shining until all the seasons of darkness are consumed and, at the season appointed by God, His exalted greatness shall shine eternally to the peace, blessing, glory, joy, and long life of all the sons of light.

On the day when the Kittim fall, there shall be battle and terrible carnage before the God of Israel, for that shall be the day appointed from ancient times for the battle of destruction of the sons of darkness. At that time, the assembly of gods and the hosts of men shall battle, causing great carnage; on the day of calamity, the sons of light shall battle with the company of darkness amid the shouts of a mighty multitude and the clamour of gods and men to (make manifest) the might of God. And it shall be a time of [great] tribulation for the people which God shall redeem; of all its afflictions none shall be as this, from its sudden beginning until its end in eternal redemption.

On the day of their battle against the Kittim [they shall set out for] carnage. In three lots shall the sons of light brace themselves in battle to strike down iniquity, and in three lots shall Satan's host gird itself to thrust back the company [of God. And when the hearts of the detach]ments of foot-soldiers faint, then shall the might of God fortify [the heart of the sons of light]. And with the seventh lot, the mighty hand of God shall bring down [the army of Satan, and all] the angels of his kingdom, and all the members [of his company in everlasting destruction] . . .

II the fifty-two heads of family in the congregation.

They shall rank the chief Priests below the High Priest and his vicar. And the twelve chief Priests shall minister at the daily sacrifice before God, whereas the twenty-six leaders of the priestly divisions shall minister in their divisions.

Below them, in perpetual ministry, shall be the chiefs of the Levites to the number of twelve, one for each tribe. The leaders of their divisions shall minister each in his place.

Below them shall be the chiefs of the tribes together with the heads of family of the congregation. They shall attend daily at the gates of the Sanctuary, whereas the leaders of their divisions, with their numbered men, shall attend at their appointed times, on new moons and on Sabbaths and on all the days of the year, their age being fifty years and over.

These are the men who shall attend at holocausts and

sacrifices to prepare sweet-smelling incense for the good pleasure of God, to atone for all His congregation, and to satisfy themselves perpetually before Him at the table of glory. They shall arrange all these things during the season of the year of Release.

During the remaining thirty-three years of the war, the men of renown, those summoned to the Assembly, together with all the heads of family of the congregation, shall choose for themselves fighting-men for all the lands of the nations. They shall arm for themselves warriors from all the tribes of Israel to enter the army year by year when they are summoned to war. But they shall arm no man for entry into the army during the years of Release, for they are Sabbaths of rest for Israel. In the thirty-five years of service, the war shall be fought during six; the whole congregation shall fight it together.

And during the remaining twenty-nine years the war shall be divided. During the first year they shall fight against Aram-Naharaim; during the second, against the sons of Lud; during the third, against the remnant of the sons of Aram, against Uz and Hul and Togar and Mesha beyond the Euphrates; during the fourth and fifth, they shall fight against the sons of Arphakshad; during the sixth and seventh, against all the sons of Assyria and Persia and the East as far as the Great Desert; during the eighth year they shall fight against the sons of Elam; during the ninth, against the sons of Ishmael and Keturah. In the ten years which follow, the war shall be divided against all the sons of Ham according to [their clans and in their ha]bitations; and during the ten years which remain, the war shall be divided against all [the sons of Japhethin] their habitations.

[The Rule for the trumpets of Summons and the trumpe]ts of Alarm according to all their duties

... [the trumpets of Summons shall sound for disposal in]
III battle formations and to summon the foot-soldiers to advance when the gates of war shall open; and the trumpets

of Alarm shall sound for massacre, and for ambush, and for pursuit when the enemy shall be smitten, and for withdrawal from battle.

On the trumpets calling the congregation they shall write, *The Called of God*.

On the trumpets calling the chiefs they shall write, *The Princes of God*.

On the trumpets of the levies they shall write, *The Army of God*.

On the trumpets of the men of renown and of the heads of family of the congregation gathered in the house of Assembly they shall write, *Summoned by God to the Council of Holiness*.

On the trumpets of the camps they shall write, *The Peace of God in the Camps of His Saints*.

And on the trumpets for breaking camp they shall write, *The mighty Deeds of God shall crush the Enemy, putting to Flight all those who hate Righteousness and bringing Shame on those who hate Him*.

On the trumpets for battle formations they shall write, *Formations of the Divisions of God for the Vengeance of His Wrath on the Sons of Darkness*.

On the trumpets summoning the foot-soldiers to advance towards the enemy formations when the gates of war are opened they shall write, *Reminder of Vengeance in God's appointed Time*.

On the trumpets of massacre they shall write, *The mighty Hand of God in War shall cause all the ungodly Slain to fall*.

On the trumpets of ambush they shall write, *The Mysteries of God shall undo Wickedness*.

On the trumpets of pursuit they shall write, *God has smitten all the Sons of Darkness; His Fury shall not end until they are utterly consumed*.

On the trumpets of withdrawal, when they withdraw from battle to the formation, they shall write, *God has re-assembled*.

On the trumpets of return from battle against the enemy

when they journey to the congregation in Jerusalem they shall write, *Rejoicings of God in the peaceful Return.*

The Rule for the standards of the whole congregation according to their levies

On the Great Standard at the head of the people they shall write, *The People of God*, together with the names of Israel and Aaron, and the names of the twelve [tribes of Israel] according to the order of their precedence.

On the standards of the camp columns formed by three tribes they shall write, . . . *of God*, together with the name of the leader of the camp . . .

On the standard of the tribe they shall write, *Banner of God*, together with the name of the leader of [the tribe and the names of the chiefs of its clans].

[On the standard of the Myriad they shall write, . . . *of God*, together with] the name of the chief of the Myriad and the names of the [leaders of its Thousands].

[On the standard of the Thousand they shall write, . . . *of God*, together with the name of the chief of the Thousand and the names of the leaders of its Hundreds].

[On the standard of the Hundred] . . .

IV On the standard of Merari they shall write, *The Votive-Offering of God*, together with the name of the chief of Merari and the names of the leaders of its Thousands.

On the standard of the Thousand they shall write, *The Wrath of God is kindled against Satan and against the Men of his Company, leaving no Remnant,* together with the name of the chief of the Thousand and the names of the leaders of its Hundreds.

On the standard of the Hundred they shall write, *From God comes the Might of War against all sinful Flesh,* together with the name of the chief of the Hundred and the names of the leaders of its Fifties.

On the standard of the Fifty they shall write, *The Stand of the Ungodly is ended by the Power of God,* together with the name of the chief of the Fifty and the names of the leaders of its Tens.

On the standard of the Ten they shall write, *Praised be God on the ten-stringed Harp*, together with the name of the chief of the Ten and the names of the nine men under his command.

When they march out to battle they shall write on their standards, *Truth of God, Justice of God, Glory of God, Judgement of God*, followed by the whole ordered list of their names.

When they approach for battle they shall write on their standards, *Right Hand of God, Appointed Time of God, Tumult of God, Slain of God*, followed by the whole list of their names.

When they return from battle they shall write on their standards, *Honour of God, Majesty of God, Splendour of God, Glory of God*, together with the whole list of their names.

The Rule for the standards of the congregation

When they set out for battle they shall write, on the first standard *Congregation of God*, on the second standard *Camps of God*, on the third standard *Tribes of God*, on the fourth standard *Clans of God*, on the fifth standard *Divisions of God*, on the sixth standard *Assembly of God*, on the seventh standard *The Called of God*, on the eighth standard *Hosts of God*; and they shall write the list of their names with all their order.

When they approach for battle they shall write on their standards, *War of God, Vengeance of God, Trial of God, Reward of God, Power of God, Retributions of God, Might of God, Extermination of God for all the Nations of Vanity*; and they shall write on them the whole list of their names.

When they return from battle they shall write on their standards, *Salvation of God, Victory of God, Help of God, Support of God, Joy of God, Thanksgivings of God, Praise of God, Peace of God*.

[The measurements of the standards.] The standard of the

whole congregation shall be fourteen cubits long; the standard [of the three tribes,] thirteen cubits long; [the standard of the tribe,] twelve cubits; [the standard of the Myriad], eleven cubits; [the standard of the Thousand, ten cubits; the standard of the Hundred,] nine cubits; [the standard of the Fifty, eight] cubits; the standard of the Ten, s[even cubits] ...

V And on the sh[ield of] the Prince of the congregation they shall write his name, together with the names of Israel, Levi, and Aaron, and the names of the twelve tribes of Israel according to the order of their precedence, with the names of their twelve chiefs.

The Rule for the ordering of the battle divisions to complete a front formation when their host has reached its full number

The formation shall consist of one thousand men ranked seven lines deep, each man standing behind the other.

They shall all hold shields of bronze burnished like mirrors. The shield shall be edged with an interlaced border and with inlaid ornament, a work of art in pure gold and silver and bronze and precious stones, a many-coloured design worked by a craftsman. The length of the shield shall be two and a half cubits and its width one and a half cubits.

In their hands they shall hold a spear and a sword. The length of the spear shall be seven cubits, of which the socket and spike shall measure half a cubit. The socket shall be edged with three embossed interlaced rings of pure gold and silver and bronze, a work of art. The inlaid ornaments on both edges of the ring shall be bordered with precious stones – patterned bands worked by a craftsman – and (embossed) with ears of corn. Between the rings, the socket shall be embossed with artistry like a pillar. The spike shall be made of brilliant white iron, the work of a craftsman; in its centre, pointing towards the tip, shall be ears of corn in pure gold.

The swords shall be made of pure iron refined by the

smelter and blanched to resemble a mirror, the work of a craftsman; on both sides (of their blades) pointing towards the tip, figured ears of corn shall be embossed in pure gold, and they shall have two straight borders on each side. The length of the sword shall be one and a half cubits and its width four fingers. The width of the scabbard shall be four thumbs. There shall be four palms to the scabbard (from the girdle), and it shall be attached (to the girdle) on both sides for a length of five palms (?). The hilt of the sword shall be of pure horn worked by a craftsman, with patterned bands in gold and silver and precious stones. ...

VI seven times and shall return to their positions.

And after them, three divisions of foot-soldiers shall advance and shall station themselves between the formations, and the first division shall hurl seven javelins of war towards the enemy formation. On the point of the javelins they shall write, *Shining Javelin of the Power of God*; and on the darts of the second division they shall write, *Bloody Spikes to bring down the Slain by the Wrath of God*; and on the javelins of the third division they shall write, *Flaming Blade to devour the Wicked struck down by the Judgement of God*. All these shall hurl their javelins seven times and shall afterwards return to their positions.

Then two divisions of foot-soldiers shall advance and shall station themselves between the two formations. The first division shall be armed with a spear and a shield, and the second with a shield and a sword, to bring down the slain by the judgement of God, and to bend the enemy formation by the power of God, to pay the reward of their wickedness to all the nations of vanity. And sovereignty shall be to the God of Israel, and He shall accomplish mighty deeds by the saints of His people.

Seven troops of horsemen shall also station themselves to right and to left of the formation; their troops shall stand on this (side) and on that, seven hundred horsemen on one flank and seven hundred horsemen on the other. Two hundred horsemen shall advance with the thousand men of the formation of foot-soldiers; and they shall likewise station themselves on both [flanks] of the camp. Altogether there shall be four thousand six hundred (men), and one thousand cavalrymen with the men of the army formations, fifty to each formation. The horsemen, together with the cavalry of the army, shall number six thousand: five hundred to each tribe.

The horses advancing into battle with the foot-soldiers shall all be stallions; they shall be swift, sensitive of mouth, and sound of wind, and of the required age, trained for war, and accustomed to noise and to every (kind of) sight. Their riders shall be gallant fighting men and skilled horsemen, and their age shall be from thirty to forty-five years. The horsemen of the army shall be from forty to fifty years old. They [and their mounts shall wear breast-plates,] helmets, and greaves; they shall carry in their hands bucklers, and a spear [eight cubits] long. [The horsemen advancing with the foot-soldiers shall carry] bows and arrows and javelins of war. They shall all hold themselves prepared . . . of God and to spill the blood of the wicked . . .

VII The men of the army shall be from forty to fifty years old.

The inspectors of the camps shall be from fifty to sixty years old.

The officers shall be from forty to fifty years old.

The despoilers of the slain, the plunderers of booty, the cleansers of the land, the keepers of the baggage, and those who furnish the provisions shall be from twenty-five to thirty years old.

No boy or woman shall enter their camps, from the time they leave Jerusalem and march out to war until they return. No man who is lame, or blind, or crippled, or afflicted with a lasting bodily blemish, or smitten with a bodily impurity, none of these shall march out to war with them. They shall all be freely enlisted for war, perfect in spirit and body and prepared for the Day of Vengeance. And no man shall go down with them on the day of battle who is impure because of his 'fount', for the holy angels shall be with their hosts. And there shall be a space of about two thousand cubits between all their camps and the place serving as a latrine, so that no indecent nakedness may be seen in the surroundings of their camps.

When the battle formations are marshalled facing the enemy, formation facing formation, seven Priests of the sons of Aaron shall advance from the middle gates to the place between the formations. They shall be clothed in vestments of white cloth of flax, in a fine linen tunic and fine linen breeches; and they shall be girdled with fine cloth of flax embroidered with blue, purple, and scarlet thread, a many-coloured design worked by a craftsman. And on their heads they shall wear mitred turbans. These shall be battle raiment; they shall not take them into the Sanctuary.

The first Priest shall advance before the men of the formation to strengthen their hand for battle, and the six other Priests shall hold in their hands the trumpets of Summons, and the trumpets of the Reminder, and the trumpets of Alarm (for massacre), and the trumpets of Pursuit, and the trumpets of Withdrawal. And when the Priests advance to the place between the formations, seven Levites shall accompany them bearing in their hands seven rams' horns; and three officers of the Levites shall walk before the Priests and Levites. The Priests shall sound the two trumpets of Sum[mons for the gates of] war to open fifty shields (wide) and the foot-soldiers shall advance, fifty from one gate [and fifty from the other. With them shall advance] the officers of the Levites, and they shall advance with every formation according to all this R[ule].

[The Priests shall sound the trumpets, and two divisions of foot-]soldiers [shall advance] from the gates [and shall]

station [themselves] between the two [formations] ...
VIII the trumpets shall sound to direct the slingers until
they have cast seven times. Afterwards, the Priests shall
sound for them the trumpets of Withdrawal and they shall
return to the flank of the first formation to take up their
position.

Then the Priests shall sound the trumpets of Summons
and three divisions of foot-soldiers shall advance from the
gates and shall station themselves between the formations;
the horsemen shall be on their flanks, to right and to left.
The Priests shall sound a sustained blast on the trumpets for
battle array, and the columns shall move to their (battle)
array, each man to his place. And when they have taken
up their stand in three arrays, the Priests shall sound a
second signal, soft and sustained, for them to advance until
they are close to the enemy formation. They shall seize their
weapons, and the Priests shall then blow a shrill staccato
blast on the six trumpets of Massacre to direct the battle,
and the Levites and all the blowers of rams' horns shall
sound a mighty alarm to terrify the heart of the enemy, and
therewith the javelins shall fly out to bring down the slain.
Then the sound of the horns shall cease, but the Priests shall
continue to blow a shrill staccato blast on the trumpets to
direct the battle until they have thrown seven times against
the enemy formation. And then they shall sound a soft, a
sustained, and a shrill sound on the trumpets of Withdrawal.

It is according to this Rule that the Priests shall sound the
trumpets for the three divisions. With the first throw, the
[Priests] shall sound [on the trumpets] a mighty alarm to
direct the ba[ttle until they have thrown seven times. Then]
the Priests [shall sound] for them on the trumpets [of Withdrawal a soft, sustained, and a shrill sound, and they shall
return] to their positions in the formation.

[Then the Priests shall blow the trumpets of Summons
and the two divisions of foot-soldiers shall advance from the
gates] and shall stand [between the formations. And the

Priests shall then blow the trumpets of] Massacre, [and the Levites and all the blowers of rams' horns shall sound an alarm, a mighty blast, and therewith] **IX** they shall set about to bring down the slain with their hands. All the people shall cease their clamour but the Priests shall continue to blow the trumpets of Massacre to direct the battle until the enemy is smitten and put to flight; and the Priests shall blow to direct the battle.

And when they are smitten before them, the Priests shall sound the trumpets of Summons and all the foot-soldiers shall rally to them from the midst of the front formations, and the six divisions, together with the fighting division, shall take up their stations. Altogether, they shall be seven formations: twenty-eight thousand fighting men and six thousand horsemen.

All these shall pursue the enemy to destroy him in an everlasting destruction in the battle of God. The Priests shall sound for them the trumpets of Pursuit, and they shall deploy against all the enemy in a pursuit to destruction; and the horsemen shall thrust them back on the flanks of the battle until they are utterly destroyed.

And as the slain men fall, the Priests shall trumpet from afar; they shall not approach the slain lest they be defiled with unclean blood. For they are holy, and they shall not profane the anointing of their priesthood with the blood of nations of vanity.

The Rule for changes in battle order to form the position of a squa[re with towers,] a concave line with towers, a convex line with towers, a shallow convex line obtained by the advance of the centre, or [by the advance of] both flanks to terrify the enemy

The shields of the towers shall be three cubits long and their spears eight cubits. The tower shall advance from the formation and shall have one hundred shields to each side; in this [manner,] the tower shall be surrounded on three sides by three hundred shields. And it shall also have two gates, [one to the right] and one to the left.

They shall write on all the shields of the towers: on the first, *Michael,* [on the second, *Gabriel,* on the third,] *Sariel,* and on the fourth, *Raphael. Michael* and *Gabriel* [shall stand on the right, and *Sariel* and *Raphael* on the left] . . . they shall set an ambush to . . .

. . . **X** our camps and to keep us from all that is indecent and evil.

Furthermore, (Moses) taught us, 'Thou art in the midst of us, a mighty God and terrible, causing all our enemies to flee before [us].' He taught our generations in former times saying, 'When you draw near to battle, the Priest shall rise and speak to the people saying, "Hear, O Israel! You draw near to battle this day against your enemies. Do not fear! Do not let your hearts be afraid! Do not be [terrified], and have no fear! For your God goes with you to fight for you against your enemies that He may deliver you"' (Deut. xx, 2–4).

Our officers shall speak to all those prepared for battle. They shall strengthen by the power of God the freely devoted of heart, and shall make all the fearful of heart withdraw; they shall fortify all the mighty men of war. They shall recount that which Thou [saidst] through Moses: 'When you go to war in your land against the oppressor who oppresses you, [you] shall blow the trumpets, and you shall be remembered before your God and shall be saved from your enemies' (Num. x, 9).

O God of Israel, who is like Thee
   in heaven or on earth?
Who accomplishes deeds and mighty works like Thine?
Who is like Thy people Israel
   which Thou hast chosen for Thyself
   from all the peoples of the lands;
the people of the saints of the Covenant,
   instructed in the laws
   and learned in wisdom . . .

who have heard the voice of Majesty
  and have seen the Angels of Holiness,
whose ear has been unstopped,
  and who have heard profound things?

[Thou, O God, hast created] the expanse of the heavens
  and the host of heavenly lights,
the tasks of the spirits
  and the dominion of the Holy Ones,
the treasury of glory
  [and the canopy of the] clouds.
(Thou art Creator of) the earth
  and of the laws dividing it into desert and grassland;
of all that it brings forth
  and of all its fruits [according to their kinds;]
of the circle of the seas
  and of the gathering-place of the rivers
  and of the divisions of the deeps;
of the beasts and birds
  and of the shape of Adam
  and of the gene[rations of] his [seed];
of the confusion of tongues
  and of the scattering of the peoples,
of the dwelling in clans
  and of the inheritance of lands;
... of the sacred seasons
  and of the cycles of the years
  and of time everlasting.

...

XI Truly, the battle is Thine! Their bodies are crushed
by the might of Thy hand and there is no man to bury
them.

Thou didst deliver Goliath of Gath, the mighty warrior,
into the hands of David Thy servant, because in place of the
sword and in place of the spear he put his trust in Thy great
Name; for Thine is the battle. Many times, by Thy great
Name, did he triumph over the Philistines. Many times hast

Thou also delivered us by the hand of our kings through Thy lovingkindness, and not in accordance with our works by which we have done evil, nor according to our rebellious deeds.

Truly the battle is Thine and the power from Thee! It is not ours. Our strength and the power of our hands accomplish no mighty deeds except by Thy power and by the might of Thy great valour. This Thou hast taught us from ancient times, saying, *A star shall come out of Jacob, and a sceptre shall rise out of Israel. He shall smite the temples of Moab and destroy all the children of Sheth. He shall rule out of Jacob and shall cause the survivors of the city to perish. The enemy shall be his possession and Israel shall accomplish mighty deeds* (Num. xxiv, 17–19).

By the hand of Thine anointed, who discerned Thy testimonies, Thou hast revealed to us the [times] of the battles of Thy hands that Thou mayest glorify Thyself in our enemies by levelling the hordes of Satan, the seven nations of vanity, by the hand of Thy poor whom Thou hast redeemed [by Thy might] and by the fulness of Thy marvellous power. (Thou hast opened) the door of hope to the melting heart: Thou wilt do to them as Thou didst to Pharaoh, and to the captains of his chariots in the Red Sea. Thou wilt kindle the downcast of spirit and they shall be a flaming torch in the straw to consume ungodliness and never to cease till iniquity is destroyed.

From ancient times Thou hast fore[told the hour] when the might of Thy hand (would be raised) against the Kittim, saying, *Assyria shall fall by the sword of no man, the sword of no mere man shall devour him* (Isa. xxxi, 8). For Thou wilt deliver into the hands of the poor the enemies from all the lands, to humble the mighty of the peoples by the hand of those bent to the dust, to bring upon the [head of Thine enemies] the reward of the wicked, and to justify Thy true judgement in the midst of all the sons of men, and to make for Thyself an everlasting Name among the people [whom Thou hast redeemed] ... of battles to be magnified and sanctified in the eyes of the remnant of the peoples, that they may know ... when Thou chastisest Gog and all his assembly gathered about him ...

For Thou wilt fight with them from heaven ... **XII** For the multitude of the Holy Ones [is with Thee] in heaven, and the host of the Angels is in Thy holy abode, praising Thy Name. And Thou hast established in [a community] for Thyself the elect of Thy holy people. [The list] of the names of all their host is with Thee in the abode of Thy holiness; [the reckoning of the saints] is in Thy glorious dwelling-place. Thou hast recorded for them, with the graving-tool of life, the favours of [Thy] blessings and the Covenant of Thy peace, that Thou mayest reign [over them] for ever and ever and throughout all the eternal ages. Thou wilt muster the [hosts of] Thine [el]ect, in their Thousands and Myriads, with Thy Holy Ones [and with all] Thine Angels, that they may be mighty in battle, [and may smite] the rebels of the earth by Thy great judgements, and that [they may triumph] together with the elect of heaven.

For Thou art [terrible], O God, in the glory of Thy kingdom, and the congregation of Thy Holy Ones is among us for everlasting succour. We will despise kings, we will mock and scorn the mighty; for our Lord is holy, and the King of Glory is with us together with the Holy Ones. Valiant [warriors] of the angelic host are among our numbered men, and the Hero of war is with our congregation; the host of His spirits is with our foot-soldiers and horsemen. [They are as] clouds, as clouds of dew (covering) the earth, as a shower of rain shedding righteousness on all that grows on the earth.

Rise up, O Hero!
Lead off Thy captives, O Glorious One!
Gather up Thy spoils, O Author of mighty deeds!
Lay Thy hand on the neck of Thine enemies
    and Thy feet on the pile of the slain!

Smite the nations, Thine adversaries,
    and devour the flesh of the sinner with Thy sword!
Fill Thy land with glory
    and Thine inheritance with blessing!
Let there be a multitude of cattle in Thy fields,
    and in Thy palaces silver and gold and precious stones!

O Zion, rejoice greatly!
O Jerusalem, show thyself amidst jubilation!
Rejoice, all you cities of Judah;
keep your gates ever open
    that the hosts of the nations
    may be brought in!

Their kings shall serve you
    and all your oppressors shall bow down before you;
    [they shall lick] the dust [of your feet].
Shout for joy, [O daughters of] my people!
Deck yourselves with glorious jewels
    and rule over [the kingdoms of the nations!
Sovereignty shall be to the Lord]
    and everlasting dominion to Israel.

. . .

. . .**XIII** (The High Priest) shall come, and his brethren the Priests and the Levites, and all the elders of the army shall be with him; and standing, they shall bless the God of Israel and all His works of truth, and shall execrate Satan there and all the spirits of his company. Speaking, they shall say:

Blessed be the God of Israel for all His holy purpose and for His works of truth! Blessed be all those who [serve] Him in righteousness and who know Him by faith!

Cursed be Satan for his sinful purpose and may he be execrated for his wicked rule! Cursed be all the spirits of his company for their ungodly purpose and may they be execrated for all their service of uncleanness! Truly they are the company of Darkness, but the company of God is one of [eternal] Light.

[Thou art] the God of our fathers; we bless Thy Name for ever. We are the people of Thine [inheritance]; Thou didst make a Covenant with our fathers, and wilt establish it with their children throughout eternal ages. And in all Thy glorious testimonies there has been a reminder of Thy mercies among us to succour the remnant, the survivors of Thy Covenant, that they might [recount] Thy works of truth and the judgements of Thy marvellous mighty deeds.

Thou [hast redeemed us] for Thyself, [O God], that we may be an everlasting people. Thou hast decreed for us a destiny of Light according to Thy truth. And the Prince of Light Thou hast appointed from ancient times to come to our support; [all the sons of righteousness are in his hand], and all the spirits of truth are under his dominion. But Satan, the Angel of Malevolence, Thou hast created for the Pit; his [rule] is in Darkness and his purpose is to bring about wickedness and iniquity. All the spirits of his company, the Angels of Destruction, walk according to the precepts of Darkness; towards them is their [inclination].

But let us, the company of Thy truth, rejoice in Thy mighty hand and be glad for Thy salvation, and exult because of Thy suc[cour and] peace. O God of Israel, who can compare with Thee in might? Thy mighty hand is with the poor. Which angel or prince can compare with Thy [redeeming] succour? [For Thou hast appointed] the day of battle from ancient times ... [to come to the aid] of truth and to destroy iniquity, to bring Darkness low and to magnify Light ... to stand for ever, and to destroy all the sons of Darkness ...

... **XIV** like the fire of His wrath against the idols of Egypt.

And when they have risen from the slain to return to the camp, they shall all sing the Psalm of Return. And in the morning, they shall wash their garments, and shall cleanse themselves of the blood of the bodies of the ungodly. And they shall return to the positions in which they stood in battle formation before the fall of the enemy slain, and there they shall all bless the God of Israel. Rejoicing together, they shall praise His Name, and speaking they shall say:

Blessed be the God of Israel
   who keeps mercy towards His Covenant,
and the appointed times of salvation
   with the people He has delivered!

He has called them that staggered
   to [marvellous mighty deeds],
and has gathered in the assembly of the nations
   to destruction without any remnant.
He has lifted up in judgement the fearful of heart
   and has opened the mouth of the dumb
     that they might praise [His mighty] works.
He has taught war [to the hand] of the feeble
   and steadied the trembling knee;
     he has braced the back of the smitten.
By the poor in spirit
   ... the hard of heart,
and by the perfect of way
   all the nations of wickedness have come to an end:
   not one of their mighty men stands.

But we, the remnant [of Thy people,
   shall praise] Thy Name, O God of mercies,
   who hast kept the Covenant with our fathers.
In all our generations Thou hast bestowed
   Thy wonderful favours on the remnant [of Thy people]
   under the dominion of Satan.
During all the mysteries of his Malevolence
   he has not made [us] stray from Thy Covenant;
Thou hast driven his spirits [of destruction]
   far from [Thine elect],

Thou hast preserved the soul of Thy redeemed
   [from all the snares] of his dominion.
Thou hast raised the fallen by Thy strength,
   but hast cut down the great in height
   [and hast brought down the lofty].
There is no rescue for all their mighty men
   and no refuge for their swift men;
Thou givest to their honoured men a reward of shame,
all their empty existence [hast Thou turned to nothing].

But we, Thy holy people, will praise Thy Name
   because of the works of Thy truth.
We will exalt Thy splendour because of Thy mighty deeds
   [in all the] seasons and appointed times for ever,
at the coming of day and at nightfall
   and at the departure of evening and morning.
For great [is the design of Thy glory]
   and of Thy wonderful mysteries on high
that [Thou shouldst raise up] dust before Thee
   and lay low the gods.

Rise up, rise up, O God of gods,
   rise up in [Thy might]!
... all the sons of Darkness.
The light of Thy greatness [shall shine forth]
   ...

XV For this shall be a time of distress for Israel, [and of the summons] to war against all the nations. There shall be eternal deliverance for the company of God, but destruction for all the nations of wickedness.

All those [who are ready] for battle shall march out and shall pitch their camp before the king of the Kittim and before all the host of Satan gathered about him for the Day [of Revenge] by the Sword of God.

Then the High Priest shall rise, with the [Priests], his brethren, and the Levites, and all the men of the army, and he shall recite aloud the Prayer in Time of War [written in the book] of the Rule concerning this time, and also all their Hymns. He shall marshal all the formations there, as is [written in the Book of War], and the priest appointed for the Day of Revenge by the voice of all his brethren shall go forward to strengthen the [hearts of the fighting men]. Speaking, he shall say:

Be strong and valiant; be warriors! Fear not! Do not be [confused and do not let your hearts be afraid!] Do not be fearful; fear them not! Do not fall back ... for they are a congregation of wickedness and all their works are in Darkness; they tend toward Darkness. [They make for themselves] a refuge [in falsehood] and their power shall vanish like smoke. All the multitudes of their community ... shall not be found. Damned as they are, all the substance of their wickedness shall quickly fade, like a flower in [the summertime].

[Be brave and] strong for the battle of God! For this day is [the time of the battle of] God against all the host of Satan, [and of the judgement of] all flesh. The God of Israel lifts His hand in His marvellous [might] against all the spirits of wickedness. [The hosts of] the warrior gods gird themselves for battle, [and the] formations of the Holy Ones [prepare themselves] for the Day [of Revenge] ... XVI ... For the God of Israel has called out the sword against all the nations, and He will do mighty deeds by the saints of His people.

And they shall obey all this Rule [on] the [day] when they stand before the camps of the Kittim

The Priests shall afterwards sound for them the trumpets of the Reminder, and the gates of war shall open; the foot-soldiers shall advance and the columns shall station themselves between the formations. The Priests shall sound for them the signal, 'Battle Array', and at the sound of the trumpets the columns [shall deploy] until every man is in his place. The Priests shall then sound a second signal [for them to advance], and when they are within throwing distance of the formation of the Kittim, each man shall seize his weapon of war. Then the six [Priests shall blow on] the trumpets of Massacre a shrill staccato blast to direct the battle, and the Levites and all the blowers of rams' horns shall sound [a battle alarm], a mighty clamour; and with this clamour they shall begin to bring down the slain from among the Kittim. All the people shall cease their clamour, [but the Priests shall continue to] sound the trumpets of Massacre, and battle shall be fought against the Kittim. And when [Satan] girds himself to come to the aid of the sons of darkness, and when the slain among the foot-soldiers begin to fall by the mysteries of God, and when all the men appointed for battle are put to ordeal by them, the Priests shall sound the trumpets of Summons for another formation of the reserve to advance into battle; and they shall take up their stand between the formations. And for those engaged [in battle] they shall sound the 'Withdrawal'.

Then the High Priest shall draw near, and standing before the formation, he shall strengthen by the power of God their hearts [and hands] in His battle. Speaking he shall say:

... **XVII** He will pay their reward with burning [fire by the hand of] those tested in the crucible. He will sharpen His weapons and will not tire until all the wicked nations are destroyed. Remember the judgement [of Nadab and Ab]ihu, sons of Aaron, by whose judgement God showed Himself holy in the eyes [of Israel. But Eleazar] and Ithamar He confirmed in an everlasting [priestly] Covenant.

Be strong and fear not; [for they tend] towards chaos and confusion, and they lean on that which is not and [shall not be. To the God] of Israel belongs all that is and shall be; [He knows] all the happenings of eternity. This is the day appointed by Him for the defeat and overthrow of the Prince of the kingdom of wickedness, and He will send eternal succour to the company of His redeemed by the might of the princely Angel of the kingdom of Michael.

With everlasting light He will enlighten with joy [the children] of Israel; peace and blessing shall be with the company of God. He will raise up the kingdom of Michael in the midst of the gods, and the realm of Israel in the midst of all flesh. Righteousness shall rejoice on high, and all the children of His truth shall jubilate in eternal knowledge.

And you, the sons of His Covenant, be strong in the ordeal of God! His mysteries shall uphold you until He moves His hand for His trials to come to an end.

After these words, the Priests shall sound to marshal them into the divisions of the formation; and at the sound of the trumpets the columns shall deploy until [every man is] in his place. Then the Priests shall sound a second signal on the trumpets for them to advance, and when the [foot-]soldiers approach throwing distance of the formation of the Kittim, every man shall seize his weapon of war. The Priests shall blow the trumpets of Massacre, [and the Levites and all] the blowers of rams' horns shall sound a battle alarm, and the foot-soldiers shall stretch out their hands against the host of the Kittim; [and at the sound of the alarm] they shall begin to bring down the slain. All the people shall cease their clamour, but the Priests shall continue to blow [the trumpets of Massacre and battle shall be fought against the Kittim.]

... and in the third lot ... that the slain may fall by the mysteries of God ...

XVIII [In the seventh lot] when the great hand of God is raised in an everlasting blow against Satan and all the hosts of his kingdom, and when Assyria is pursued [amidst the shouts of Angels] and the clamour of the Holy Ones, the sons of Japheth shall fall to rise no more. The Kittim shall be crushed without [remnant, and no man shall be saved from among them].

[At that time, on the day] when the hand of the God of Israel is raised against all the multitude of Satan, the Priests shall blow [the six trumpets] of the Reminder and all the battle formations shall rally to them and shall divide against all the [camps of the] Kittim to destroy them utterly. [And as] the sun speeds to its setting on that day, the High Priest shall stand, together [with the Levites] who are with him and the [tribal] chiefs [and the elders] of the army, and they shall bless the God of Israel there. Speaking they shall say:

Blessed be Thy Name, O God [of gods], for Thou hast worked great marvels [with Thy people]! Thou hast kept Thy Covenant with us from of old, and hast opened to us the gates of salvation many times. For the [sake of Thy Covenant Thou hast removed our misery, in accordance with] Thy [goodness] towards us. Thou hast acted for the sake of Thy Name, O God of righteousness ... [Thou hast worked a marvellous] miracle [for us], and from ancient times there never was anything like it. For Thou didst know the time appointed for us and it has appeared [before us] this day ... [Thou hast shown] us [Thy merciful hand] in everlasting redemption by causing [the dominion of] the enemy to fall back for ever. (Thou hast shown us) Thy mighty hand in [a stroke of destruction in the war against all] our enemies.

And now the day speeds us to the pursuit of their multitude ... Thou hast delivered up the hearts of the brave so that they stand no more.

For Thine is the power, and the battle is in Thy hands! ... **XIX** For our Sovereign is holy and the King of Glory is with us; the [host of his spirits is with our foot-soldiers and horsemen. They are as clouds, as clouds of dew] covering the earth, and as a shower of rain shedding righteousness on [all that grows there].

[Rise up, O Hero!
Lead off Thy captives, O Glorious One!
Gather up] Thy spoils, O Author of mighty deeds!
Lay Thy hand on the neck of Thine enemies
   and Thy feet [on the pile of the slain!
Smite the nations, Thine adversaries],
   and devour flesh with Thy sword!

Fill Thy land with glory
    and Thine inheritance with blessing!
[Let there be a multitude of cattle in Thy fields,
    and in] Thy palaces
    [silver and gold and precious stones]!

O Zion, rejoice greatly!
    Rejoice all you cities of Judah!
[Keep your gates ever open
    that the] hosts of the nations
    [may be brought in]!
Their kings shall serve you
    and all your oppressors shall bow down before you;
    [they shall lick the dust of your feet.
Shout for joy, O daughters of] my people!
Deck yourselves with glorious jewels
    [and rule over the kingdom of the nations!
Sovereignty shall be to the Lord]
    and everlasting dominion to Israel.

... that night to rest until the morning. And in the morning [they shall go to the place where the formation stood before the] warriors of the Kittim fell, and the multitudes of Assyria, and the hosts of all the nations [assembled with them] ... [slain, for] they fell there under the Sword of God. And the High Priest shall draw near, [with his vicar, and the chief Priests and the Levites] ... of battle, and all the chiefs of the formations and their numbered men; [they shall return to the positions which they held before the] slain [began to fall] from among the Kittim, and there they shall praise the God [of Israel] ...

· 8 ·

THE HYMNS

THE Hymns Scroll was published by E. L. Sukenik in 1954–5 (*The Dead Sea Scrolls of the Hebrew University*, Jerusalem). It has suffered a good deal of deterioration and the translator has difficulty, not only in making sense of the poems, but also in determining where one ends and the other begins.

I have counted twenty-five compositions similar to the biblical Psalms. They are all hymns of thanksgiving, individual prayers as opposed to those intended for communal worship, expressing a rich variety of spiritual and doctrinal detail. But the two fundamental themes running through the whole collection are those of salvation and knowledge. The sectary thanks God continually for having been saved from the 'lot' of the wicked, and for his gift of insight into the divine mysteries. He, a 'creature of clay', has been singled out by his Maker to receive favours of which he feels himself unworthy and he alludes again and again to his frailty and total dependence on God.

Whereas some of the Hymns give expression to thoughts and sentiments common to all the members of the sect, others, particularly nos. 1, 2, and 7–11, appear to refer to the experiences of a teacher abandoned by his friends and persecuted by his enemies. Several scholars tend to ascribe the authorship of these to the Teacher of Righteousness, and even consider that he may be responsible for all the Hymns. But although this hypothesis is not improbable, no sure conclusion can yet be reached.

Nor are we in a position to date any particular composition. The most we can say is that the collection as such probably attained its final shape during the last century of the sect's history.

Philo's account of the banquet celebrated by the contemplative Essenes, or Therapeutae, on the Feast of Pentecost may indicate the use to which the Hymns were put. He reports that when the President of the meeting had ended his commentary on the Scriptures, he rose and chanted a hymn, either one of his own making or an old one, and after him each of his brethren did likewise (*The*

Contemplative Life, § 80). Similarly, it is probable that the psalms of this Scroll were recited by the Guardian and newly initiated members at the Feast of the Renewal of the Covenant. Hymn 21 expressly refers to the oath of the Covenant, and Hymn 22 appears to be a poetic commentary on the liturgy of the entry into the Community. Indeed, the relative poverty of principal themes may be due to the fact that all this poetry was intended for a special occasion and its inspirational scope thereby limited.

I

I ...
  Thou art long-suffering in Thy judgements
    and righteous in all Thy deeds.

By Thy wisdom [all things exist from] eternity,
    and before creating them Thou knewest their works
    for ever and ever.
[Nothing] is done [without Thee]
    and nothing is known unless Thou desire it.

Thou hast created all the spirits
    [and hast established a statute] and law
    for all their works.
Thou hast spread the heavens for Thy glory
    and hast [appointed] all [their hosts]
    according to Thy will;
the mighty winds according to their laws
    before they became angels [of holiness]
    ... and eternal spirits in their dominions;
the heavenly lights to their mysteries,
    the stars to their paths,
[the clouds] to their tasks,
    the thunderbolts and lightnings to their duty,
and the perfect treasuries (of snow and hail)
    to their purposes,
    ... to their mysteries.

Thou hast created the earth by Thy power
    and the seas and deeps [by Thy might].

Thou hast fashioned [all] their [inhabi]tants
   according to Thy wisdom,
and hast appointed all that is in them
   according to Thy will.

[And] to the spirit of man
   which Thou hast formed in the world,
[Thou hast given dominion over the works of Thy hands]
   for everlasting days and unending generations.
... in their ages
Thou hast allotted to them tasks
   during all their generations,
and judgement in their appointed seasons
   according to the rule [of the two spirits.
For Thou hast established their ways]
   for ever and ever,
[and hast ordained from eternity]
   their visitation for reward and chastisements;
Thou hast allotted it to all their seed
   for eternal generations and everlasting years ...
In the wisdom of Thy knowledge
   Thou didst establish their destiny before ever they were.
All things [exist] according to [Thy will]
   and without Thee nothing is done.

These things I know
   by the wisdom which comes from Thee,
for Thou hast unstopped my ears
   to marvellous mysteries.

And yet I, a shape of clay
   kneaded in water,
a ground of shame
   and a source of pollution,
a melting-pot of wickedness
   and an edifice of sin,
a straying and perverted spirit
   of no understanding,

151

fearful of righteous judgements,
what can I say that is not foreknown,
    and what can I utter that is not foretold?
All things are graven before Thee
    on a written Reminder
    for everlasting ages,
and for the numbered cycles
    of the eternal years
    in all their seasons;
they are not hidden or absent from Thee.

What shall a man say
    concerning his sin?
And how shall he plead
    concerning his iniquities?
And how shall he reply
    to righteous judgement?
For thine, O God of knowledge,
    are all righteous deeds
    and the counsel of truth;
but to the sons of men is the work of iniquity
    and deeds of deceit.

It is Thou who hast created breath for the tongue
    and Thou knowest its words;
Thou didst establish the fruit of the lips
    before ever they were.
Thou dost set words to measure
    and the flow of breath from the lips to metre.
Thou bringest forth sounds
    according to their mysteries,
and the flow of breath from the lips
    according to its reckoning,
that they may tell of Thy glory
    and recount Thy wonders
in all Thy works of truth
    and [in all Thy] righteous [judgements];
and that Thy Name be praised

by the mouth of all men,
and that they may know Thee
   according to their understanding
   and bless Thee for ever.

By Thy mercies and by Thy great goodness,
Thou hast strengthened the spirit of man
   in the face of the scourge,
and hast purified [the erring spirit]
   of a multitude of sins,
that it may declare Thy marvels
   in the presence of all Thy creatures.
[I will declare to the assembly of the simple]
   the judgements by which I was scourged,
and to the sons of men, all Thy wonders
   by which Thou hast shown Thyself mighty [in me
   in the presence of the sons of Adam].

Hear, O you wise men, and meditate on knowledge;
   O you fearful, be steadfast!
Increase in prudence, [O all you simple];
   O just men, put away iniquity!
Hold fast [to the Covenant],
   O all you perfect of way;
[O all you afflicted with] misery,
   be patient and despise no righteous judgement!

...

[but the foo]lish of heart
   shall not comprehend these things.

   ...

II   ... Upon my [uncircumcised] lips
   Thou hast laid a reply.
Thou hast upheld my soul,
   strengthening my loins and restoring my power;
my foot has stood in the realm of ungodliness.
I have been a snare to those who rebel,
   but healing to those of them who repent,
prudence to the simple,

153

and steadfastness to the fearful of heart.
To traitors Thou hast made of me
    a mockery and scorn,
but a counsel of truth and understanding
    to the upright of way.
I have been iniquity for the wicked,
    ill-repute on the lips of the fierce,
    the scoffers have gnashed their teeth.
I have been a byword to traitors,
    the assembly of the wicked has raged against me;
they have roared like turbulent seas
    and their towering waves have spat out mud and slime.
But to the elect of righteousness
    Thou hast made me a banner,
and a discerning interpreter of wonderful mysteries,
    to try [those who practise] truth
    and to test those who love correction.
To the interpreters of error I have been an opponent,
    [but a man of peace] to all those who see truth.
To all those who seek smooth things
    I have been a spirit of zeal;
like the sound of the roaring of many waters
    so have [all] the deceivers thundered against me;
    [all] their thoughts were devilish [schemings].

They have cast towards the Pit the life of the man
    whose mouth Thou hast confirmed,
and into whose heart
    Thou hast put teaching and understanding,
that he might open a fountain of knowledge
    to all men of insight.
They exchanged them for lips of uncircumcision,
    and for the foreign tongue
    of a people without understanding,
    that they might come to ruin in their straying.

2

I thank Thee, O Lord,
   for Thou hast placed my soul
   in the bundle of the living,
and hast hedged me about
   against all the snares of the Pit.

Violent men have sought after my life
   because I have clung to Thy Covenant.
For they, an assembly of deceit,
   and a horde of Satan,
know not that my stand
   is maintained by Thee,
and that in Thy mercy Thou wilt save my soul
   since my steps proceed from Thee.
From Thee it is
   that they assail my life,
that Thou mayest be glorified
   by the judgement of the wicked,
and manifest Thy might through me
   in the presence of the sons of men;
for it is by Thy mercy that I stand.

And I said, Mighty men
   have pitched their camps against me,
and have encompassed me
   with all their weapons of war.
They have let fly arrows
   against which there is no cure,
and the flame of (their) javelins
   is like a consuming fire among trees.
The clamour of their shouting
   is like the bellowing of many waters,
like a storm of destruction
   devouring a multitude of men;
as their waves rear up,
   Naught and Vanity spout upward to the stars.

But although my heart melted like water,
   my soul held fast to Thy Covenant,
and the net which they spread for me
   has taken their own foot;
they have themselves fallen
   into the snares which they laid for my life.
But my foot remains upon level ground;
   apart from their assembly I will bless Thy Name.

3

I thank Thee, O Lord,
   for Thou hast [fastened] Thine eye upon me.
Thou hast saved me from the zeal
   of lying interpreters,
and from the congregation of those
   who seek smooth things.
Thou hast redeemed the soul of the poor one
   whom they planned to destroy
   by spilling his blood because he served Thee.

Because [they knew not]
   that my steps were directed by Thee,
they made me an object of shame and derision
   in the mouth of all the seekers of falsehood.
But Thou, O my God, hast succoured
   the soul of the poor and the needy
   against one stronger than he;
Thou hast redeemed my soul
   from the hand of the mighty.
Thou hast not permitted their insults to dismay me
   so that I forsook Thy service
   for fear of the wickedness of the [ungodly],
or bartered my steadfast heart for folly
. . .

4

III ...
They caused [me] to be
    like a ship on the deeps of the [sea],
and like a fortified city
  before [the aggressor],
[and] like a woman in travail
  with her first-born child,
upon whose belly pangs have come
  and grievous pains,
filling with anguish her child-bearing crucible.

For the children have come to the throes of Death,
  and she labours in her pains who bears the Man.
For amid the throes of Death
  she shall bring forth a man-child,
and amid the pains of Hell
  there shall spring from her child-bearing crucible
  a Marvellous Mighty Counsellor;
and the Man shall be delivered from out of the throes.

When he is conceived
  all wombs shall quicken,
and the time of their delivery
  shall be in grievous pains;
they shall be appalled
  who are with child.
And when he is brought forth
  every pang shall come upon the child-bearing crucible.

And they, the conceivers of Vanity,
  shall be prey to terrible anguish;
the wombs of the Pit
  shall be prey to all the works of horror.
The foundations of the wall shall rock
  like a ship upon the face of the waters;
the heavens shall roar
  with a noise of roaring,

and those who dwell in the dust
  as well as those who sail the seas
  shall be appalled by the roaring of the waters.

All their wise men
  shall be like sailors on the deeps,
for all their wisdom shall be swallowed up
  in the midst of the howling seas.
As the Abysses boil
  above the fountains of the waters,
the towering waves and billows shall rage
  with the voice of their roaring;
and as they rage,
  [Hell and Abaddon] shall open
[and all] the flying arrows of the Pit
  shall send out their voice to the Abyss.

And the gates [of Hell] shall open
  [on all] the works of Vanity;
and the doors of the Pit shall close
  on the conceivers of wickedness;
and the everlasting bars shall be bolted
  on all the spirits of Naught.

5

I thank Thee, O Lord,
  for Thou hast redeemed my soul from the Pit,
and from the Hell of Abaddon
  Thou hast raised me up to everlasting height.

I walk on limitless level ground,
and I know there is hope for him
  whom Thou hast shaped from dust
  for the everlasting Council.
Thou hast cleansed a perverse spirit of great sin
  that it may stand with the host of the Holy Ones,
and that it may enter into community
  with the congregation of the Sons of Heaven.

Thou hast allotted to man an everlasting destiny
   amidst the spirits of knowledge,
that he may praise Thy Name in a common rejoicing
   and recount Thy marvels before all Thy works.

And yet I, a creature of clay,
   what am I?
Kneaded with water,
   what is my worth and my might?
For I have stood in the realm of wickedness
   and my lot was with the damned;
the soul of the poor one was carried away
   in the midst of great tribulation.
Miseries of torment dogged my steps
while all the snares of the Pit were opened
   and the lures of wickedness were set up
   and the nets of the damned (were spread) on the waters;
while all the arrows of the Pit
   flew out without cease,
   and striking, left no hope;
while the rope beat down in judgement
   and a destiny of wrath (fell) upon the abandoned
   and a venting of fury upon the cunning.
It was a time of the wrath of all Satan
   and the bonds of death tightened without any escape.

The torrents of Satan shall reach
   to all sides of the world.
In all their channels
   a consuming fire shall destroy
   every tree, green and barren, on their banks;
unto the end of their courses
   it shall scourge with flames of fire,
and shall consume the foundations of the earth
   and the expanse of dry land.
The bases of the mountains shall blaze
   and the roots of the rocks shall turn
   to torrents of pitch;

it shall devour as far as the great Abyss.

The torrents of Satan shall break into Abaddon,
   and the deeps of the Abyss shall groan
   amid the roar of heaving mud.
The land shall cry out because of the calamity
   fallen upon the world,
   and all its deeps shall howl.
And all those upon it shall rave
   and shall perish amid the great misfortune.
For God shall sound His mighty voice,
   and His holy abode shall thunder
   with the truth of His glory.
The heavenly hosts shall cry out
   and the world's foundations
   shall stagger and sway.
The war of the heavenly warriors shall scourge the earth;
   and it shall not end before the appointed destruction
   which shall be for ever and without compare.

6

I thank Thee, O Lord,
   for Thou art as a fortified wall to me,
   and as an iron bar against all destroyers
   ...
Thou hast set my feet upon rock ...
   that I may walk in the way of eternity
   and in the paths which Thou hast chosen
   ...

7

IV ...
I thank Thee, O Lord,
   for Thou hast illumined my face by Thy Covenant.
...
I seek Thee,
   and sure as the dawn
   Thou appearest as [perfect Light] to me.

Teachers of lies [have smoothed] Thy people [with words],
    and [false prophets] have led them astray;
they perish without understanding
    for their works are in folly.
For I am despised by them
    and they have no esteem for me
    that Thou mayest manifest Thy might through me.
They have banished me from my land
    like a bird from its nest;
all my friends and brethren are driven far from me
    and hold me for a broken vessel.

And they, teachers of lies and seers of falsehood,
    have schemed against me a devilish scheme,
to exchange the Law engraved on my heart by Thee
    for the smooth things (which they speak) to Thy people.
And they withhold from the thirsty the drink of Knowledge,
    and assuage their thirst with vinegar,
that they may gaze on their straying,
    on their folly concerning their feast-days,
    on their fall into their snares.

But Thou, O God,
    dost despise all Satan's designs;
it is Thy purpose that shall be done
    and the design of Thy heart
    that shall be established for ever.

As for them, they dissemble,
    they plan devilish schemes.
They seek Thee with a double heart
    and are not confirmed in Thy truth.
A root bearing poisoned and bitter fruit
    is in their designs;
they walk in stubbornness of heart
    and seek Thee among idols,
and they set before them
    the stumbling-block of their sin.

They come to inquire of Thee
   from the mouth of lying prophets deceived by error
who speak [with strange] lips to Thy people,
   and an alien tongue,
that they may cunningly turn
   all their works to folly.

For [they hearken] not [to] Thy [voice],
   nor do they give ear to Thy word;
of the vision of Knowledge they say, 'It is unsure',
   and of the way of Thy heart, 'It is not (the way)'.
But Thou, O God, wilt reply to them,
chastising them in Thy might
   because of their idols
   and because of the multitude of their sins,
that they who have turned aside from Thy Covenant
   may be caught in their own designs.
Thou wilt destroy in Judgement
   all men of lies,
   and there shall be no more seers of error;
for in Thy works is no folly,
   no guile in the design of Thy heart.
But those who please Thee
   shall stand before Thee for ever;
those who walk in the way of Thy heart
   shall be established for evermore.

Clinging to Thee, I will stand.
I will rise against those who despise me
   and my hand shall be turned
   against those who deride me;
for they have no esteem for me
   [that Thou mayest] manifest Thy might through me.
Thou hast revealed Thyself to me in Thy power
   as perfect Light,
   and Thou hast not covered my face with shame.
All those who are gathered in Thy Covenant
   inquire of me,

and they hearken to me who walk in the way of Thy heart,
  who array themselves for Thee
  in the Council of the holy.

Thou wilt cause their law to endure for ever
  and truth to go forward unhindered,
and Thou wilt not allow them to be led astray
  by the hand of the damned
  when they plot against them.
Thou wilt put the fear of them into Thy people
  and (wilt make of them) a hammer
  to all the peoples of the lands,
that at the Judgement they may cut off
  all those who transgress Thy word.

Through me Thou hast illumined
  the face of the Congregation
  and hast shown Thine infinite power.
For Thou hast given me knowledge
  through Thy marvellous mysteries,
and hast shown Thyself mighty within me
  in the midst of Thy marvellous Council.
Thou hast done wonders before the Congregation
  for the sake of Thy glory,
that they may make known Thy mighty deeds
  to all the living.

But what is flesh (to be worthy) of this?
What is a creature of clay
  for such great marvels to be done,
whereas he is in iniquity from the womb
  and in guilty unfaithfulness until his old age?
Righteousness, I know, is not of man,
  nor is perfection of way of the son of man:
to the Most High God belong all righteous deeds.
The way of man is not established
  except by the spirit which God created for him
  to make perfect a way for the children of men,

that all His creatures might know
   the might of His power,
and the abundance of His mercies
   towards all the sons of His grace.

As for me, shaking and trembling seize me
   and all my bones are broken;
my heart dissolves like wax before fire
   and my knees are like water
     pouring down a steep place.
For I remember my sins
   and the unfaithfulness of my fathers.
When the wicked rose against thy Covenant
   and the damned against Thy word,
I said in my sinfulness,
   'I am forsaken by Thy Covenant.'
But calling to mind the might of Thy hand
   and the greatness of Thy compassion,
I rose and stood,
   and my spirit was established
     in face of the scourge.

I lean on Thy grace
   and on the multitude of Thy mercies,
for Thou wilt pardon iniquity,
   and through Thy righteousness
     [Thou wilt purify man] of his sin.
Not for his sake wilt Thou do it,
   [but for the sake of Thy glory].
For Thou hast created the just and the wicked
...V...

8

'I thank Thee, O Lord,
   for Thou hast not abandoned me
   whilst I sojourned among a people [burdened with sin].

[Thou hast not] judged me
   according to my guilt,

nor hast Thou abandoned me
  because of the designs of my inclination;
but Thou hast saved my life from the Pit.
Thou hast brought [Thy servant deliverance]
  in the midst of lions destined to the guilty,
and of lionesses which crush the bones of the mighty
  and drink the blood of the brave.

Thou hast caused me to dwell with the many fishers
  who spread a net upon the face of the waters,
  and with the hunters of the children of iniquity;
Thou hast established me there for justice.
Thou hast confirmed the counsel of truth in my heart
  and the waters of the Covenant for those who seek it.
Thou hast closed up the mouth of the young lions
  whose teeth are like a sword,
  and whose great teeth are like a pointed spear,
  like the venom of dragons.
All their design is for robbery
  and they have lain in wait;
but they have not opened their mouth against me.

For Thou, O God, hast sheltered me
  from the children of men,
and hast hidden Thy Law [within me]
  against the time when Thou shouldst reveal
  Thy salvation to me.
For Thou hast not forsaken me
  in my soul's distress,
and Thou hast heard my cry
  in the bitterness of my soul;
and when I groaned,
  Thou didst consider my sorrowful complaint.
Thou hast preserved the soul of the poor one
  in the den of lions
  which sharpened their tongue like a sword.
Thou hast closed up their teeth, O God,
  lest they rend the soul of the poor and needy.

Thou hast made their tongue go back
   like a sword to its scabbard
   [lest] the soul of Thy servant [be blotted out].

Thou hast dealt wondrously with the poor one
   to manifest Thy might within me
   in the presence of the sons of men.
Thou hast placed him in the melting-pot,
   [like gold] in the fire,
and like silver refined
   in the melting-pot of the smelters,
   to be purified seven times.
The wicked and fierce have stormed against me
   with their afflictions;
   they have pounded my soul all day.
But Thou, O my God,
   hast changed the tempest to a breeze;
Thou hast delivered the soul of the poor one
   like [a bird from the net
   and like] prey from the mouth of lions.

9

I thank Thee (corrected: Blessed art Thou) O Lord,
   for Thou hast not abandoned the fatherless
   or despised the poor.
For Thy might [is boundless]
   and Thy glory beyond measure
   and wonderful Heroes minister to Thee;
yet [hast Thou done marvels] among the humble
   in the mire underfoot,
   and among those eager for righteousness,
causing all the well-loved poor
   to rise up together from the trampling.

But I have been [iniquity to] those who contend with me,
dispute and quarrelling to my friends,
wrath to the members of my Covenant

and murmuring and protest to all my companions.

[All who have ea]ten my bread
  have lifted their heel against me,
and all those joined to my Council
  have mocked me with wicked lips.
The members of my [Covenant] have rebelled
  and have murmured round about me;
they have gone as talebearers
   before the children of mischief
    concerning the mystery which Thou hast hidden in me.

And to show Thy great[ness] through me,
  and because of their guilt,
Thou hast hidden the fountain of understanding
  and the counsel of truth.

They consider but the mischief of their heart;
[with] devilish [schemings] they unsheath
  a perfidious tongue
  from which ever springs the poison of dragons.
And like (serpents) which creep in the dust,
  so do they let fly [their poisonous darts],
  viper's [venom] against which there is no charm;
and this has brought incurable pain,
  a malignant scourge
  within the body of Thy servant,
causing [his spirit] to faint
  and draining his strength
  so that he maintains no firm stand.

They have overtaken me in a narrow pass without escape
  and there is no [rest for me in my trial].
They sound my censure upon a harp
  and their murmuring and storming upon a zither.
Anguish [seizes me]
  like the pangs of a woman in travail,
  and my heart is troubled within me.
I am clothed in blackness

and my tongue cleaves to the roof [of my mouth];
[for I fear the mischief of] their heart
    and their inclination (towards evil)
    appears as bitterness before me.
The light of my face is dimmed to darkness
    and my radiance is turned to decay.

For Thou, O God, didst widen my heart,
    but they straiten it with affliction
    and hedge me about with darkness.
I eat the bread of wailing
    and drink unceasing tears;
truly, my eyes are dimmed by grief,
    and my soul by daily bitterness.
[Groaning] and sorrow encompass me
    and ignominy covers my face.
My bread is turned into an adversary
    and my drink into an accuser;
it has entered into my bones
    causing my spirit to stagger
    and my strength to fail.
According to the mysteries of sin,
    they change the works of God by their transgression.

Truly, I am bound with untearable ropes
    and with unbreakable chains.
A thick wall [fences me in],
    iron bars and gates [of bronze];
my [prison] is counted with the Abyss
    as being without [any escape]
...
[The torrents of Satan] have encompassed my soul
    [leaving me without deliverance]
...

10

VI ...
Thou hast unstopped my ears
    [to the correction] of those who reprove with justice

...

[Thou hast saved me] from the congregation of [vanity]
   and from the assembly of violence;
Thou hast brought me into the Council of ...
   [and hast purified me of] sin.
And I know there is hope
   for those who turn from transgression
   and for those who abandon sin

...

and to walk without wickedness
   in the way of Thy heart.
I am consoled for the roaring of the peoples,
   and for the tumult of k[ing]doms when they assemble;
[for] in a little while, I know,
   Thou wilt raise up survivors among Thy people
   and a remnant within Thine inheritance.
Thou wilt purify and cleanse them of their sin
   for all their deeds are in Thy truth.
Thou wilt judge them in Thy great lovingkindness
   and in the multitude of Thy mercies
   and in the abundance of Thy pardon,
   teaching them according to Thy word;
and Thou wilt establish them in Thy Council
   according to the uprightness of Thy truth.

Thou wilt do these things for Thy glory
   and for Thine own sake,
to [magnify] the Law and [the truth
   and to enlighten] the members of Thy Council
   in the midst of the sons of men,
that they may recount Thy marvels
   for everlasting generations
   and [meditate] unceasingly upon Thy mighty deeds
All the nations shall acknowledge Thy truth,
   and all the people Thy glory.

For Thou wilt bring Thy glorious [salvation]
   to all the men of Thy Council,

to those who share a common lot
with the Angels of the Face.
And among them shall be no mediator to [invoke Thee],
and no messenger [to make] reply;
for ...
They shall reply according to Thy glorious word
and shall be Thy princes in the company [of the Angels].

They shall send out a bud [for ever]
like a flower [of the fields],
and shall cause a shoot to grow
into the boughs of an everlasting Plant.
It shall cover the whole [earth] with its shadow
[and its crown] (shall reach) to the [clouds];
its roots (shall go down) to the Abyss
[and all the rivers of Eden shall water its branches].

...
A source of light
shall become an eternal ever-flowing fountain,
and in its bright flames
all the [sons of iniquity] shall be consumed;
[it shall be] a fire to devour all sinful men
in utter destruction.

They who bore the yoke of my testimony
have been led astray [by teachers of lies],
[and have rebelled] against the service of righteousness.
Whereas Thou, O my God, didst command them
to mend their ways
[by walking] in the way of [holiness]
where no man goes who is uncircumcised
or unclean or violent,
they have staggered aside from the way of Thy heart
and languish in [great] wretchedness.
A counsel of Satan is in their heart
[and in accordance with] their wicked design
they wallow in sin.

[I am] as a sailor in a ship

amid furious seas;
their waves and all their billows
    roar against me.
[There is no] calm in the whirlwind
    that I may restore my soul,
no path that I may straighten my way
    on the face of the waters.
The deeps resound to my groaning
    and [my soul has journeyed] to the gates of death.

But I shall be as one who enters a fortified city,
    as one who seeks refuge behind a high wall
    until deliverances (comes);
    I will [lean on] Thy truth, O my God.
For Thou wilt set the foundation on rock
    and the framework by the measuring-cord of justice;
and the tried stones [Thou wilt lay]
    by the plumb-line [of truth],
to [build] a mighty [wall] which shall not sway;
    and no man entering there shall stagger.

For no enemy shall ever invade [it
    since its doors shall be] doors of protection
    through which no man shall pass;
and its bars shall be firm
    and no man shall break them.
No rabble shall enter in with their weapons of war
    until all the [arrows] of the war of wickedness
    have come to an end.

And then at the time of Judgement
    the Sword of God shall hasten,
and all the sons of His truth shall awake
    to [overthrow] wickedness;
all the sons of iniquity shall be no more.
The Hero shall bend his bow;
the fortress shall open on to endless space
and the everlasting gates shall send out weapons of war.

They shall be mighty
  from end to end [of the earth
and there shall be no escape]
  for the guilty of heart [in their battle];
they shall be utterly trampled down
  without any [remnant.
There shall be no] hope
  in the greatness [of their might],
  no refuge for the mighty warriors;
for [the battle shall be] to the Most High God
. . .

Hoist a banner,
  O you who lie in the dust!
O bodies gnawed by worms,
  raise up an ensign for [the destruction of wickedness]!
[The sinful shall] be destroyed
  in the battles against the ungodly.

The scourging flood when it advances
  shall not invade the stronghold
. . .

VII ... As for me, I am dumb ...
[my arm] is torn from its shoulder
  and my foot has sunk into the mire.
My eyes are closed by the spectacle of evil,
  and my ears by the crying of blood.
My heart is dismayed by the mischievous design,
  for Satan is manifest in their (evil) inclination.
All the foundations of my edifice totter
  and my bones are pulled out of joint;
my bowels heave like a ship in a violent tempest
  and my heart is utterly distressed.
A whirlwind engulfs me
  because of the mischief of their sin.

I thank Thee, O Lord,
  for Thou hast upheld me by Thy strength.
Thou hast shed Thy Holy Spirit upon me
  that I may not stumble.

Thou hast strengthened me
  before the battles of wickedness,
and during all their disasters
  Thou hast not permitted that fear
  should cause me to desert Thy Covenant.
Thou hast made me like a strong tower, a high wall,
  and hast established my edifice upon rock;
eternal foundations
  serve for my ground,
and all my ramparts are a tried wall
  which shall not sway.

Thou hast placed me, O my God,
  among the branches of the Council of Holiness;
Thou hast [established my mouth] in Thy Covenant,
  and my tongue is like that of Thy disciples;
  whereas the spirit of disaster is without a mouth
  and all the sons of iniquity without a reply;
  for the lying lips shall be dumb.
For Thou wilt condemn in Judgement
  all those who assail me,
distinguishing through me
  between the just and the wicked.
For Thou knowest the whole intent of a creature,
  Thou discernest every reply,
and Thou hast established my heart
  [on] Thy teaching and truth,
directing my steps into the paths of righteousness
  that I may walk before Thee
  in the land [of the living],
into paths of glory and [infinite] peace
  which shall [never] end.

For thou knowest the inclination of Thy servant,
that I have not relied [upon the works of my hands]
    to raise up [my heart],
nor have I sought refuge
    in my own strength.
I have no fleshly refuge,
[and Thy servant has] no righteous deeds
    to deliver him from the [Pit of no] forgiveness.
But I lean on the [abundance of Thy mercies]
    and hope [for the greatness] of Thy grace,
that Thou wilt bring [salvation] to flower
    and the branch to growth,
providing refuge in (Thy) strength
    [and raising up my heart].

[For in] Thy righteousness
    Thou hast appointed me for Thy Covenant,
and I have clung to Thy truth
    and [gone forward in Thy ways].

Thou hast made me a father to the sons of grace,
    and as a foster-father to men of marvel;
they have opened their mouths like little babes ...
    like a child playing in the lap of its nurse.
Thou hast lifted my horn above those who insult me,
    and those who attack me
    [sway like the boughs] (of a tree);
my enemies are like chaff before the wind,
    and my dominion is over the sons [of iniquity.
For] Thou hast succoured my soul, O my God,
    and hast lifted my horn on high.
And I shall shine in a seven-fold light
    in [the Council appointed by] Thee for Thy glory;
for Thou art an everlasting heavenly light to me
    and wilt establish my feet
    [upon level ground for ever].

12

I [thank Thee, O Lord],
   for Thou hast enlightened me through Thy truth.
In Thy marvellous mysteries,
and in Thy lovingkindness to a man [of vanity,
and] in the greatness of Thy mercy to a perverse heart
   Thou hast granted me knowledge.

Who is like Thee among the gods, O Lord,
   and who is according to Thy truth?
Who, when he is judged,
   shall be righteous before Thee?
For no spirit can reply to Thy rebuke
   nor can any withstand Thy wrath.

Yet Thou bringest all the sons of Thy truth
   in forgiveness before Thee,
[to cleanse] them of their faults
   through Thy great goodness,
and to establish them before Thee
   through the multitude of Thy mercies
   for ever and ever.

For Thou art an eternal God;
   all Thy ways are determined for ever [and ever]
   and there is none other beside Thee.
And what is a man of Naught and Vanity
   that he should understand Thy marvellous mighty deeds?

...

13

[I thank] Thee, O God,
   for Thou hast not cast my lot
   in the congregation of Vanity,
nor hast Thou placed my portion
   in the council of the cunning.

[Thou hast] led me to Thy grace and forgiveness
... VIII ...

I [thank Thee, O Lord,
   for] Thou hast placed me beside a fountain of streams
      in an arid land,
and close to a spring of waters
      in a dry land,
and beside a watered garden
      [in a wilderness].

[For Thou didst set] a plantation
   of cypress, pine, and cedar for Thy glory,
trees of life beside a mysterious fountain
   hidden among the trees by the water,
and they put out a shoot
   of the everlasting Plant.
But before they did so, they took root
   and sent out their roots to the watercourse
that its stem might be open to the living waters
   and be one with the everlasting spring.

And all [the beasts] of the forest
   fed on its leafy boughs;
its stem was trodden by all who passed on the way
   and its branches by all the birds.
And all the [trees] by the water rose above it
   for they grew in their plantation;
but they sent out no root to the watercourse.

And the bud of the shoot of holiness
   for the Plant of truth
   was hidden and was not esteemed;
and being unperceived,
   its mystery was sealed.
Thou didst hedge in its fruit, [O God],
   with the mystery of mighty Heroes
   and of spirits of holiness
   and of the whirling flame of fire.
No [man shall approach] the well-spring of life

or drink the waters of holiness
   with the everlasting trees,
   or bear fruit with [the Plant] of heaven,
who seeing has not discerned,
   and considering has not believed
   in the fountain of life,
who has turned [his hand against] the everlasting [bud].

And I was despised by tumultuous rivers
   for they cast up their slime upon me.

But Thou, O my God, hast put into my mouth
   as it were rain for all [those who thirst]
   and a fount of living waters which shall not fail.
When they are opened they shall not run dry;
they shall be a torrent [overflowing its banks]
   and like the [bottom]less seas.
They shall suddenly gush forth
   which were hidden in secret,
[and shall be like the waters of the Flood
   to every tree], both the green and the barren;
   to every beast and bird [they shall be an abyss.
The trees shall sink like] lead in the mighty waters,
   fire [shall burn among them]
and they shall be dried up;
but the fruitful Plant
   [by the] everlasting [spring
shall be] an Eden of glory
   [bearing] fruits [of life].

By my hand Thou hast opened for them
   a well-spring and ditches,
[that all their channels] may be laid out
   according to a certain measuring-cord,
and the planting of their trees
   according to the plumb-line of the sun,
that [their boughs may become
   a beautiful] Branch of glory.

When I lift my hand to dig its ditches
  its roots shall run deep into hardest rock
  and its stem ... in the earth;
  in the season of heat it shall keep its strength.
But if I take away my hand
  it shall be like a thistle [in the wilderness];
its stem shall be like nettles in a salty land,
    and thistles and thorns shall grow from its ditches,
    and brambles and briars.
Its border [trees] shall be like the wild grapevine
    whose foliage withers before the heat,
    and its stem shall not be open to [the spring].

[Behold, I am] carried away with the sick;
  [I am acquainted] with scourges.
I am forsaken in [my sorrow] ...
  and without any strength.
For my sore breaks out in bitter pains
  and in incurable sickness impossible to stay;
[my heart laments] within me
  as in those who go down to Hell.
My spirit is imprisoned with the dead
  for [my life] has reached the Pit;
my soul languishes [within me]
  day and night without rest.

My wound breaks out like burning fire
  shut up in [my bones],
whose flames devour me for days on end,
    diminishing my strength for times on end
    and destroying my flesh for seasons on end.
The pains fly out [towards me]
  and my soul within me languishes even to death.
My strength has gone from my body
  and my heart runs out like water;
my flesh is dissolved like wax
  and the strength of my loins is turned to fear.

My arm is torn from its socket
   [and I can] lift my hand [no more];
My [foot] is held by fetters
   and my knees slide like water;
   I can no longer walk.
I cannot step forward lightly,
   [for my legs and arms] are bound by shackles
   which cause me to stumble.
The tongue has gone back which Thou didst make
   marvellously mighty within my mouth;
   it can no longer give voice.
[I have no word] for my disciples
   to revive the spirit of those who stumble
   and to speak words of support to the weary.
My circumcised lips are dumb.

. . .

IX . . .

[For] the throes of death [encompass me]
   and Hell is upon my bed;
my couch utters a lamentation
   [and my pallet] the sound of a complaint.
My eyes are like fire in the furnace
   and my tears like rivers of water;
my eyes grow dim with waiting,
   [for my salvation] is far from me
   and my life is apart from me.

But behold,
   from desolation to ruin,
   and from the pain to the sore,
   and from the travail to the throes,
my soul meditates on Thy marvellous works.
In Thy mercies Thou hast not cast me aside;
season by season, my soul shall delight
   in the abundance of mercy.
I will reply to him who slanders me
   and I will rebuke my oppressor;

I will declare his sentence unjust
  and declare Thy judgement righteous.

For I know by Thy truth,
  and I choose Thy judgement upon me;
I delight in my scourges
  for I hope for Thy lovingkindness.
Thou hast put a supplication
  in the mouth of Thy servant,
and Thou hast not threatened my life
  nor rejected my peace.
Thou hast not failed my expectation,
  but hast upheld my spirit in face of the scourge.

For it is Thou who hast founded my spirit
  and Thou knowest my intent;
  in my distress Thou hast comforted me.
I delight in forgiveness,
  and am consoled for the former transgression;
for I know there is hope in Thy grace
  and expectation in Thy great power.
For no man can be just in Thy judgement
  or [righteous in] Thy trial.
Though one man be more just than another,
  one person [more] wise [than another],
one mortal more glorious
  than another creature [of clay],
  yet is there no power to compare with Thy might.
There is no [bound] to Thy glory,
  and to Thy wisdom, no measure;
[to Thy truth] there is no . . .
  and all who forsake it . . .

. . .

  and my oppressor shall [not] prevail against me.
I will be a stumbling-block to [those who swallow me up,
  and a snare to] all those who battle against me;
[I will be for my enemies a] cause of shame,

and a cause of disgrace
　　to those who murmur against me.
For Thou, O my God ...
　　Thou wilt plead my cause;
for it is according to the mystery of Thy wisdom
　　that Thou hast rebuked me.

Thou wilt conceal the truth until [its] time,
　　[and righteousness] until its appointed moment.
Thy rebuke shall become my joy and gladness,
　　and my scourges shall turn to [eternal] healing
　　and everlasting [peace].
The scorn of my enemies shall become a crown of glory,
　　and my stumbling (shall change) to everlasting might.

For in Thy ...
　　and my light shall shine forth in Thy glory.
For as a light from out of the darkness,
　　so wilt Thou enlighten me.
[Thou wilt bring healing to] my wound,
　　and marvellous might in place of my stumbling,
　　and everlasting space to my straitened soul.
For Thou art my refuge, my high mountain,
　　my stout rock and my fortress;
in Thee will I shelter
　　from all the [designs of ungodliness,
for Thou wilt succour me] with eternal deliverance.

For Thou hast known me from (the time of) my father,
　　[and hast chosen me] from the womb.
[From the belly of] my mother
　　Thou hast dealt kindly with me,
and from the breast of her who conceived me
　　have Thy mercies been with me.
[Thy grace was with me] in the lap of her who reared me,
　　and from my youth Thou hast illumined me
　　with the wisdom of Thy judgement.

Thou hast upheld me with certain truth;

Thou hast delighted me with Thy Holy Spirit
  and [hast opened my heart] till this day.
Thy just rebuke accompanies my [faults]
  and Thy safeguarding peace delivers my soul.
The abundance of (Thy) forgiveness is with my steps
    and infinite mercy accompanies Thy judgement of me.
Until I am old Thou wilt care for me;
  for my father knew me not
  and my mother abandoned me to Thee.
For Thou art a father
  to all [the sons] of Thy truth,
and as a woman who tenderly loves her babe,
  so dost Thou rejoice in them;
and as a foster-father bearing a child in his lap,
  so carest Thou for all Thy creatures.

15

[I thank Thee, O Lord]
. . .
X . . . and nothing exists except by Thy will;
none can consider [Thy deep secrets]
  or contemplate Thy [mysteries].

What then is man that is earth,
  that is shaped [from clay] and returns to the dust,
that Thou shouldst give him to understand such marvels
  and make known to him the counsel of [Thy truth]?

Clay and dust that I am,
  what can I devise unless Thou wish it,
  and what contrive unless Thou desire it?
What strength shall I have
  unless Thou keep me upright,
and how shall I understand
  unless by (the spirit) which Thou hast shaped for me?
What can I say unless Thou open my mouth
  and how can I answer unless Thou enlighten me?

Behold, Thou art Prince of gods
   and King of majesties,
Lord of all spirits,
   and Ruler of all creatures;
nothing is done without Thee,
   and nothing is known without Thy will.
Beside Thee there is nothing,
   and nothing can compare with Thee in strength;
in the presence of Thy glory there is nothing,
   and Thy might is without price.

Who among Thy great and marvellous creatures
   can stand in the presence of Thy glory?
   How then can he who returns to his dust?
For Thy glory's sake alone hast Thou made all these things.

16

Blessed art Thou, O Lord,
   God of mercy [and abundant] grace,
for Thou hast made known [Thy wisdom to me
   that I should recount] Thy marvellous deeds,
   keeping silence neither by day nor [by night]!

[For I have trusted] in Thy grace.
In Thy great goodness,
   and in [the multitude of Thy mercies]
. . .
For I have leaned on Thy truth
. . .
[And unless] Thou rebuke,
   there is no stumbling;
unless Thou foreknow it,
   [there is no] scourge;
   [nothing is done without] Thy [will].

[I will cling to Thy ways]
   according to my knowledge [of Thy] truth;

contemplating Thy glory
   I will recount Thy wonderful works,
and understanding [Thy goodness
   I will lean on the] multitude of Thy mercies
   and hope for Thy forgiveness.

For Thou Thyself hast shaped [my spirit]
   and established me [according to Thy will];
and Thou hast not placed my support in gain,
   [nor does] my [heart delight in riches];
   Thou hast given me no fleshly refuge.
The might of warriors (rests) on abundant delights,
   [and on plenty of corn] and wine and oil;
   they pride themselves in possessions and wealth.
[But the righteous is like a] green [tree]
   beside streams of water,
   bringing forth leaves and multiplying its branches;
for [Thou hast chosen them
   from among the children of] men
   that they may all grow fat from the land.

Thou wilt give to the children of Thy truth
   [unending joy and] everlasting [gladness],
and according to the measure of their knowledge,
   so shall they be honoured one more than another.

And likewise for the son of man ...
   Thou wilt increase his portion
   in the knowledge of Thy truth,
and according to the measure of his knowledge,
   so shall he be honoured ...
[For the soul] of Thy servant has loathed [riches] and gain,
   and he has not [desired] exquisite delights.
My heart rejoices in Thy Covenant
   and Thy truth delights my soul.
I shall flower [like the lily]
   and my heart shall be open to the everlasting fountain;
   my support shall be in the might from on high.

But . . .
   and withers like a flower before [the heat].
My heart is stricken with terror,
   and my loins with trembling;
my groaning goes down to the Abyss,
   and is shut up in the chambers of Hell.
I am greatly afraid when I hear of Thy judgement
   of the mighty Heroes,
and of Thy trial of the host
   of Thy Holy Ones

. . . XI . . .

17

I thank Thee, my God,
   for Thou hast dealt wondrously to dust,
   and mightily towards a creature of clay!
I thank Thee, I thank Thee!

What am I, that Thou shouldst [teach] me
   the counsel of Thy truth,
and give me understanding
   of Thy marvellous works;
that Thou shouldst lay hymns of thanksgiving
   within my mouth
   and [praise] upon my tongue,
and that of my circumcised lips
   (Thou shouldst make) a seat of rejoicing?

I will sing Thy mercies,
   and on Thy might I will meditate all day long.
I will bless Thy Name evermore.
I will declare Thy glory in the midst of the sons of men
   and my soul shall delight in Thy great goodness.

I know that Thy word is truth,
   and that righteousness is in Thy hand;
that all knowledge is in Thy purpose,
   and that all power is in Thy might,
   and that every glory is Thine.

In Thy wrath are all chastisements,
   but in Thy goodness is much forgiveness
   and Thy mercy is towards the sons of Thy goodwill.
For Thou hast made known to them
   the counsel of Thy truth,
and hast taught them Thy marvellous mysteries.

For the sake of Thy glory
   Thou hast purified man of sin
that he may be made holy for Thee,
   with no abominable uncleanness
   and no guilty wickedness;
that he may be one [with] the children of Thy truth
   and partake of the lot of Thy Holy Ones;
that bodies gnawed by worms may be raised from the dust
   to the counsel [of Thy truth],
and that the perverse spirit (may be lifted)
   to the understanding [which comes from Thee];
that he may stand before Thee
   with the everlasting host
   and with [Thy] spirits [of holiness],
to be renewed together with all the living
   and to rejoice together with them that know.

18

I thank Thee, my God!
I praise Thee, my Rock!
. . .

For Thou hast made known to me the counsel of Thy truth
   [and hast taught me Thy marvellous mysteries;]
. . .
   and hast revealed Thy [wonders] to me.
I have beheld [Thy deeds towards the children] of grace,
   and I know [that] righteousness is Thine,
that in Thy mercies there is [hope for me],
   but without Thy grace [destruction] without end.

But a fountain of bitter mourning opens for me,
   [and my tears fall down].
Distress is not hidden from my eyes
   when I think of the (evil) inclinations of man,
of his return [to dust,
   and of his leaning] towards sin and the sorrow of guilt.
They enter my heart and reach into my bones
   to ...
   and to meditate in sorrowful meditation.
I will groan with the zither of lamentation
   in all grief-stricken mourning and bitter complaint
until iniquity and [wickedness] are consumed
   and the disease-bringing scourge is no more.
Then will I play on the zither of deliverance
   and the harp of joy,
[on the tabors of prayer] and the pipe of praise
   without end.

Who among all Thy creatures
   is able to recount [Thy wonders]?
May Thy Name be praised
   by the mouth of all men!
May they bless Thee for ever
   in accordance with [their understanding],
and proclaim Thee with the voice of praise
   in the company of [the Sons of Heaven]!
There shall be neither groaning nor complaint
   and wickedness [shall be destroyed for ever];
Thy truth shall be revealed in eternal glory
   and in everlasting peace.

Blessed art [Thou, O my Lord],
who hast given to [Thy servant]
   the knowledge of wisdom
that he may comprehend Thy wonders,
   and recount Thy ...
   in Thy abundant grace!

Blessed art Thou,
  O God of mercy and compassion,
for the might of Thy [power]
  and the greatness of Thy truth,
and for the multitude of Thy favours
  in all Thy works!
Rejoice the soul of Thy servant with Thy truth
  and cleanse me by Thy righteousness.
Even as I have hoped in Thy goodness,
  and waited for Thy grace,
so hast Thou freed me from my calamities
  in accordance with Thy forgiveness;
and in my distress Thou hast comforted me
  for I have leaned on Thy mercy.

Blessed art Thou, O Lord,
  for it is Thou who hast done these things!
Thou hast set [hymns of praise]
  within the mouth of Thy servant,
and hast established for me a response of the tongue.
...

19

XII...
I will praise Thy Name among them that fear Thee.
Bowing down in prayer I will beg Thy favours
  [from generation to generation]
  and from season to season without end:

when light emerges from [its dwelling-place],
and when the day reaches its appointed end
  in accordance with the laws
  of the Great Light of heaven;
when evening falls and light departs
  at the beginning of the dominion of darkness,
at the hour appointed for night,
and at its end when morning returns
  and (the shadows) retire to their dwelling-place
  before the approach of light;

always,
  at the genesis of every period
  and at the beginning of every age
  and at the end of every season,
according to the statute and signs
  appointed to every dominion
  by the certain law from the mouth of God,
by the precept which is and shall be
  for ever and ever without end.
Without it nothing is nor shall be,
  for the God of knowledge established it
  and there is no other beside Him.

I, the Master, know Thee O my God,
  by the spirit which Thou hast given to me,
and by Thy Holy Spirit I have faithfully hearkened
  to Thy marvellous counsel.
In the mystery of Thy wisdom
  Thou hast opened knowledge to me,
and in Thy mercies
  [Thou hast unlocked for me] the fountain of Thy might.
. . .

Before Thee no man is just . . .
[that he may] understand all Thy mysteries
  or give answer [to Thy rebuke.
But the children of Thy grace
  shall delight in] Thy correction
  and watch for Thy goodness,
for in Thy mercies [Thou wilt show Thyself to them]
  and they shall know Thee;
at the time of Thy glory
  they shall rejoice.
[Thou hast caused them to draw near]
  in accordance [with their knowledge],
and hast admitted them
  in accordance with their understanding,
and in their divisions they shall serve Thee

throughout their dominion
[without ever turning aside] from Thee
  or transgressing Thy word.

Behold, [I was taken] from dust
  [and] fashioned [out of clay]
as a source of uncleanness,
  and a shameful nakedness,
a heap of dust,
  and a kneading [with water,]
. . .
  and a house of darkness,
  a creature of clay returning to dust,
returning [at the appointed time
  to dwell] in the dust whence it was taken.

How then shall dust reply [to its Maker,
  and how] understand His [works]?
How shall it stand before Him who reproves it?
. . .
  [and the Spring of] Eternity,
the Well of Glory
  and the Fountain of Knowledge.
Not even [the wonderful] Heroes [can] declare all Thy glory
  or stand in face of Thy wrath,
and there is none among them
  that can answer Thy rebuke;
for Thou art just and none can oppose Thee.
How then can (man) who returns to his dust?

I hold my peace;
  what more shall I say than this?
I have spoken in accordance with my knowledge,
  out of the righteousness given to a creature of clay.
And how shall I speak unless Thou open my mouth;
  how understand unless Thou teach me?
How shall I seek Thee unless Thou uncover my heart,
  and how follow the way that is straight

    unless [Thou guide me?
How shall my foot] stay on [the path
    unless Thou] give it strength;
and how shall I rise . . .

20

XIII . . .

All these things [Thou didst establish in Thy wisdom.
Thou didst appoint] all Thy works
    before ever creating them:
the host of Thy spirits
    and the Congregation [of Thy Holy Ones,
the heavens and all] their hosts
    and the earth and all it brings forth.
In the seas and deeps . . .
    . . . and an everlasting task;
for Thou hast established them from before eternity.

And the work of . . .
    and they shall recount Thy glory
    throughout all Thy dominion.
For Thou hast shown them that
    which they had not [seen
by removing all] ancient things
    and creating new ones,
by breaking asunder things anciently established,
    and raising up the things of eternity.
For [Thou art from the beginning]
    and shalt endure for ages without end.
And Thou hast [appointed] all these things
    in the mysteries of Thy wisdom
    to make known Thy glory [to all].

[But what is] the spirit of flesh
    that it should understand all this,
and that it should comprehend
    the great [design of Thy wisdom]?
What is he that is born of woman
    in the midst of all Thy terrible [works]?

He is but an edifice of dust,
  and a thing kneaded with water,
whose beginning [is sinful iniquity],
  and shameful nakedness,
  [and a fount of uncleanness],
and over whom a spirit of straying rules.
If he is wicked he shall become [a sign for] ever,
  and a wonder to (every) generation,
  [and an object of horror to all] flesh.

By Thy goodness alone is man righteous,
  and with Thy many mercies [Thou strengthenest him].
Thou wilt adorn him with Thy splendour
  and wilt [cause him to reign amid] many delights
  with everlasting peace and length of days.
[For Thou hast spoken],
  and Thou wilt not take back Thy word.

And I, Thy servant,
  I know by the spirit which Thou hast given to me
  [that Thy words are truth],
and that all Thy works are righteousness,
  and that Thou wilt not take back Thy word
...XIV...

21

[Blessed art Thou,] O Lord,
  who hast given understanding
  to the heart of [Thy] servant
that he may ...
  and resist [the works] of wickedness
  and bless [Thy Name always,
and that he may choose all] that Thou lovest
  and loathe all that Thou [hatest]

...

[For Thou hast divided men] into good and evil
  in accordance with the spirits of their lot;

[in accordance with] their [divisions
    do they accomplish] their task.
And I know through the understanding
    which comes from Thee,
that in Thy goodwill towards [ashes
    Thou hast shed] Thy Holy Spirit [upon me]
      and thus drawn me near to understanding of Thee.
And the closer I approach,
    the more am I filled with zeal
    against all the workers of iniquity
    and the men of deceit.

For none of those who approach Thee
    rebels against Thy command,
nor do any of those who know Thee
    alter Thy words;
for Thou art just,
    and all Thine elect are truth.
Thou wilt blot out all wickedness [and sin] for ever,
    and Thy righteousness shall be revealed
    before the eyes of all Thy creatures.

I know through Thy great goodness;
and with an oath I have undertaken
    never to sin against Thee,
nor to do anything evil in Thine eyes.
And thus do I bring into community
    all the men of my Council.

I will cause each man to draw near
    in accordance with his understanding,
and according to the greatness of his portion
    so will I love him.
I will not honour an evil man,
    nor consider [the bribes of the wicked];
I will [not] barter Thy truth for riches,
    nor one of Thy precepts for bribes.
But according as [Thou drawest a man near to Thee,
    so will I love] him,

and according as Thou removest him far from Thee,
   so will I hate him;
and none of those who have turned [from] Thy [Covenant]
   will I bring into the Council [of Thy truth].

22

[I thank] Thee, O Lord,
   as befits the greatness of Thy power
   and the multitude of Thy marvels for ever and ever.

[Thou art a merciful God] and rich in [favours],
   pardoning those who repent of their sin
   and visiting the iniquity of the wicked.
[Thou delightest in] the free-will offering [of the righteous]
   but iniquity Thou hatest always.
Thou hast favoured me, Thy servant,
   with a spirit of knowledge,
[that I may choose] truth [and goodness]
   and loathe all the ways of iniquity.
And I have loved Thee freely
   and with all my heart;
[contemplating the mysteries of] Thy wisdom
   [I have sought Thee].
For this is from Thy hand
   and [nothing is done] without [Thy will].
...XV...

I have loved Thee freely
   and with all my heart and soul.
I have purified ...
   [that I might not] turn aside from any of Thy commands.
I have clung to the Congregation ...
   that I might not be separated from any of Thy laws.

I know through the understanding which comes from Thee
   that righteousness is not in a hand of flesh,
   [that] man [is not master of] his way
   and that it is not in mortals to direct their step.

I know that the inclination of every spirit
   [is in Thy hand];
Thou didst establish [all] its [ways] before ever creating it,
   and how can any man change Thy words?
Thou alone didst [create] the just
   and establish him from the womb
   for the time of goodwill,
that he might hearken to Thy Covenant
   and walk in all (Thy ways),
and that [Thou mightest show Thyself great] to him
   in the multitude of Thy mercies,
and enlarge his straitened soul to eternal salvation,
   to perpetual and unfailing peace.
Thou wilt raise up his glory
   from among flesh.

But the wicked Thou didst create
   for [the time] of Thy [wrath],
Thou didst vow them from the womb
   to the Day of Massacre,
   for they walk in the way which is not good.
They have despised [Thy Covenant]
   and their souls have loathed Thy [truth];
they have taken no delight in all Thy commandments
   and have chosen that which Thou hatest.

[For according to the mysteries] of Thy [wisdom],
   Thou hast ordained them for great chastisements
   before the eyes of all Thy creatures,
that [for all] eternity
   they may serve as a sign [and a wonder],
and that [all men] may know Thy glory
   and Thy tremendous power.

But what is flesh
   that it should understand [these things]?
   And how should [a creature of] dust direct his steps?
It is Thou who didst shape the spirit

and establish its work [from the beginning];
   the way of all the living proceeds from Thee.
I know that no riches equal Thy truth,
   and [have therefore desired
   to enter the Council of] Thy holiness.
I know that Thou hast chosen them before all others
   and that they shall serve Thee for ever.
Thou wilt [take no bribe for the deeds of iniquity],
   nor ransom for the works of wickedness;
for Thou art a God of truth
   and [wilt destroy] all iniquity [for ever,
   and] no [wickedness] shall exist before Thee.

...

XVI...

Because I know all these things
   my tongue shall utter a reply.
Bowing down and [confessing all] my transgressions,
   I will seek [Thy] spirit [of knowledge];
cleaving to Thy spirit of [holiness],
   I will hold fast to the truth of Thy Covenant,
that [I may serve] Thee in truth and wholeness of heart,
   and that I may love [Thy Name].

Blessed art Thou, O Lord,
   Maker [of all things and mighty in] deeds:
   all things are Thy work!
Behold, Thou art pleased to favour [Thy servant],
   and hast graced me with Thy spirit of mercy
   and [with the radiance] of Thy glory.
Thine, Thine is righteousness,
   for it is Thou who hast done all [these things]!

I know that Thou hast marked the spirit of the just,
   and therefore I have chosen to keep my hands clean
   in accordance with [Thy] will;
the soul of Thy servant [has loathed]
   every work of iniquity.

And I know that man is not righteous
   except through Thee,
and therefore I implore Thee
   by the spirit which Thou hast given [me]
   to perfect Thy [favours] to Thy servant [for ever],
purifying me by Thy Holy Spirit,
   and drawing me near to Thee by Thy grace
   according to the abundance of Thy mercies

...

[Grant me] the place [of Thy lovingkindness]
   which [Thou hast] chosen for them that love Thee
   and keep [Thy commandments,
that they may stand] in Thy presence [for] ever.

...

Let no scourge [come] near him
   lest he stagger aside from the laws of Thy Covenant.

...

I [know, O Lord,
   that Thou art merciful] and compassionate,
   [long]-suffering and [rich] in grace and truth,
   pardoning transgression [and sin].
Thou repentest of [evil against them that love Thee]
   and keep [Thy] commandments,
[that] return to Thee with faith
   and wholeness of heart
... to serve Thee
   [and to do that which is] good in Thine eyes.
Reject not the face of Thy servant
... XVII ...

23

...

As Thou hast said by the hand of Moses,
   Thou forgivest transgression, iniquity, and sin,
   and pardonest rebellion and unfaithfulness.

For the bases of the mountains shall melt
   and fire shall consume the deep places of Hell,

but Thou wilt deliver
    all those that are corrected by Thy judgements,
that they may serve Thee faithfully
    and that their seed may be before Thee for ever.
Thou wilt keep Thine oath
    and wilt pardon their transgression;
    Thou wilt cast away all their sins.
Thou wilt cause them to inherit all the glory of Adam
    and abundance of days,

24

[I give Thee thanks]
    because of the spirits which Thou hast given to me!
I [will bring forth] a reply of the tongue
    to recount Thy righteous deeds,
and the forbearance ...
    and the works of Thy mighty right hand,
    and [the pardon] of the sins of the forefathers.
[I will bow down] and implore Thy mercy
    [on my sins and wicked] deeds,
    and on the perversity of [my heart],
for I have wallowed in uncleanness,
    and have [turned aside] from the counsel [of Thy truth],
and I have not laboured ...

[For] Thine, Thine is righteousness,
    and an everlasting blessing be upon Thy Name!
[According to] Thy righteousness,
    let [Thy servant] be redeemed
    [and] the wicked be brought to an end.

For I have understood that [it is Thou
    who dost establish] the path of whomsoever Thou choosest;
Thou dost hedge him in with [true] discernment
    that he may not sin against Thee,
and that his humility [may bear fruit]
    through Thy chastisement.
[Thou dost purify] his heart in [Thy trials].

[Preserve] Thy servant, [O God], lest he sin against Thee,
   or stagger aside from any word of Thy will.
Strengthen the [loins of Thy servant
   that he may] resist the spirits [of falsehood,
that] he may walk in all that Thou lovest,
   and despise all that Thou loathest,
   [that he may do] that which is good in Thine eyes.
[Destroy] their [dominion] in my bowels,
   for [within] Thy servant is a spirit of [flesh].

25

[I thank Thee, O Lord,
   for] Thou didst shed [Thy] Holy Spirit upon Thy Servant
. . .

XVIII . . .

they are confirmed in [the ears] of Thy servant for ever
. . . [to announce] Thy marvellous tidings
. . .
Withdraw not Thy hand . . .
   that he may be confirmed in Thy Covenant
   and stand before Thee [for ever].

[For Thou, O my God,] didst open a [fountain]
   in the mouth of Thy Servant.
Thou didst engrave by the measuring-cord
   [Thy mysteries] upon his tongue,
[that] out of his understanding
   [he might] preach to a creature,
and interpret these things
   to dust like myself.

Thou didst open [his fountain]
   that he might rebuke the creature of clay for his way,
and him who is born of woman
   for the guilt of his deeds;
that he might open [the fount of] Thy truth
   to a creature whom Thou upholdest by Thy might;

[that he might be], according to Thy truth,
  a messenger [in the season] of Thy goodness;
that to the humble he might bring
  glad tidings of Thy great mercy,
[proclaiming salvation]
  from out of the fountain [of holiness
  to the contrite] of spirit,
and everlasting joy to those who mourn.

...

[How] shall I look,
  unless Thou open my eyes?
Or hear,
  [unless Thou unstop my ears]?
My heart is astounded,
for to the uncircumcised ear
  a word has been disclosed,
and a heart [of stone
  has understood the right precepts].

I know it is for Thyself
  that Thou hast done these things, O God;
for what is flesh
  [that Thou shouldst act] marvellously [towards it]?
It is Thy purpose to do mightily
  and to establish all things for Thy glory.
[Thou hast created] the host of knowledge
  to declare (Thy) mighty deeds to flesh,
  and the right precepts to him that is born [of woman].
Thou hast [caused the perverse heart to enter]
  into a Covenant with Thee,
and hast uncovered the heart of dust
that it may be preserved from evil,
  and saved from the snares of Judgement
  in accordance with Thy mercies.

And I, a creature [of clay
  kneaded with water,

a heap of dust]
   and a heart of stone,
for what am I reckoned to be worthy of this?
For into an ear of dust [Thou hast put a new word]
   and hast engraved on a heart of [stone] things everlasting.
Thou hast caused [the straying spirit] to return
   that it may enter into a Covenant with Thee,
and stand [before Thee for ever]
   in the everlasting abode,
illumined with perfect Light for ever,
   with [no more] darkness,
   [for un]ending [seasons of joy]
   and un[numbered] ages of peace.
   . . .

· 9 ·

LITURGICAL FRAGMENTS

The Words of the Heavenly Lights

I N 1961 M. Baillet published in *Revue Biblique* two long fragments of a liturgical composition (*Un recueil liturgique de Qumrân, Grotte 4: 'Les paroles des luminaires'*, pp. 195–250). The precise significance of the mysterious title, 'The Words of the Heavenly Lights', is so far uncertain, but the prayers and hymns included under this heading were apparently intended for various days of the week. One of the unpublished fragments mentions 'the fourth day' (Wednesday) and column VII contains the rubric 'Hymns for the Sabbath Day'. It is reasonable to assume, therefore, that the long penitential prayer immediately preceding the Sabbath Hymns was meant for recital on a Friday. Each section appears to conclude with the old liturgical formula 'Amen! Amen!'

Baillet, on palaeographical grounds, dates the manuscript from the middle of the second century B.C. and draws attention to the complete absence of any sectarian bias. 'The Words of the Heavenly Lights' may consequently be ascribed to the earliest, pre-Essene, stage of Qumran literature.

I ... Amen! Amen!

...II... We pray Thee, O Lord, do in accordance with Thyself, in accordance with the greatness of Thy might, Thou who didst pardon our fathers when they rebelled against Thy word. Thou wert angry with them so as to wish to destroy them, but because of Thy love for them and for the sake of Thy Covenant – for Moses had atoned for their sin – and in order that Thy great might and the abundance of Thy mercy might be known to everlasting generations, Thou didst take pity on them. So let Thine anger and wrath against all [their] sin turn away from Thy people Israel.

Remember Thy marvels which Thou didst in the sight

of the nations. For we were called by Thy Name ... to [cause] us [to repent] with all (our) heart and soul and to plant Thy Law in our heart [that we might never depart from it, straying neither] to right nor to left. For Thou wilt heal us of foolishness and of blindness and confusion [of heart ... Behold] we were sold because of our iniquities but despite our offences Thou didst call us ... Thou wilt save us from sinning against Thee ...

III ... Behold, all the nations are as nothing beside Thee, they are counted as void and nought before Thee. We have called on Thy Name alone. Thou hast created us for Thy glory and made us Thy children in the sight of all the nations. For Thou hast named Israel 'My son, my first-born', and hast chastised us as a man chastises his son. Thou hast caused us to grow throughout the years of our generations [by means of] evil diseases, famine, thirst, pestilence, and the sword ... of Thy Covenant. Because Thou hast chosen us [from all] the earth [to be Thy people,] therefore hast Thou poured out Thine anger [and jealousy] upon us together with all the fury of Thy wrath. Thou hast caused [the scourge] of Thy [plagues] to cleave to us of which Moses wrote, and Thy servants the Prophets, that Thou wouldst send evil against us in the last days ...

IV ... Thy dwelling-place ... a resting-place in Jerus[alem, the city which] Thou hast [chosen] from all the earth that Thy [Name] might remain there for ever. For Thou hast loved Israel above all the peoples. Thou hast chosen the tribe of Judah and hast established Thy Covenant with David that he might be as a princely shepherd over Thy people and sit before Thee on the throne of Israel for ever. All the nations have seen Thy glory, Thou who hast sanctified Thyself in the midst of Thy people Israel. They brought their offering to Thy great Name, silver and gold and precious stones together with all the treasures of their lands, that they might glorify Thy people, and Zion Thy holy city, and the House of Thy majesty. And there was neither adversary nor misfortune, but peace and blessing . . . and they ate and were satisfied and grew fat . . .

V . . . [they forsook] the fount of living waters and served a strange god in their land. Also, their land was ravaged by their enemies; for Thy fury and the heat of Thy wrath overflowed, together with the fire of Thy jealousy, making of it a desert where no man came nor went. Yet notwithstanding all this, Thou didst not reject the seed of Jacob neither didst Thou cast away Israel to destruction, breaking Thy Covenant with them. For Thou alone art a living God and there is none beside Thee. Thou didst remember Thy Covenant, Thou who didst rescue us in the presence of all the nations, and didst not forsake us amid the nations. Thou wert gracious towards Thy people Israel in all the lands to which Thou didst banish them, that they might remember to return to Thee and to hearken to Thy voice [according to] all Thou hadst commanded by the hand of Moses Thy servant.

For Thou hast shed Thy Holy Spirit upon us, bringing upon us Thy blessings, that we might seek Thee in our distress [and mur]mur (prayers) in the ordeal of Thy chastisement. We have entered into distress, have been [stri]cken and tried by the fury of the oppressor. For we also have tired God with our iniquity, we have wearied the Rock with [our] sins. [But] in order that we may profit, Thou hast not wearied us who leadest [us] in the way in [which we must walk. But] we have not heeded . . .

VI . . . [Thou hast taken away] all our transgressions and hast purified us of our sin for Thine own sake. Thine, Thine is righteousness, O Lord, for it is Thou who hast done all this! Now, on the day when our heart is humbled, we expiate our iniquity and the iniquity of our fathers, together with our unfaithfulness and rebellion. We have not rejected Thy trials and scourges; our soul has not despised them to the point of breaking Thy Covenant despite all the distress of our soul. For Thou, who hast sent our enemies against us, strengthenest our heart that we may recount Thy mighty deeds to everlasting generations. We pray Thee O Lord, since Thou workest marvels from everlasting to everlasting, to let Thine anger and wrath turn away from us. Look on [our affliction] and trouble and distress, and deliver Thy people Israel [from all] the lands, near and far, [to which Thou hast banished them], every man who is inscribed in the Book of Life ... serve Thee and give thanks to [Thy holy Name] ...

VII ... who deliverest us from all distress. Amen! [Amen!]

HYMNS FOR THE SABBATH DAY

Give thanks ...
[Bless] His holy Name unceasingly
... all the angels of the holy firmament
... [above] the heavens,
the earth and all its deep places,
the great [Abyss] and Abaddon
and the waters and all that is [in them.]
[Let] all His creatures [bless Him] unceasingly
for everlasting [ages. Amen! Amen!]

A Liturgical Prayer

The following fragments, published by J. T. Milik (*Qumran Cave I*, Oxford, 1955, pp. 153-5), belong to a collection of prayers for Jewish festivals. The title of the present section is lost, but reference to the Renewal of the Covenant seems to indicate that we have here another part of the sect's Pentecostal liturgy.

I ... Thou wilt cause the wicked to be our ransom and the unfaithful to be our redemption. [Thou wilt] blot out all our oppressors and we shall praise Thy Name for ever [and ever]. For this hast Thou created us and [to say to Thee] this: Blessed art Thou ...

II ... the Great Light (of heaven) for the [day]time, [and the Little Light (of heaven) for the night] ... without transgressing their laws, ... and their dominion is over all the world.

But the seed of man did not understand all that Thou caused them to inherit; they did not discern Thee in all Thy words and wickedly turned aside from every one. They heeded not Thy great power and therefore Thou didst reject them. For wickedness pleases Thee not, and the ungodly shall not be established before Thee.

But in the time of Thy goodwill Thou didst choose for Thyself a people. Thou didst remember Thy Covenant and [granted] that they should be set apart for Thyself from among all the peoples as a holy thing. And Thou didst renew for them Thy Covenant (founded) on a glorious vision and the words of Thy Holy [Spirit], on the works of Thy hands and the writing of Thy Right Hand, that they might know the foundations of glory and the steps towards eternity . . . [Thou didst raise up] for them a faithful shepherd . . .

The Blessings

These fragments from a collection of blessings were originally attached to the Scroll of the Community Rule and the Messianic Rule. They have been skilfully pieced together by J. T. Milik (*Qumran Cave I*, Oxford, 1955, pp. 118–29).

The Blessings were to be recited by the Master or Guardian, and were, as it seems, intended for the Messianic age, and perhaps for the ceremony of the institution of the new Community. It is however possible that they were actually used during the course of some liturgy anticipating and symbolizing the coming of the Messianic era. All the members of the Covenant are blessed first, followed by someone who seems to be the priestly head of the Community, the Messiah of Aaron. The next blessing is addressed to the sons of Zadok, the Priests (and Levites?), and finally the Prince of the Congregation, the Messiah of Israel, is blessed. The rest of the document is lost.

THE BLESSING OF THE FAITHFUL

I Words of blessing. The Master shall bless them that fear [God and do] His will, that keep His commandments, and hold fast to His holy [Covenant], and walk perfectly [in all the ways of] His [truth]; whom He has chosen for an eternal Covenant which shall endure for ever.

May the [Lord bless you from the Abode of His holiness];
may He open for you from heaven an eternal fountain
which [shall not fail]!

...

May He [favour] you with every [heavenly] blessing;
[may He teach you] the knowledge of the Holy Ones!

[May He unlock for you the] everlasting [fountain; may
He not withhold the waters of life from] them that
thirst!

...

THE BLESSING OF THE HIGH PRIEST

II ...

III May the Lord lift His countenance towards you;
[may He delight in the] sweet odour [of your sacrifices]!

May He choose [all] them that sit in your pries[tly
college]; may He store up all your sacred offerings, and
in the [season of] ... all your seed!

May He [lift] His countenance towards all your congregation!

May He place upon your head [a diadem] ... in [ever-
lasting] glory; may He sanctify your seed in glory without
end!

May He grant you everlasting [peace] ...

May He fight [at the head of] your Thousands [until the
generation of falsehood is ended] ... [to bend] many
peoples before you ... all the riches of the world ...

For God has established all the foundations of ... may He
lay the foundation of your peace for ever!

THE BLESSING OF THE PRIESTS

Words of blessing. The M[aster shall bless] the sons of
Zadok the Priests, whom God has chosen to confirm His
Covenant for [ever, and to inquire] into all His precepts in
the midst of His people, and to instruct them as He commanded; who have established [His Covenant] on truth
and watched over all His laws with righteousness and
walked according to the way of His choice.

May the Lord bless you from His holy [Abode]; may He set you as a splendid jewel in the midst of the congregation of the saints!

May He [renew] for you the Covenant of the [everlasting] priesthood; may He sanctify you [for the House] of Holiness!

May He [judge all] the leaders by your works, and all [the princes] of the peoples by the words from out of your lips!

May He give you as your portion the first-fruits of [all delectable things]; may He bless by your hand the counsel of all flesh!

IV ... may everlasting blessings be the crown upon your head! ...

[For] He has chosen you [to] ... and to number the saints and to [bless] your people ... the men of the Council of God by your hand, and not by the hand of a prince ...

... May you be as an Angel of the Presence in the Abode of Holiness to the glory of the God of [hosts] ...

May you attend upon the service in the Temple of the Kingdom and decree destiny in company with the Angels of the Presence, in common council [with the Holy Ones] for everlasting ages and time without end; for [all] His judgements are [truth]!

May He make you holy among His people, and an [eternal] light [to illumine] the world with knowledge and to enlighten the face of the Congregation [with wisdom]!

[May He] consecrate you to the Holy of Holies! For [you are made] holy for Him and you shall glorify His Name and His holiness ...

V ...

THE BLESSING OF THE PRINCE
OF THE CONGREGATION

The Master shall bless the Prince of the Congregation ... and shall renew for him the Covenant of the Community that he may establish the kingdom of His people for ever, [that he may judge the poor with righteousness and]

dispense justice with [equity to the oppressed] of the land,
and that he may walk perfectly before Him in all the ways
[of truth], and that he may establish His holy Covenant at
the time of the affliction of those who seek God.

May the Lord raise you up to everlasting heights, and as
    a fortified tower upon a high wall!
[May you smite the peoples] with the might of your hand
    and ravage the earth with your sceptre; may you bring
    death to the ungodly with the breath of your lips!
[May He shed upon you the spirit of counsel] and everlasting
    might, the spirit of knowledge and of the fear of God;
    may righteousness be the girdle [of your loins] and may
    your reins be girdled [with faithfulness]!
May He make your horns of iron and your hooves of
    bronze; may you toss like a young bull [and trample the
    peoples] like the mire of the streets!
For God has established you as the sceptre. The rulers ...
    [and all the kings of the] nations shall serve you. He shall
    strengthen you with His holy Name and you shall be as a
    [lion; and you shall not lie down until you have de-
    voured the] prey which nought shall deliver ...

The Triumph of Righteousness

Originally entitled *The Book of Mysteries* by J. T. Milik (*Qumran
Cave I*, pp. 102–5), these fragments expound the familiar theme of
the struggle between good and evil but their nature is difficult to
determine. Perhaps they derive from a sermon, or from an
apocalyptical writing.

I ... the mysteries of sin ... They know not the mystery to
come, nor do they understand the things of the past. They
know not that which shall befall them, nor do they save
their soul from the mystery to come.

    And this shall be the sign for you that these things shall
come to pass.

    When the breed of iniquity is shut up, wickedness shall

then be banished by righteousness as darkness is banished by the light. As smoke clears and is no more, so shall wickedness perish for ever and righteousness be revealed like a sun governing the world. All who cleave to the mysteries of sin shall be no more; knowledge shall fill the world and folly shall exist no longer.

This word shall surely come to pass; this prophecy is true. And by this may it be known to you that it shall not be taken back.

Do not all the peoples loathe iniquity? And yet it is spread by them all. Does not the fame of truth issue from the mouth of all the nations? Yet is there a lip or tongue which holds to it? Which nation likes to be oppressed by another stronger than itself, or likes its wealth to be wickedly seized? And yet which nation has not oppressed another, and where is there a people which has not seized [another]'s wealth?

The Angelic Liturgy

Two fragments of a strange and important document concerned with angelic worship were published by J. Strugnell in 1960 under the title, *The Angelic Liturgy at Qumran* (*Congress Volume, Oxford,* Supplements to Vetus Testamentum vii, Leiden, pp. 318–45).

In fragment 1, the seven 'sovereign Princes' are the seven chief angels, and the object of their blessings appears to be the community of the saints, earthly and heavenly. Its original title, Songs of the Sabbath Sacrifice, seems to indicate that this angelic liturgy was thought to coincide with the Sabbath offering. If so, it testifies to the Community's belief in the union of heavenly and terrestrial worship.

The second fragment, The Divine Throne-Chariot, draws its inspiration from Ezekiel (i, x) and is related to the book of Revelation (iv). It depicts the appearance and movement of the *Merkabah,* the divine Chariot supported and drawn by the Cherubim, which is at the same time a throne and a vehicle. The 'small voice' of blessing is drawn from 1 Kings (xix, 12): it was in a 'still small voice' that God manifested Himself to Elijah. In our Qumran text this voice is uttered by the Cherubim and it is interesting to note that although the Bible does not define the source of the voice, the ancient Aramaic translation of 1 Kings (Targum of Jonathan) ascribes it to angelic beings called 'they who bless silently'.

The Throne-Chariot was a central subject of meditation in ancient as well as in medieval Jewish esotericism and mysticism, but the guardians of Rabbinic orthodoxy tended to discourage such speculation. The liturgical use of Ezekiel's chapter on the Chariot is expressly forbidden in the Mishnah; it even lays down that no wise man is to share his understanding of the *Merkabah* with a person less enlightened than himself. As a result, there is very little ancient literary material extant on the subject, and the Qumran text is therefore of great importance to the study of the origins of Jewish mysticism.

THE ANGELIC BLESSINGS

In the name of the King's majesty,
  [the fourth sovereign] Prince shall bless
  with seven [majestic] words
  [all who] walk [up]rightly.
He shall bless all who lay the foundations of [truth]
  with seven [marvellous] words.
He shall bless all the gods [who exalt] true knowledge
  [with seven] righteous words
  (that they may obtain) His glorious favours.

In the name of His marvellous deeds,
  the fifth [sovereign] Prince shall bless
  with seven [words] of His exalted truth
  [all who walk in] purity.
[He shall bless] all who eagerly do His will
  with seven [marvellous words.
He shall bless] all who glorify Him
  with seven majestic words
  that they may praise [Him for ever].

In the name [of the might of the God] of gods,
  the sixth sovereign Prince shall bless
  with seven words of His marvellous mighty deeds
  all who are mighty in wisdom.
He shall bless all the perfect of way

with seven marvellous words
that they may stand with them that live for [ever].
He shall bless all who wait for Him
with seven marvellous words
that they may obtain the return
of the [grace] of His favours.

In the name of His holiness,
the seventh sovereign Prince shall bless
with seven words of His marvellous holiness
all the holy founders [of knowledge.
He shall bless] all who exalt His Statutes
with seven marvellous words
that they may be for them stout shields.
He shall bless all the [companions] of righteousness
who endlessly [praise] His glorious kingship
with seven [marvellous words]
(that they may obtain) everlasting peace.

In the name of ...
all the [sovereign] Princes [shall bless] the God of gods
. . .

THE DIVINE THRONE-CHARIOT

... the [ministers] of the Glorious Face in the abode of [the gods] of knowledge fall down before Him, [and the Cheru]-bim utter blessings. And as they rise up, there is a divine small voice ... and loud praise; (there is) a divine [small] voice as they fold their wings.

The Cherubim bless the image of the Throne-Chariot above the firmament, and they praise the [majesty] of the fiery firmament beneath the seat of His glory. And between the turning wheels, Angels of Holiness come and go, as it were a fiery vision of most holy spirits; and about them (flow) seeming rivulets of fire, like gleaming bronze, a radiance of many gorgeous colours, of marvellous pigments magnificently mingled.

The spirits of the Living God move perpetually with the

glory of the wonderful Chariot. The small voice of blessing accompanies the tumult as they depart, and on the path of their return they worship the Holy One. Ascending, they rise marvellously; settling, they [stay] still. The sound of joyful praise is silenced and there is a small voice of blessing in all the camp of God. And a voice of praise [resounds] from the midst of all their divisions in [worship of] . . . and each one in his place, all their numbered ones sing hymns of praise.

BIBLE INTERPRETATION

THREE types of biblical Commentary have been recovered from the Qumran caves.

The first, represented by Genesis Apocryphon, sets out to render the Bible story more intelligible and attractive by giving it more substance, by reconciling conflicting statements, and also by reinterpreting in the light of contemporary standards and beliefs any passages which might seem to give offence.

The second type of Commentary departs from the biblical text and, relying on one or several passages, creates a new story. The Words of Moses and the Prayer of Nabonidus, inspired by Deuteronomy and Daniel, come into this category.

The third and most characteristic form of exegesis applies prophetic texts to the past, present, and future of the sect. Normally the commentator expounds a biblical book verse by verse, but one work – A Midrash on the Last Days – follows the traditional Jewish example and assembles passages from different parts of Scripture in order to develop a common theme.

The following is a list of the Qumran Commentaries as originally published.

THE GENESIS APOCRYPHON	N. Avigad and Y. Yadin, *A Genesis Apocryphon* (Jerusalem, 1956).
THE BLESSINGS OF JACOB	J. M. Allegro, 'Further Messianic References in Qumran Literature' (*Journal of Biblical Literature*, 1956), pp. 174–6.
THE WORDS OF MOSES	J. T. Milik, *Qumran Cave I* (Oxford, 1955), pp. 91–7.

ISAIAH	J. M. Allegro, A. A. Anderson, *DJD* v (Oxford, 1968), pp. 11–28.
THE PRAYER OF NABONIDUS	J. T. Milik, 'Prière de Nabonide' (*Revue Biblique*, 1956), pp. 407–11.
HOSEA	J. M. Allegro, A. A. Anderson, *op. cit.*, pp. 31–2.
MICAH	J. T. Milik, *Qumran Cave I* (Oxford, 1955), p. 78.
NAHUM	J. M. Allegro, A. A. Anderson, *op. cit.*, pp. 37–42.
HABAKKUK	M. Burrows, *The Dead Sea Scrolls of St Mark's Monastery*, *I* (New Haven, 1950).
PSALM 37	J. M. Allegro, A. A. Anderson, *op. cit.*, pp. 42–9.
A MIDRASH ON THE LAST DAYS	J. M. Allegro, A. A. Anderson, *op. cit.*, pp. 53–5.
A MESSIANIC ANTHOLOGY	J. M. Allegro, A. A. Anderson, *op. cit.*, pp. 57–60.
BIBLICAL LAWS	J. M. Allegro, A. A. Anderson, *op. cit.*, pp. 6–7.

The Genesis Apocryphon

The first section (col. II), refers to the miraculous birth of Noah. His father, Lamech, suspects that his wife has consorted with one of the angels who descended from heaven and married the 'daughters of men' (Gen. vi, 1–4). Her emphatic denial does not convince him and he asks his father, Methuselah, to find his own father, the omniscient Enoch who lives at Parwain, the site of Paradise, in order to discover the truth from him. A story parallel to this appears in the Book of Enoch.

The second section (cols. XIX–XXII) develops Genesis (xii–xv) with its account of Abraham's journey to Egypt, his return to Canaan, the war against the Mesopotamian kings, and the renewal of the divine promise. This lively and delightful narrative, devoid of sectarian bias, throws valuable light on the Bible interpretation current in Palestine during the inter-Testamental period.

Although this Aramaic work was discovered in cave I fifteen years ago, so far only five of its twenty-two columns have been published, mainly because of its poor state of preservation.

... **II** Behold, I thought then within my heart that conception was (due) to the Watchers and the Holy Ones ... and to the Giants ... and my heart was troubled within me because of this child. Then I, Lamech, approached Bathenosh [my] wife in haste and said to her, '... by the Most High, the Great Lord, the King of all the worlds and Ruler of the Sons of Heaven, until you tell me all things truthfully, if ... Tell me [this truthfully] and not falsely ... by the King of all the worlds until you tell me truthfully and not falsely.'

Then Bathenosh my wife spoke to me with much heat [and] ... and said, 'O my brother, O my lord, remember my pleasure ... the lying together and my soul within its body. [And I tell you] all things truthfully.'

My heart was then greatly troubled within me, and when Bathenosh my wife saw that my countenance had changed ... Then she mastered her anger and spoke to me saying 'O my lord, O my [brother, remember] my pleasure! I swear to you by the Holy Great One, the King of [the heavens] ... that this seed is yours and that [this] conception is from you. This fruit was planted by you ... and by no stranger or Watcher or Son of Heaven ... [Why] is your countenance thus changed and dismayed, and why is your spirit thus distressed ... I speak to you truthfully.'

Then I, Lamech, ran to Methuselah my father, and [I

told] him all these things. [And I asked him to go to Enoch] his father for he would surely learn all things from him. For he was beloved, and he shared the lot [of the angels], who taught him all things. And when Methuselah heard [my words . . . he went to] Enoch his father to learn all things truthfully from him . . . his will.

He went at once to Parwain and he found him there . . . [and] he said to Enoch his father, 'O my father, O my lord, to whom I . . . And I say to you, lest you be angry with me because I come here . . .

XIX . . . And I said, 'Thou art . . .' . . . '. . . until now you have not come to the Holy Mountain.'

And I departed . . . and I travelled towards the south . . . until I came to Hebron [at the time when Hebron] was being built; and I dwelt there [two years].

Now there was famine in all this land, and hearing that there was prosperity in Egypt I went . . . to the land of Egypt . . . I [came to] the river Karmon, one of the branches of the River . . . and I crossed the seven branches of the River . . . We passed through our land and entered the land of the sons of Ham, into the land of Egypt.

And on the night of our entry into Egypt, I, Abram, dreamt a dream; [and behold], I saw in my dream a cedar tree and a palm tree . . . men came and they sought to cut down the cedar tree and to pull up its roots, leaving the palm tree (standing) alone. But the palm tree cried out saying, 'Do not cut down this cedar tree, for cursed be he who shall fell [it].' And the cedar tree was spared because of the palm tree and [was] not felled.

And during the night I woke from my dream, and I said to Sarai my wife, 'I have dreamt a dream . . . [and I am] fearful [because of] this dream.' She said to me, 'Tell me your dream that I may know it.' So I began to tell her this dream . . . [the interpretation] of the dream . . . '. . . that they will seek to kill me, but will spare you . . . [Say to them] of me, He is my brother, and because of you I shall live, and because of you my life shall be saved . . .'

And Sarai wept that night on account of my words ...

Then we journeyed towards Zoan, I and Sarai ... by her life that none should see her ...

And when those five years had passed, three men from among the princes of Egypt [came at the command] of Pharaoh of Zoan to inquire after [my] business and after my wife and they gave ... goodness, wisdom, and truth. And I exclaimed before them ... because of the famine ... And they came to ascertain ... with much food and drink ... the wine ...

(During the party, the Egyptians must have seen Sarai, and on their return they praised her to the king.)

XX ... '... and beautiful is her face! How ... fine are the hairs of her head! How lovely are her eyes! How desirable her nose and all the radiance of her countenance ... How fair are her breasts and how beautiful all her whiteness! How pleasing are her arms and how perfect her hands, and how [desirable] all the appearance of her hands! How fair are her palms and how long and slender are her fingers! How comely are her feet, how perfect her thighs! No virgin or bride led into the marriage chamber is more beautiful than she; she is fairer than all other women. Truly, her beauty is greater than theirs. Yet together with all this grace she possesses abundant wisdom, so that whatever she does is perfect (?).'

When the king heard the words of Harkenosh and his two companions, for all three spoke as with one voice, he desired her greatly and sent out at once to take her. And seeing her, he was amazed by all her beauty and took her to be his wife, but me he sought to kill. Sarai said to the king, 'He is my brother,' that I might benefit from her, and I, Abram, was spared because of her and I was not slain.

And I, Abram, wept aloud that night, I and my nephew Lot, because Sarai had been taken from me by force. I prayed that night and I begged and implored, and I said in my sorrow while my tears ran down: 'Blessed art Thou, O Most High God, Lord of all the worlds, Thou who art Lord and King of all things and who rulest over all the kings of the earth and judgest them all! I cry now before Thee, my Lord, against Pharaoh of Zoan the king of Egypt, because of my wife who has been taken from me by force. Judge him for me that I may see Thy mighty hand raised against him and against all his household, and that he may not be able to defile my wife this night (separating her) from me, and that they may know Thee, my Lord, that Thou art Lord of all the kings of the earth.' And I wept and was sorrowful.

And during that night the Most High God sent a spirit to scourge him, an evil spirit to all his household; and it scourged him and all his household. And he was unable to approach her, and although he was with her for two years he knew her not.

At the end of those two years the scourges and afflictions grew greater and more grievous upon him and all his household, so he sent for all [the sages] of Egypt, for all the magicians, together with all the healers of Egypt, that they might heal him and all his household of this scourge. But not one healer or magician or sage could stay to cure him, for the spirit scourged them all and they fled.

Then Harkenosh came to me, beseeching me to go to the king and to pray for him and to lay my hands upon him that he might live, for the king had dreamt a dream ... But Lot said to him, 'Abram my uncle cannot pray for the king while Sarai his wife is with him. Go, therefore, and tell the king to restore his wife to her husband; then he will pray for him and he shall live.'

When Harkenosh had heard the words of Lot, he went to the king and said, 'All these scourges and afflictions with which my lord the king is scourged and afflicted are because of Sarai the wife of Abram. Let Sarai be restored to Abram her husband, and this scourge and the spirit of festering shall vanish from you.'

And he called me and said, 'What have you done to me with regard to [Sarai]? You said to me, She is my sister, whereas she is your wife; and I took her to be my wife.

Behold your wife who is with me; depart and go hence from all the land of Egypt! And now pray for me and my house that this evil spirit may be expelled from it.'

So I prayed [for him] ... and I laid my hands on his [head]; and the scourge departed from him and the evil [spirit] was expelled [from him], and he lived. And the king rose to tell me ... and the king swore an oath to me that ... and the king gave her much [silver and gold] and much raiment of fine linen and purple ... And Hagar also ... and he appointed men to lead [me] out [of all the land of Egypt]. And I, Abram, departed with very great flocks and with silver and gold, and I went up from [Egypt] together with my nephew [Lot]. Lot had great flocks also, and he took a wife for himself from among [the daughters of Egypt.

I pitched my camp] **XXI** [in] every place in which I had formerly camped until I came to Bethel, the place where I had built an altar. And I built a second altar and laid on it a sacrifice and an offering to the Most High God. And there I called on the name of the Lord of worlds and praised the Name of God and blessed God, and I gave thanks before God for all the riches and favours which He had bestowed on me. For He had dealt kindly towards me and had led me back in peace into this land.

After that day, Lot departed from me on account of the deeds of our shepherds. He went away and settled in the valley of the Jordan, together with all his flocks; and I myself added more to them. He kept his sheep and journeyed as far as Sodom, and he bought a house for himself in Sodom and dwelt in it. But I dwelt on the mountain of Bethel and it grieved me that my nephew Lot had departed from me.

And God appeared to me in a vision at night and said to me, 'Go to Ramath Hazor which is north of Bethel, the place where you dwell, and lift up your eyes and look to the east and to the west and to the south and to the north; and behold all this land which I give to you and your seed for ever.'

The next morning, I went up to Ramath Hazor and from

that high place I beheld the land from the River of Egypt to Lebanon and Senir, and from the Great Sea to Hauran, and all the land of Gebal as far as Kadesh, and all the Great Desert to the east of Hauran and Senir as far as Euphrates. And He said to me, 'I will give all this land to your seed and they shall possess it for ever. And I will multiply your seed like the dust of the earth which no man can number; neither shall any man number your seed. Rise and go! Behold the length and breadth of the land for it is yours; and after you, I will give it to your seed for ever.'

And I, Abram, departed to travel about and see the land. I began my journey at the river Gihon and travelled along the coast of the Sea until I came to the Mountain of the Bull (Taurus). Then I travelled from the coast of the Great Salt Sea and journeyed towards the east by the Mountain of the Bull, across the breadth of the land, until I came to the river Euphrates. I journeyed along the Euphrates until I came to the Red Sea (Persian Gulf) in the east, and I travelled along the coast of the Red Sea until I came to the tongue of the Sea of Reeds (the modern Red Sea) which flows out from the Red Sea. Then I pursued my way in the south until I came to the river Gihon, and returning, I came to my house in peace and found all things prosperous there. I went to dwell at the Oaks of Mamre, which is at Hebron, north-east of Hebron; and I built an altar there, and laid on it a sacrifice and an oblation to the Most High God. I ate and drank there, I and all the men of my household, and I sent for Mamre, Ornam, and Eshkol, the three Amorite brothers, my friends, and they ate and drank with me.

Before these days, Kedorlaomer king of Elam had set out with Amrafel king of Babylon, Ariok king of Kaptok, and Tidal king of the nations which lie between the rivers; and they had waged war against Bera king of Sodom, Birsha king of Gomorrah, Shinab king of Admah, Shemiabad king of Zeboim, and against the king of Bela. All these had made ready for battle in the valley of Siddim, and the king of Elam and the other kings with him had prevailed over the king of Sodom and his companions and had imposed a tribute upon them.

For twelve years they had paid their tribute to the king of Elam, but in the thirteenth year they rebelled against him. And in the fourteenth year, the king of Elam placed himself at the head of all his allies and went up by the Way of the Wilderness; and they smote and pillaged from the river Euphrates onward. They smote the Refaim who were at Ashteroth Karnaim, the Zumzamim who were at Ammon, the Emim [who were at] Shaveh ha-Keriyyoth, and the Horites who were in the mountains of Gebal, until they came to El Paran which is in the Wilderness. And they returned ... at Hazazon Tamar.

The king of Sodom went out to meet them, together with the king [of Gomorrah], the king of Admah, the king of Zeboim, and the king of Bela, [and they fought] a battle in the valley [of Siddim] against Kedorlaomer [king of Elam and the kings] who were with him. But the king of Sodom was vanquished and fled, and the king of Gomorrah fell into the pits ... [And] the king of Elam [carried off] all the riches of Sodom and [Gomorrah] ... and they took Lot the nephew **XXII** of Abram who dwelt with them in Sodom, together with all his possessions.

Now one of the shepherds of the flocks which Abram had given to Lot escaped from captivity and came to Abram: at that time Abram dwelt in Hebron. He told him that Lot his nephew had been taken, together with all his possessions, and that he had not been slain, and that the kings had gone by the Way of the Great Valley (of the Jordan) in the direction of their land, taking captives and plundering and smiting and slaying, and that they were journeying towards the land of Damascus.

Abram wept because of Lot his nephew. Then he braced himself; he rose up and chose from among his servants three hundred and eighteen fighting men trained for war, and Ornam and Eshkol and Mamre went with him also.

He pursued them until he came to Dan, and came on them while they were camped in the valley of Dan. He fell on them at night from four sides and during the night he slew them; he crushed them and put them to flight, and all of them fled before him until they came to Helbon which is north of Damascus. He rescued from them all their captives, and all their booty and possessions. He also delivered Lot his nephew, together with all his possessions, and he brought back all the captives which they had taken.

When the king of Sodom learned that Abram had brought back all the captives and all the booty, he came out to meet him; and he went to Salem, which is Jerusalem.

Abram camped in the valley of Shaveh, which is the valley of the king, the valley of Beth-ha-Kerem; and Melchizedek king of Salem brought out food and drink to Abram and to all the men who were with him. He was the Priest of the Most High God. And he blessed Abram and said, 'Blessed be Abram by the Most High God, Lord of heaven and earth! And blessed be the Most High God who has delivered your enemies into your hand!' And Abram gave him the tithe of all the possessions of the king of Elam and his companions.

Then the king of Sodom approached and said to Abram, 'My lord Abram, give me the souls which are mine, which you have delivered from the king of Elam and taken captive, and you may have all the possessions.'

Then said Abram to the king of Sodom, 'I raise my hand this day to the Most High God, Lord of heaven and earth! I will take nothing of yours, not even a shoe-lace or shoe-strap, lest you say, Abram's riches come from my possessions! I will take nothing but that which the young men with me have eaten already, and the portion of the three men who have come with me. They shall decide whether they will give you their portion.' And Abram returned all the possessions and all the captives and gave them to the king of Sodom; he freed all the captives from this land who were with him, and sent them all back.

After these things, God appeared to Abram in a vision and said to him, 'Behold, ten years have passed since you departed from Haran. For two years you dwelt here and you spent seven years in Egypt, and one year has passed since you returned from Egypt. And now examine and count all you have, and see how it has grown to be double that which came out with you from Haran. And now do not fear, I am with you; I am your help and your strength. I am a shield above you and a mighty safeguard round about you. Your wealth and possessions shall multiply greatly.' But Abram said, 'My Lord God, I have great wealth and possessions but what good shall they do to me? I shall die naked, childless shall I go hence. A child from my household shall inherit from me. Eliezer son ... shall inherit from me.' And He said to him, 'He shall not be your heir, but one who shall spring [from your body shall inherit from you].' ...

The Blessings of Jacob

The subject of this interpretation is the blessing of Judah, i.e. of the tribe from which David was born. The commentator emphasizes that the royal power will belong for ever to the descendants of David, thereby implying that all non-Davidic rulers, such as the contemporary Hasmonean priest-kings, occupy the throne unlawfully.

The sceptre shall not depart from the tribe of Judah, nor the ruler's staff from between his feet, until he comes to whom it belongs. And the peoples shall be in obedience to him (Gen. xlix, 10)

Whenever Israel rules there shall [not] fail to be a descendant of David upon the throne. For the *ruler's staff* is the Covenant of kingship, [and the clans] of Israel are the *feet*, until the Messiah of Righteousness comes, the Branch of David. For to him and to his seed was granted the Covenant of kingship over his people for everlasting generations ...

The Words of Moses

This farewell discourse takes its inspiration from various passages of Deuteronomy and is chiefly remarkable for the emphasis laid on the appointment of special teachers, or interpreters, of the Law (Levites and Priests).

[God spoke] to Moses in the [fortieth] year after [the children of] Israel had come [out of the land of] Egypt, in the eleventh month, on the first day of the month, saying:

'[Gather together] all the congregation and go up to [Mount Nebo] and stand [there], you and Eleazar son of Aaron. Inter[pret to the heads] of family of the Levites and to all the [Priests], and proclaim to the children of Israel the words of the Law which I proclaimed [to you] on Mount Sinai. Proclaim care[fully] into their ears all that I [require] of them. And [call] heaven and [earth to witness against] them; for they will not love what I have commanded [them to do], neither [they] nor their children, [during all] the days they shall [live upon the earth].

[For] I say that they will abandon [me, and will choose the abominations of the nations,] their horrors [and their idols. They will serve] false gods which shall be for them a snare and a pitfall. [They will sin against the] holy [days], and against the Sabbath and the Covenant, [and against the commandments] which I command you to keep this day.

[Therefore I will smite] them with a mighty [blow] in the midst of the land [which they] cross the Jordan [to possess]. And when all the curses come upon them and catch up with them to destroy them and [blot] them out, then shall they know that the truth has been [fulfilled] with regard to them.'

Then Moses called Eleazar son of [Aaron] and Joshua [son of Nun and said to them,] 'Speak [all these words to the people] ...:

[Be still] II O Israel, and hear! This [day shall you

become the people] of God, your [God. You shall keep my laws] and my testimonies [and my commandments which I] command you to [keep this] day. [And when you] cross the [Jordan so that I may give] you great [and good cities], and houses filled with all [pleasant things, and vines and olives] which [you have not planted, and] wells which you have not dug, [beware,] when you have eaten and are full, that your hearts be not lifted up, and that [you do not forget what I have commanded you to do this day. For] it is this that will bring you life and length of [days].'

And Moses [spoke to the children] of Israel [and said to them]:

'[Behold,] forty [years have passed since] the day we came out of the land [of Egypt, and today has God], our God, [uttered these words] from out of His mouth: [all] His [precepts and] all [His] precepts.

'[But how shall I carry] your loads [and burdens and disputes alone]? When I have [established] the Covenant and commanded [the way] in which you shall walk, [appoint wise men whose] work it shall be to expound [to you and your children] all these words of the Law. [Watch carefully] for your own sakes [that you keep them, lest] the wrath [of your God] kindle and burn against you, and He stop the heavens above from shedding rain [upon you], and [the water beneath the earth from] giving you [harvest].'

And Moses [spoke further] to the children of Israel.

'Behold the commandments [which God has] commanded you to keep . . .'

Commentaries on Isaiah

Fragments i and iv are of particular interest. The former expounds the celebrated Messianic passage from chapter xi; the latter applies to the Community the prophetic vision of the new Jerusalem. A similar bias appears in the New Testament (Rev. xxi, 9–27).

(i)

[And there shall come forth a rod from the stem of Jesse and a

*Branch shall grow out of its roots. And the spirit of the Lord shall
rest upon him, the spirit of wisdom and understanding, the spirit of
counsel and might, the spirit of knowledge and of the fear of the
Lord. And his delight shall be in the fear of the Lord. He shall not
judge by what his eyes see, or pass sentence by what his ears hear;
he shall judge the poor righteously and shall pass sentence justly on
the humble of the earth]* (xi, 1–3).

[Interpreted, this concerns the Branch] of David who
shall arise at the end [of days] ... God will uphold him
with [the spirit of might, and will give him] a throne of
glory and a crown of [holiness] and many-coloured garments ... [He will put a sceptre] in his hand and he shall
rule over all the [nations]. And Magog ... and his sword
shall judge [all] the peoples.

And as for that which He said, *He shall not [judge by what
his eyes see] or pass sentence by what his ears hear;* interpreted,
this means that ... [the Priests] ... As they teach him, so
will he judge; and as they order, [so will he pass sentence].
One of the Priests of renown shall go out, and garments of
... shall be in his hands ...

(ii)

[*For ten acres of vineyard shall produce only one* bath, *and an
omer of seed shall yield but one* ephah] (v, 10).

Interpreted, this saying concerns the last days, the deva-
station of the land by sword and famine. At the time of the
Visitation of the land there shall be *Woe to those who rise
early in the morning to run after strong drink, to those who linger in
the evening until wine inflames them. They have zither and harp
and timbrel and flute and wine at their feasts, but they do not
regard the work of the Lord or see the deeds of His hand. Therefore
my people go into exile for want of knowledge, and their noblemen
die of hunger and their multitude is parched with thirst. Therefore
Hell has widened its gullet and opened its mouth beyond measure,
and the nobility of Jerusalem and her multitude go down, her tumult
and he who rejoices in her* (v, 11–14).

These are the Scoffers in Jerusalem who have *despised*

the Law of the Lord and scorned the word of the Holy One of Israel. Therefore the wrath of the Lord was kindled against His people. He stretched out His hand against them and smote them; the mountains trembled and their corpses were like sweepings in the middle of the streets. And [His wrath] has not relented for all these things [and His hand is stretched out still] (v, 24–25).

This is the congregation of Scoffers in Jerusalem ...

(iii)

Thus said the Lord, the Holy One of Israel, 'You shall be saved by returning and resting; your strength shall be in silence and trust.' But you would not. You [said], 'No. We will flee upon horses and will ride on swift steeds.' Therefore your pursuers shall be speedy also. A thousand shall flee [before] the threat of one; at the threat of five you shall flee [till] you are left like a flagstaff on top of a mountain and like a signal on top of a hill. Therefore the Lord waits to be [gracious to] you; therefore He exalts Himself to have mercy on you. For the Lord is a God of justice. How blessed are all those who wait for Him! (xxx, 15–18)

Referring to the last days, this saying concerns the congregation of those who seek smooth things in Jerusalem ... [who despise the] Law and do not [trust in God] ... As robbers lie in wait for a man ... they have despised [the words of] the Law ...

O people of Zion [who live in Jerusalem, you shall weep no more. At the sound of] your crying [He will be gracious to you; He will answer you] when He [hears it. Although the Lord give you bread of oppression and water of distress, your Teacher] shall be hidden [no more and your eyes shall see your Teacher] ... (xxx, 19–20).

(iv)

Behold, I will set your stones in antimony (liv, 11b).

[Interpreted, this saying concerns] ... all Israel sought Thee according to Thy command.

And I will lay your foundations with sapphires (liv, 11c).

Interpreted, this concerns the Priests and the people who

laid the foundations of the Council of the Community ...
the congregation of His elect (shall sparkle) like a sapphire
among stones.

[*And I will make*] *all your pinnacles* [*of agate*] (liv, 12a).
Interpreted, this concerns the twelve [chief Priests] who
shall enlighten by judgement of the Urim and Tummim ...
which are absent from them, like the sun with all its light,
and like the moon ...

[*And all your gates of carbuncles*] (liv, 12b).
Interpreted, this concerns the chiefs of the tribes of
Israel ...

The Prayer of Nabonidus

Whilst the book of Daniel (iv) writes of the miraculous recovery of
Nebuchadnezzar after an illness which lasted seven years, this
interesting composition tells a similar story about the last king of
Babylon, Nabonidus. The principal difference between the two is
that Nebuchadnezzar was cured by God Himself when he recognized His sovereignty, whereas a Jewish exorcist healed Nabonidus
by teaching him the truth and forgiving his sins.

The words of the prayer uttered by Nabunai king of
Babylon, [the great] king, [when he was afflicted] with
an evil ulcer in Teiman by decree of the [Most High
God].
    I was afflicted [with an evil ulcer] for seven years ... and
an exorcist pardoned my sins. He was a Jew from among the
[children of the exile of Judah, and he said], 'Recount this
in writing to [glorify and exalt] the Name of the [Most High
God'. And I wrote this]:
    'I was afflicted with an [evil] ulcer in Teiman [by decree
of the Most High God]. For seven years [I] prayed to the gods
of silver and gold, [bronze and iron], wood and stone and
clay, because [I believed] that they were gods ...'

Commentary on Hosea

In this interpretation, the unfaithful wife is the Jewish people, and her lovers are the Gentiles who have led the nation astray.

[*She knew not that*] *it was I who gave her* [*the new wine and oil*], *who lavished* [*upon her silver*] *and gold which they* [*used for Baal*] (ii, 8).

Interpreted, this means that [they ate and] were filled, but they forgot God who ... They cast His commandments behind them which He had sent [by the hand of] His servants the Prophets, and they listened to those who led them astray. They revered them, and in their blindness they feared them as though they were gods.

Therefore I will take back my corn in its time and my wine [*in its season*]. *I will take away my wool and my flax lest they cover* [*her nakedness*]. *I will uncover her shame before the eyes of* [*her*] *lovers* [*and*] *no man shall deliver her from out of my hand* (ii, 9–10).

Interpreted, this means that He smote them with hunger and nakedness that they might be shamed and disgraced in the sight of the nations on which they relied. They will not deliver them from their miseries.

I will put an end to her rejoicing, [*her feasts*], *her* [*new*] *moons, her Sabbaths, and all her festivals* (ii, 11).

Interpreted, this means that [they have rejected the ruling of the law, and have] followed the festivals of the nations. But [their rejoicing shall come to an end and] shall be changed into mourning.

I will ravage [*her vines and her fig trees*], *of which she said,* '*They are my wage* [*which my lovers have given me*'.] *I will make of them a thicket and the* [*wild beasts*] *shall eat them* ... (ii, 12).

Commentary on Micah

Although the prophet's words are intended to castigate Samaria and Jerusalem, the Qumran commentator interprets the final phrase favourably and relates it to the Teacher of Righteousness.

[All this is] for the transgression [of Jacob and for the sins of the House of Israel. What is the transgression of Jacob?] Is it not [Samaria? And what is the high place of Judah? It is not Jerusalem? I will make of Samaria a ruin in the fields, and of Jerusalem a plantation of vines] (i, 5–6).

Interpreted, this concerns the Spouter of Lies [who led the] Simple [astray].

And what is the high place of Judah? [Is it not Jerusalem?] (i, 5).

[Interpreted, this concerns] the Teacher of Righteousness who [expounded the Law to] his [Council] and to all who freely pledged themselves to join the elect of [God to keep the Law] in the Council of the Community; who shall be saved on the Day [of Judgement] ...

Commentary on Nahum

The historical significance of this fragment is discussed in Chapter 3 (pp. 58ff).

For a correct understanding of the interpretation of Nahum ii, 12, the reader should bear in mind the biblical order that only the corpses of executed criminals should be hanged (Deut. xxi, 21). Hanging men alive, i.e. crucifixion, was a sacrilegious novelty. Some translators consider the mutilated final sentence unfinished, and render it: 'For a man hanged alive on a tree shall be called ...' The version given here seems more reasonable.

I *[Where is the lions' den and the cave of the young lions?]* (ii, 11)'
[Interpreted, this concerns] ... a dwelling-place for the ungodly of the nations.

Whither the lion goes, there is the lion's cub, [with none to disturb it] (ii, 11b).

[Interpreted, this concerns Deme]trius king of Greece who sought, on the counsel of those who seek smooth things, to enter Jerusalem. [But God did not permit the city to be delivered] into the hands of the kings of Greece, from the time of Antiochus until the coming of the rulers of the Kittim. But then she shall be trampled under their feet ...

The lion tears enough for its cubs and it chokes prey for its lionesses (ii, 12a).

[Interpreted, this] concerns the furious young lion who strikes by means of his great men, and by means of the men of his council.

[*And chokes prey for its lionesses; and it fills*] *its caves* [*with prey*] *and its dens with victims* (ii, 12a–b).

Interpreted, this concerns the furious young lion [who executes revenge] on those who seek smooth things and hangs men alive, [a thing never done] formerly in Israel. Because of a man hanged alive on [the] tree, He proclaims, '*Behold I am against* [*you, says the Lord of Hosts*'].

[*I will burn up your multitude in smoke*], *and the sword shall devour your young lions. I will* [*cut off*] *your prey* [*from the earth*] (ii, 13).

[Interpreted] ... *your multitude* is the bands of his army ... and his *young lions* are ... his *prey* is the wealth which [the Priests] of Jerusalem have [amassed], which ... Israel shall be delivered ...

[*And the voice of your messengers shall no more be heard*] (ii, 13b).

[Interpreted] **II** ... his *messengers* are his envoys whose voice shall no more be heard among the nations.

Woe to the city of blood; it is full of lies and rapine (iii, 1ab).

Interpreted, this is the city of Ephraim, those who seek smooth things during the last days, who walk in lies and falsehood.

The prowler is not wanting, noise of whip and noise of rattling wheel, prancing horse and jolting chariot, mounting horsemen, flame and glittering spear, a multitude of slain and a heap of carcases. There is no end to the corpses; they stumble upon their corpses (iii, 1c–3).

Interpreted, this concerns the dominion of those who seek smooth things, from the midst of whose assembly the sword of the nations shall never be wanting. Captivity, looting, and burning shall be among them, and exile from dread of the enemy. A multitude of guilty corpses shall fall in their days; there shall be no end to the sum of their slain. They shall also stumble upon their body of flesh because of their guilty counsel.

Because of the many harlotries of the well-favoured harlot, the mistress of seduction, she who sells nations through her harlotries and families through her seductions (iii, 4).

Interpreted, this concerns those who lead Ephraim astray, who lead many astray through their false teaching, their lying tongue, and deceitful lips – kings, princes, priests, and people, together with the stranger who joins them. Cities and families shall perish through their counsel; honourable men and rulers shall fall through their tongue's [decision].

Behold, I am against you – oracle of the Lord of hosts – and I will life up your skirts to your face and expose your nakedness to the nations and your shame to the kingdoms (iii, 5).

Interpreted ... cities of the east. For the *skirts* are ... **III** and the nations shall ... among them their filthy idols.

I will cast filth upon you and treat you with contempt and render you despicable, so that all who look upon you shall flee from you (iii, 6–7a).

Interpreted, this concerns those who seek smooth things, whose evil deeds shall be uncovered to all Israel at the end of time. Many shall understand their iniquity and treat them with contempt because of their guilty presumption. When the glory of Judah shall arise, the simple of Ephraim shall flee from their assembly; they shall abandon those who lead them astray and shall join Israel.

They shall say, Niniveh is laid waste; who shall grieve over her? Whence shall I seek comforters for you? (iii, 7b.).

Interpreted, this concerns those who seek smooth things, whose Council shall perish and whose congregation shall be dispersed. They shall lead the assembly astray no more, and the simple shall support their Council no more.

Are you better than Amon which lay among the rivers? (iii, 8a).

Interpreted, *Amon* is Manasseh, and the *rivers* are the great men of Manasseh, the honourable men of ...

Which was surrounded by waters, whose rampart was the sea and whose walls were waters? (iii, 8b).

Interpreted, these are her valiant men, her almighty warriors.

Ethiopia [and Egypt] were her [limitless] strength (iii, 9a). [Interpreted] ...

[Put and the Lybians were your helpers] (iii, 9b).

IV Interpreted, these are the wicked of [Judah], the House of Separation, who joined Manasseh.

Yet she was exiled; she went into captivity. Her children were crushed at the top of all the streets. They cast lots for her honourable men, and all her great men were bound with chains (iii, 10).

Interpreted, this concerns Manasseh in the final age, whose kingdom shall be brought low by [Israel ...] his wives, his children, and his little ones shall go into captivity. His mighty men and honourable men [shall perish] by the sword.

[You shall be drunk] and shall be stupified (iii, 11a).

Interpreted, this concerns the wicked of E[phraim ...] whose cup shall come after Manasseh ...

[*You shall also seek*] *refuge in the city because of the enemy* (iii, 11b).

Inter[preted, this concerns ...] their enemies in the city ...

[*All your strongholds shall be*] *like fig trees with newly-ripe figs* (iii, 12a).

...

Commentary on Habakkuk

The doctrinal and historical references contained in this detailed interpretation of Habakkuk are analysed in Chapters 2 and 3.

I [*Oracle of Habakkuk the prophet. How long, O Lord, shall I cry*] *for help and Thou wilt not* [*hear*]? (i, 1–2).

[Interpreted, this concerns the beginning] of the [final] generation ...

[*Or shout to Thee 'Violence', and Thou wilt not deliver?*] (i, 2b)
...

[*Why dost Thou cause me to see iniquity and to look upon trouble? Desolation and violence are before me*] (i, 3).

... God with oppression and unfaithfulness ... they rob riches.

[*There is quarrelling and contention*] (i, 3b).
...

So the law is weak [*and justice never goes forth*] (i, 4a–b).
[Interpreted] this concerns those who have despised the Law of God ...

[*For the wicked encompasses*] *the righteous* (i, 4c).
[*The wicked* is the Wicked Priest, and *the righteous*] is the Teacher of Righteousness ...

[*So*] *justice goes forth* [*perverted*] (i, 4d).
...

[Behold the nations and see, marvel and be astonished; for I accomplish a deed in your days but you will not believe it when] **II** told (i, 5).

[Interpreted, this concerns] those who were unfaithful together with the Liar, in that they [did] not [listen to the word received by] the Teacher of Righteousness from the mouth of God. And it concerns the unfaithful of the New [Covenant] in that they have not believed in the Covenant of God [and have profaned] His holy Name. And likewise, this saying is to be interpreted [as concerning those who] will be unfaithful at the end of days. They, the men of violence and the breakers of the Covenant, will not believe when they hear all that [is to happen to] the final generation from the Priest [in whose heart] God set [understanding] that he might interpret all the words of His servants the Prophets, through whom He foretold all that would happen to His people and [His land].

For behold, I rouse the Chaldeans, that [bitter and hasty] nation (i, 6a).

Interpreted, this concerns the Kittim [who are] quick and valiant in war, causing many to perish. [All the world shall fall] under the dominion of the Kittim, and the [wicked . . .] they shall not believe in the laws of [God . . .]

[Who march through the breadth of the earth to take possession of dwellings which are not their own] (i, 6b).
. . . **III** they shall march across the plain, smiting and plundering the cities of the earth. For it is as He said, *To take possession of dwellings which are not their own.*

They are fearsome and terrible; their justice and grandeur proceed from themselves (i, 7).

Interpreted, this concerns the Kittim who inspire all the nations with fear [and dread]. All their evil plotting is done with intention and they deal with all the nations in cunning and guile.

Their horses are swifter than leopards and fleeter than evening wolves. Their horses step forward proudly and spread their wings;

they fly from afar like an eagle avid to devour. All of them come for violence; the look on their faces is like the east wind (i, 8-9a).

[Interpreted, this] concerns the Kittim who trample the earth with their horses and beasts. They come *from afar*, from the islands of the sea, to devour all the peoples *like an eagle* which cannot be satisfied, and they address [all the peoples] with anger and [wrath and fury] and indignation. For it is as He said, *The look on their faces is like the east wind.*

[*They heap up*] *captives* [*like sand*] (i, 9b).

. . .

IV *They scoff* [*at kings*], *and princes are their laughing-stock* (i, 10a).

Interpreted, this means that they mock the great and despise the venerable; they ridicule kings and princes and scoff at the mighty host.

They laugh at every fortress; they pile up earth and take it (i, 10b).

Interpreted, this concerns the commanders of the Kittim who despise the fortresses of the peoples and laugh at them in derision. To capture them, they encircle them with a mighty host, and out of fear and terror they deliver themselves into their hands. They destroy them because of the sins of their inhabitants.

The wind then sweeps on and passes; and they make of their strength their god (i, 11).

Interpreted, [this concerns] the commanders of the Kittim who, on the counsel of [the] House of Guilt, pass one in front of the other; one after another [their] commanders come to lay waste the earth. [*And they make*] *of their strength their god*: interpreted, this concerns [. . . all] the peoples . . .

[*Art Thou not from everlasting, O Lord, my God, my Holy One? We shall not die.*] *Thou hast ordained them,* [*O Lord*], **V** *for judgement; Thou hast established them, O Rock, for chastisement. Their eyes are too pure to behold evil; and Thou canst not look on distress* (i, 12-13a).

Interpreted, this saying means that God will not destroy His people by the hand of the nations; God will execute the judgement of the nations by the hand of His elect. And through their chastisement all the wicked of His people shall expiate their guilt who keep His commandments in their distress. For it is as He said, *Too pure of eyes to behold evil:* interpreted, this means that they have not lusted after their eyes during the age of wickedness.

O traitors, why do you stare and stay silent when the wicked swallows up one more righteous than he? (i, 13b).

Interpreted, this concerns the House of Absalom and the members of its council who were silent at the time of the chastisement of the Teacher of Righteousness and gave him no help against the Liar who flouted the Law in the midst of their whole [congregation].

Thou dealest with men like the fish of the sea, like creeping things, to rule over them. They draw [them all up with a fish-hook], and drag them out with their net, and gather them in [their seine. Therefore they sacrifice] to their net. Therefore they rejoice [and exult and burn incense to their seine; for by them] their portion is fat [and their sustenance rich] (i, 14–16).

... **VI** the Kittim. And they shall gather in their riches, together with all their booty, *like the fish of the sea.* And as for that which He said, *Therefore they sacrifice to their net and burn incense to their seine:* interpreted, this means that they sacrifice to their standards and worship their weapons of war. *For through them their portion is fat and their sustenance rich:* interpreted, this means that they divide their yoke and their tribute – *their sustenance* – over all the peoples year by year, ravaging many lands.

Therefore their sword is ever drawn to massacre nations mercilessly (i, 17).

Interpreted, this concerns the Kittim who cause many to perish by the sword – youths, grown men, the aged, women and children – and who even take no pity on the fruit of the womb.

I will take my stand to watch and will station myself upon my fortress. I will watch to see what He will say to me and how [He will answer] my complaint. And the Lord answered [and said to me, 'Write down the vision and make it plain] upon the tablets, that [he who reads] may read it speedily (ii, 1–2).

... **VII** and God told Habakkuk to write down that which would happen to the final generation, but He did not make known to him when time would come to an end. And as for that which He said, *That he who reads may read it speedily,* interpreted this concerns the Teacher of Righteousness, to whom God made known all the mysteries of the words of His servants the Prophets.

For there shall be yet another vision concerning the appointed time. It shall tell of the end and shall not lie (ii, 3a).

Interpreted, this means that the final age shall be prolonged, and shall exceed all that the Prophets have said; for the mysteries of God are astounding.

If it tarries, wait for it, for it shall surely come and shall not be late (ii, 3b).

Interpreted, this concerns the men of truth who keep the Law, whose hands shall not slacken in the service of truth when the final age is prolonged. For all the ages of God reach their appointed end as He determines for them in the mysteries of His wisdom.

Behold, [his soul] is puffed up and is not upright (ii, 4a).

Interpreted, this means that [the wicked] shall double their guilt upon themselves [and it shall not be forgiven] when they are judged ...

[But the righteous shall live by his faith] (ii, 4b).

VIII Interpreted, this concerns all those who observe the Law in the House of Judah, whom God will deliver from the House of Judgement because of their suffering and because of their faith in the Teacher of Righteousness.

Moreover, the arrogant man seizes wealth without halting. He widens his gullet like Hell and like Death he has never enough. All the nations are gathered to him and all the peoples are assembled to him. Will they not all of them taunt him and jeer at him saying, 'Woe to him who amasses that which is not his! How long will he load himself up with pledges?' (ii, 5–6).

Interpreted, this concerns the Wicked Priest who was called by the name of truth when he first arose. But when he ruled over Israel his heart became proud, and he forsook God and betrayed the precepts for the sake of riches. He robbed and amassed the riches of the men of violence who rebelled against God, and he took the wealth of the peoples, heaping sinful iniquity upon himself. And he lived in the ways of abominations amidst every unclean defilement.

Shall not your oppressors suddenly arise and your torturers awaken; and shall you not become their prey? Because you have plundered many nations, all the remnant of the peoples shall plunder you (ii, 7–8a).

[Interpreted, this concerns] the Priest who rebelled [and violated] the precepts [of God ... to command] **IX** his chastisement by means of the judgements of wickedness. And they inflicted horrors of evil diseases and took vengeance upon his body of flesh. And as for that which He said, *Because you have plundered many nations, all the remnant of the peoples shall plunder you*, interpreted this concerns the last Priests of Jerusalem, who shall amass money and wealth by plundering the peoples. But in the last days, their riches and booty shall be delivered into the hands of the army of the Kittim, for it is they who shall be the *remnant of the peoples*.

Because of the blood of men and the violence done to the land, to the city, and to all its inhabitants (ii, 8b).

Interpreted, this concerns the Wicked Priest whom God delivered into the hands of his enemies because of the iniquity committed against the Teacher of Righteousness and the men of his Council, that he might be humbled by means of a destroying scourge, in bitterness of soul, because he had done wickedly to His elect.

Woe to him who gets evil profit for his house; who perches his nest high to be safe from the hand of evil! You have devised shame to your house; by cutting off many peoples you have forfeited your own soul. For the [stone] cries out [from] the wall [and] the beam from the woodwork replies (ii, 9–11).

[Interpreted, this] concerns the [Priest] who ... **X** that its stones might be laid in oppression and the beam of its woodwork in robbery. And as for that which He said, *By cutting off many peoples you have forfeited your own soul,* interpreted this concerns the condemned House whose judgement God will pronounce in the midst of many peoples. He will bring him thence for judgement and will declare him guilty in the midst of them, and will chastise him with fire of brimstone.

Woe to him who builds a city with blood and founds a town upon falsehood! Behold, is it not from the Lord of Hosts that the peoples shall labour for fire and the nations shall strive for naught? (ii, 12–13).

Interpreted, this concerns the Spouter of Lies who led many astray that he might build his city of vanity with blood and raise a congregation on deceit, causing many thereby to perform a service of vanity for the sake of its glory, and to be pregnant with [works] of deceit, that their labour might be for nothing and that they might be punished with fire who vilified and outraged the elect of God.

For as the waters cover the sea, so shall the earth be filled with the knowledge of the glory of the Lord (ii, 14).

Interpreted, [this means that] when they return ... **XI** the lies. And afterwards, knowledge shall be revealed to them abundantly, like the waters of the sea.

Woe to him who causes his neighbours to drink; who pours out his venom to make them drunk that he may gaze on their feasts! (ii, 15).

Interpreted, this concerns the Wicked Priest who pursued the Teacher of Righteousness to the house of his exile that he might confuse him with his venomous fury. And at the time appointed for rest, for the Day of Atonement, he appeared before them to confuse them, and to cause them to stumble on the Day of Fasting, their Sabbath of repose.

You have filled yourself with ignominy more than with glory. Drink also, and stagger! The cup of the Lord's right hand shall come round to you and shame shall come on your glory (ii, 16).

Interpreted, this concerns the Priest whose ignominy was greater than his glory. For he did not circumcise the foreskin of his heart, and he walked in the ways of drunkenness that he might quench his thirst. But the cup of the wrath of God shall confuse him, multiplying his . . . and the pain of . . .

[*For the violence done to Lebanon shall overwhelm you, and the destruction of the beasts*] **XII** *shall terrify you, because of the blood of men and the violence done to the land, the city, and all its inhabitants* (ii, 17).

Interpreted, this saying concerns the Wicked Priest, inasmuch as he shall be paid the reward which he himself tendered to the Poor. For *Lebanon* is the Council of the Community; and the *beasts* are the Simple of Judah who keep the Law. As he himself plotted the destruction of the Poor, so will God condemn him to destruction. And as for that which He said, *Because of the blood of the city and the violence done to the land:* interpreted, *the city* is Jerusalem where the Wicked Priest committed abominable deeds and defiled the Temple of God. *The violence done to the land:* these are the cities of Judah where he robbed the Poor of their possessions.

Of what use is an idol that its maker should shape it, a molten image, a fatling of lies? For the craftsman puts his trust in his own creation when he makes dumb idols (ii, 18).

Interpreted, this saying concerns all the idols of the nations which they make so that they may serve and worship them. But they shall not deliver them on the Day of Judgement.

*Woe [to him who says] to wood, 'Awake', and to dumb [stone,
'Arise'! Can such a thing give guidance? Behold, it is covered with
gold and silver but there is no spirit within it. But the Lord is in His
holy Temple]: let all the earth be silent before Him!* (ii, 19–20).

Interpreted, this concerns all the nations which serve
stone and wood. But on the Day of Judgement, God will
destroy from the earth all idolatrous and wicked men.

Commentary on Psalm 37

The Psalm's description of the destiny of the righteous and the
wicked is applied to that of the sect and its enemies, and more particularly to the struggle of the Teacher of Righteousness against
the Wicked Priest.

The author introduces an important change into the text of
verse 20b, rendering it 'those who *love* the Lord' instead of 'those
who *hate* the Lord'. The artificiality of this alteration is evident
from the broken context.

*[Do not be angry against the man who prospers, against him who
carries out evil devices]* (7).

. . . they shall perish by the sword and famine and plague.

*Relent from anger and abandon wrath. Do not be angry, it tends
only to evil; for the wicked shall be cut off* (8–9a).

Interpreted, this concerns all those who return to the
Law, to those who do not refuse to turn away from their
evil. For all those who are stubborn in turning away from
their iniquity shall be cut off.

But those who wait for the Lord shall possess the land (9b).
Interpreted, this is the congregation of His elect who do
His will.

*A little while and the wicked shall be no more; I will look
towards his place but he shall not be there* (10).

Interpreted, this concerns all the wicked. At the end of
the forty years they shall be blotted out and not an [evil]
man shall be found on the earth.

*But the humble shall possess the land and delight in abundant
peace* (11).

Interpreted, this concerns [the congregation of the] Poor who shall accept the season of penance and shall be delivered from all the snares [of Satan . . .]

The wicked draw the sword and bend their bow to bring down the poor and needy and to slay the upright of way. Their sword shall enter their own heart and their bows shall be broken (14–15).

Interpreted, this concerns the wicked of Ephraim and Manasseh, who shall seek to lay hands on the Priest and the men of his Council at the time of trial which shall come upon them. But God will redeem them from out of their hand. And afterwards, they shall be delivered into the hand of the violent among the nations for judgement . . .

[*The Lord knows the days of the perfect and their portion shall be for ever. In evil times they shall not be shamed*] (18–19a).
. . . to the penitents of the desert who shall live for a thousand generations . . . [and to whom all the glory] of Adam [shall belong], as also to their seed for ever.

And in the days of famine they shall be [*satisfied, but the wicked*] *shall perish* (19b–20a).

Interpreted, this [means that] He will keep them alive during the famine and the time [of trial, whereas the wicked] shall perish from famine and plague, all those who have not departed [from the land of Judah].

And those who love the Lord shall be like the pride of pastures (20b).

Interpreted, [this concerns] the congregation of His elect, who shall be leaders and princes . . . of the flock among their herds.

Like smoke they shall all of them vanish away (20c).

Interpreted, [this] concerns the princes [of wickedness] who have oppressed His holy people, and who shall perish like smoke [blown away by the wind].

The wicked borrows and does not repay, but the righteous is

generous and gives. Truly, those whom He [blesses shall possess]
the land, but those whom He curses [shall be cut off] (21–22).

Interpreted, this concerns the congregation of the Poor,
who [shall possess] the portion of all . . . They shall possess
the High Mountain of Israel [for ever], and shall enjoy
[everlasting] delights in His Sanctuary. [But those who]
shall be *cut off*, they are the violent [of the nations and] the
wicked of Israel; they shall be cut off and blotted out for
ever.

The steps of the Man are confirmed by the Lord and He delights
in all his ways; though [he stumble, he shall not fall, for the Lord
shall support his hand] (23–24).

Interpreted, this concerns the Priest, the Teacher of
[Righteousness . . . whom] He established to build for Himself the congregation of . . .

The wicked watches out for the righteous and seeks [to slay him.
The Lord will not abandon him into his hand or] let him be con-
demned when he is tried (32–33).

Interpreted, this concerns the Wicked [Priest] who [rose
up against the Teacher of Righteousness] that he might put
him to death [because he served the truth] and the Law,
[for which reason] he laid hands upon him. But God will
not *abandon [him into his hand and will not let him be condemned*
when he is] tried. And [God] will pay him his reward by
delivering him into the hand of the violent of the nations,
that they may execute upon him [the judgements of
wickedness].

A Midrash on the Last Days

This collection of texts assembled from 2 Samuel and the Psalter,
and combined with other scriptural passages, serves to present the
sectarian doctrine identifying the Community with the Temple,
and to announce the coming of the two Messiahs, the 'Branch of
David' and the 'Interpreter of the Law'.

I . . . [*I will appoint a place for my people Israel and will plant*
them that they may dwell there and be troubled no more by their]

*enemies. No son of iniquity [shall afflict them again] as formerly,
from the day that [I set judges] over my people Israel* (2 Sam. vii,
10).

This is the House which [He will build for them in the]
last days, as it is written in the book of Moses, *In the sanctuary
which Thy hands have established, O Lord, the Lord shall reign for
ever and ever* (Exod. xv, 17–18). This is the House into which
[the unclean shall] never [enter, nor the uncircumcised,]
nor the Ammonite, nor the Moabite, nor the half-breed,
nor the foreigner, nor the stranger, ever; for there shall My
Holy Ones be. [Its glory shall endure] forever; it shall
appear above it perpetually. And strangers shall lay it
waste no more, as they formerly laid waste the Sanctuary
of Israel because of its sin. He has commanded that a
Sanctuary of men be built for Himself, that there they
may send up, like the smoke of incense, the works of the
Law.

And concerning His words to David, *And I [will give] you
[rest] from all your enemies* (2 Sam. vii, 11), this means that He
will give them rest from all the children of Satan who cause
them to stumble so that they may be destroyed [by their
errors,] just as they came with a [devilish] plan to cause
the [sons] of light to stumble and to devise against them a
wicked plot, that [they might become subject] to Satan in
their [wicked] straying.

The Lord declares to you that He will build you a House (2
Sam. vii, 11c). *I will raise up your seed after you* (2 Sam. vii,
12). *I will establish the throne of his kingdom [for ever]* (2 Sam.
vii, 13). *I [will be] his father and he shall be my son* (2 Sam.
vii, 14). He is the Branch of David who shall arise with the
Interpreter of the Law [to rule] in Zion [at the end] of
time. As it is written, *I will raise up the tent of David that is
fallen* (Amos ix, 11). That is to say, the fallen *tent of David* is
he who shall arise to save Israel.

Explanation of *How blessed is the man who does not walk in
the counsel of the wicked* (Ps. i, 1). Interpreted, this saying
[concerns] those who turn aside from the way [of the

people]; as it is written in the book of Isaiah the Prophet concerning the last days, *It came to pass that [the Lord turned me aside, as with a mighty hand, from walking in the way of] this people* (Isa. viii, 11). They are those of whom it is written in the book of Ezekiel the Prophet, *The Levites [strayed far from me, following] their idols* (Ezek. xliv, 10). They are the sons of Zadok who [seek their own] counsel and follow [their own inclination] apart from the Council of the Community.

[*Why*] *do the nations [rage] and the peoples meditate [vanity, the kings of the earth] rise up, [and the] princes take counsel together against the Lord and against [His Messiah]?* (Ps. ii, 1). Interpreted, this saying concerns [the kings of the nations] who shall [rage against] the elect of Israel in the last days. **II** This shall be the time of the trial to come ...

A Messianic Anthology

This short document, similar in literary style to the Christian *Testimonia*, or collection of Messianic proof-texts, includes five quotations arranged in four groups, the last being followed by a particular interpretation.

The first group consists of two texts from Deuteronomy referring to the Prophet similar to Moses; the second is an extract from a prophecy of Balaam about the royal Messiah; the third is a blessing of the Levites and, implicitly, of the Priest-Messiah.

The last group opens with a verse from Joshua which is then expounded by means of a quotation from the sectarian Psalms of Joshua. Most experts hold that the commentator, bearing in mind the biblical passage, is alluding to three characters, a father ('an accursed man') and his two sons. However, the verb 'arose' in the second sentence is in the singular, and it would seem correct to interpret this text as referring to the two brothers only.

The Lord spoke to Moses saying:

You have heard the words which this people have spoken to you; all they have said is right. O that their heart were always like this, to fear me and to keep my commandments always, that it might be well with them and their children for ever! (Deut. v, 28–9). *I will*

*raise up for them a Prophet like you from among their brethren. I
will put my words into his mouth and he shall tell them all that I
command him. And I will require a reckoning of whoever will not
listen to the words which the Prophet shall speak in my Name*
(Deut. xviii, 18–19).

He took up his discourse and said:

*Oracle of Balaam son of Beor. Oracle of the man whose eye is
penetrating. Oracle of him who has heard the words of God, who
knows the wisdom of the Most High and sees the vision of the
Almighty, who falls and his eyes are opened. I see him but not now.
I behold him but not near. A star shall come out of Jacob and a
sceptre shall rise out of Israel; he shall crush the temples of Moab
and destroy all the children of Sheth* (Num. xxiv, 15–17).

And of Levi he said:

*Give Thy Tummim to Levi, and Thy Urim to Thy pious one
whom Thou didst test at Massah, and with whom Thou didst
quarrel at the waters of Meribah; who said to his father and mother,
'I know you not', and who did not acknowledge his brother, or know
his sons. For they observed Thy word and kept Thy Covenant. They
shall cause Thy precepts to shine before Jacob and Thy Law
before Israel. They shall send up incense towards Thy nostrils
and place a burnt offering upon Thine altar. Bless his power, O
Lord, and delight in the work of his hands. Smite the loins of
his adversaries and let his enemies rise no more* (Deut. xxxiii,
8–11).

When Joshua had finished offering praise and thanksgiving, he said:

*Cursed be the man who rebuilds this city! May he lay its
foundation on his first-born, and set its gate upon his youngest son*
(Josh. vi, 26). Behold, an accursed man, a man of Satan,
has risen to become a fowler's net to his people, and a cause
of destruction to all his neighbours. And [his brother] arose
[and ruled], both being instruments of violence. They have
rebuilt [Jerusalem and have set up] a wall and towers to
make of it a stronghold of ungodliness ... In Israel, and a

horror in Ephraim, and in Judah ... They have committed an abomination in the land, and a great blasphemy among the children [of Israel. They have shed blood] like water upon the ramparts of the daughter of Zion and within the precincts of Jerusalem.

A Commentary on Biblical Laws

Although the general context of the document is not clear, two statutes can be recognized relating to Deuteronomy xxiii, 25–6 and to Exodus xxx, 11–16 (xxxviii, 25–6) respectively.

In the first, the Bible allows a man crossing another person's field to pluck the ears of corn and to eat them, but forbids him to cut the grain with his sickle. Applying this law to the case of a man who is destitute, the Qumran interpreter stipulates that although he may eat while in the field, nothing must be taken home. On the other hand, he may both eat and gather provisions for his family from the threshing floor.

The second statute refers to the tax of half a shekel to be contributed to the upkeep of the place of worship by every Israelite aged twenty. Later Jewish tradition interpreted this passage as instituting a yearly tax to be paid by every male Israelite (cf. Neh. x, 32; Matt. xvii, 24–7; see also the treatise *Shekalim* or *Shekel Dues* in the Mishnah). The Qumran ordinance, however, insists on one single payment, thereby complying with the scriptural rule and at the same time refusing regular support to the Temple of Jerusalem.

II ... Any destitute [Israelite] who goes into a threshing-floor may eat there and gather for himself and for [his] hou[sehold. But should he walk among corn standing in] the field, he may eat but may not bring it to his house to store it.

Concerning ... the money of valuation that a man gives as ransom for his life, it shall be half [a shekel ...] He shall give it only once in his life. Twenty gerahs make one shekel according to [the shekel of the Temple (cf. Exod. xxx, 12–13) ...] For the 600,000, one hundred talents; for the 3,000, half a talent = 30 minahs); [for the 500, five minahs;] and for the 50, half a minah, (which is) twenty-five shekels (cf. Exod. xxxviii, 25–6) ...

ADDENDA

I RULES

The Temple Scroll

THE *Temple Scroll*, over twenty-eight feet long, and the largest of all the Qumran manuscripts, emerged from semi-clandestinity almost immediately after the end of the 'Six Day War' in the summer of 1967. It came into the hands of Professor Yigael Yadin and is expected to appear in print in the very near future. A preliminary description of the scroll was published by the same scholar in the December 1967 issue of *The Biblical Archaeologist*, and reprinted in D. N. Freedman and J. C. Greenfield's *New Directions in Biblical Archaeology*, New York, 1971, pp. 156–66.

Yadin distinguishes four main subjects in the document: (1) rules regarding ritual cleanness, etc. (2) the ceremonial for festivals; (3) the building of the Temple; (4) the king and the army. Altogether sixty-six columns have survived.

The two short extracts so far released come from the final section of the scroll. The first, column LVII, lines 17–19, imposes a monogamous marriage on the king (see above, pp. 36–7, 101). Cf. Y. Yadin, 'L'attitude essénienne envers la polygamie et le divorce', *Revue Biblique*, 1972, pp. 98–9; G. Vermes, 'Sectarian Matrimonial Halakhah in the Damascus Rule', *Journal of Jewish Studies*, 1974, pp. 197–202.

The second, column LXIV, lines 6–13, decrees that an Israelite guilty of treason, or a similar crime against the Jewish state, is to die by 'hanging on the tree', i.e. most probably by crucifixion (cf. above pp. 60–61, 231–2). See Y. Yadin, 'Pesher Nahum (4Q pNahum) Reconsidered', *Israel Exploration Journal*, 1971, pp. 1–12; E. Schürer, G. Vermes, F. Millar, *The History of the Jewish People in the Age of Jesus Christ*, vol. 1, Edinburgh, 1973, p. 225.

LVII He (the king) shall not take another wife in addition to her, for she (the first wife) shall be with him all the days of her life. But if she dies, he shall marry another.

LXIV If a man slanders his people, and delivers his people to a foreign nation, and does evil to his people, you shall hang him on a tree and he shall die. On the testimony of two witnesses, and on the testimony of three witnesses he shall be put to death, and they shall hang him (on) the tree.

If a man is guilty of a capital crime and he flees (abroad) to the Gentiles, and curses his people, and the sons of Israel, you shall hang him also on the tree, and he shall die. But their bodies shall not stay overnight on the tree. Indeed, you shall bury him on the same day, for he who is hanged on the tree is accursed of God and men, and you shall not pollute the ground which I give you to possess.

The Wicked and the Holy

The first fragment of a document (4Q **181**), which its editor has left untitled, describes in a manner similar to Community Rule IV, the respective destinies of the damned and the chosen. See J. M. Allegro, A. A. Anderson, *Discoveries in the Judaean Desert of Jordan*, vol. V, Oxford, 1968, pp. 79–80; cf. J. Strugnell, 'Notes en marge du volume V des *Discoveries in the Judaean Desert of Jordan*', *Revue de Qumrân*, 1970, pp. 254–5; J. T. Milik, '*Milkî-sedeq* and *Milkî-resha'* dans les anciens écrits juifs et chrétiens', *Journal of Jewish Studies*, 1972, pp. 114–18.

... for guilt with the congregation of his people, for it has wallowed in the sin of the sons of men; (and it was appointed) for great judgements and evil diseases in the flesh according to the mighty deeds of God and in accordance with their wickedness. In conformity with their congregation of uncleanness, (they are to be separated) as a community of wickedness until (wickedness) ends.

In accordance with the mercies of God, according to His goodness and wonderful glory, He caused some of the sons of the world to draw near (Him) ... to be counted with Him in the com[munity of the g]ods as a congregation of holiness in service for eternal life and (sharing) the lot of

His holy ones ... each man according to his lot which He has cast for ... for eternal life ...

Ordinances

Further fragments belonging to *A Commentary on Biblical Laws* (see above, pp. 249–50) have been published by J. M. Allegro. They deal with the prohibition on selling an Israelite as a slave (cf. Lev. xxv, 39–46); with a case to be judged by a court of twelve judges; with the forbidden interchange of garments between men and women (cf. Deut. xxii, 5); and with the charge laid by a husband against his wife that she was not a virgin when he married her (Deut. xxii, 13–21). See J. M. Allegro, A. A. Anderson, *DJD* v, p. 8; cf. J. Strugnell, *Revue de Qumrân*, 1970, pp. 175–8.

... before Isra[el] shall [n]ot serve Gentiles among foreign[ers, for I have brought them out from the land of] Egypt, and I have commanded concerning them that none shall be sold as a slave ...

... [t]en men and two priests, and they shall be judged before these twelve ... spoke in Israel against a person, they shall inquire in accordance with them. Whosoever shall rebel ..., shall be put to death for he has acted wilfully.

Let no man's garment be on a woman all [the days of her life]. Let him [not] be covered with a woman's mantle, nor wear a woman's tunic, for this is an abomination.

If a man slanders a virgin of Israel, if in ... when he married her, let him say so. And they shall examine her [concerning her] trustworthiness, and if he has not lied concerning her, she shall be put to death. But if he has humiliated her [false]ly, he shall be fined two minas, and shall not divorce her all his life.

Curses of Satan and his lot

J. T. Milik published two fragments from cave IV in 1972, containing liturgical curses. One of these, designated as 4Q **286–7**, and provisionally entitled 'Blessings (and Curses)', is paralleled by War Rule XIII and Community Rule II. The other (4Q **280-2**) depends mainly on Community Rule II, but reveals Satan's specific name, *Melkiresha'* (My king is wickedness), the counterpart of *Melkizedek* (My king is justice), chief of the Army of Light (cf. below, pp. 260-1, 265-8). See Milik, *Journal of Jewish Studies*, 1972, pp. 126-35.

Blessings and Curses

... council of the Community shall all say together, Amen, amen.

Afterwards [they] shall damn Satan and all his guilty lot. They will answer and say, Cursed be [S]atan in his hostile design, and damned in his guilty dominion. Cursed be all the spirits of his [lo]t in their wicked design, and damned in their thoughts of unclean impurity. For they are the lot of darkness and their visitation is for eternal destruction. Amen, amen.

Cursed be the Wicke[d One in all ...] of his dominions, and may all the sons of Satan be damned in all the works of their service until their annihilation [for ever. Amen, amen.]

And [they will continue to say: Be cursed, Ang]el of Perdition and Spir[it of Dest]ruction, in all the thoughts of your g[uilty] inclination [and all your abomina]ble [plots] and [your] wicked design, [and] may you be [da]mned ... Amen, am[en].

[Cursed be a]ll those who practi[ce] their [wicked designs] and establish [in their heart] your (evil) devices, [plotting against Go]d'[s Covenant] ... to exchange the judgemen[ts of truth for folly.]

Melkiresha‘

[May God set him apart] for evil from the midst of the Sons of Li[ght because he has turned away from following Him.

And they will continue saying: Be cur]sed, Melkiresha‘, in all the thou[ghts of your guilty inclination. May] God [deliver you up] for torture at the hands of the vengeful Avengers. May God not heed [when] you call on Him. [May He raise His angry face] towards you. May there be no (greeting of) 'Peace' for you in the mouth of all those who hold fast to the Father[s. May you be cursed] with no remnant, and damned without escape.

Cursed be those who practi[ce their wicked designs] and [es]tablish in their heart your (evil) devices, plotting against the Covenant of God . . . , seers of [His] truth.

[Who]ever refuses to enter [His Covenant, walking in the stubbornness of his heart] . . .

II POETIC TEXTS

A Lamentation

Several fragments of a poem inspired by the biblical Book of Lamentations have been preserved in cave IV (4Q **179**). Only fragment 2 offers a text long enough for intelligible translation. See J. M. Allegro, A. A. Anderson, *DJD* v, pp. 75-7; cf. J. Strugnell, *Revue de Qumrân*, 1970, pp. 250-2.

. . .

[How] solitary [lies] the city,

. . .

    the princess of all the peoples is desolate
    like a forsaken woman;

and all her [dau]ghters are forsak[en]
  [like] a forsaken woman;
like a woman hurt and forsaken
  by her [husband].
All her palaces and [her] wal[ls] are
  like a barren woman;
and like a sheltered woman,
  all [her] paths;
[all her] . . .
  like a woman of bitterness,
  and all her daughters are like women
  mourning for [their] hus[bands];
[all her] . . . like women
  deprived of their only children.
Weep, weep, Jer[usalem]
. . .
[her tears flow] upon her cheeks
  because of her sons . . .

The Seductress

A long and relatively well-preserved Wisdom poem from cave IV
(4Q 184) depicts by means of the metaphor of the harlot the dan-
gers and attraction of false doctrine. See J. M. Allegro, A. A.
Anderson, *DJD* v, pp. 82–5; J. Strugnell, *Revue de Qumrân*, 1970,
pp. 263–8.

. . . speaks vanity
  and . . . errors.
She is ever prompt to oil her words,
  and she flatters with irony,
  deriding with iniquitous l[ips].
Her heart is set up as a snare,
  and her kidneys as a fowler's nets.
Her eyes are defiled with iniquity,
  her hands have seized hold of the pit.
Her legs go down to work wickedness,

and to walk in wrong-doings.
Her . . . are foundations of darkness,
 and a multitude of sins is in her skirts.
Her . . . are darkness of night,
 and her garments . . .
Her clothes are shades of twilight,
 and her ornaments plagues of corruption.
Her couches are beds of corruption,
 and her . . . depths of the pit.
Her inns are couches of darkness,
 and her dominions in the midst of the night.
She pitches her dwelling on the foundations of darkness,
 she abides in the tents of silence.
Amid everlasting fire is her inheritance,
 not among those who shine brightly.
She is the beginning of all the ways of iniquity.
Woe (and) disaster to all who possess her!
 And desolation to all who hold her!
For her ways are ways of death,
 and her paths are roads of sin,
 and her tracks are pathways to iniquity,
 and her bye-ways are rebellious wrong-doings.
Her gates are gates of death,
and from the entrance of the house
 she sets out toward the underworld.
None of those who enter there will ever return,
 and all who possess her will descend to the Pit.
She lies in wait in secret places,
 . . .
In the city's squares she veils herself,
 and she stands at the gates of towns.
She will never re[st] from wh[orin]g,
 her eyes glance hither and thither.
She lifts her eyelids naughtily
 to stare at a virtuous one and join him,
 and an important one to trip him up,
 at upright men to pervert their way,

and the righteous elect to keep them from the
                                    commandment,
    at the firmly established to bring them down wantonly,
    and those who walk in uprightness to alter the statute.
To cause the humble to rebel against God,
    and turn their steps away from the ways of justice,
    to bring insolence to their heart,
    so that they march no more in the paths of uprightness;
    to lead man astray to the ways of the Pit,
    and seduce with flatteries every son of man.

Exhortation to seek Wisdom

Large fragments of a Wisdom poem in which a teacher encourages
his 'people', his 'sons', the 'Simple', to search for Wisdom have
been preserved in cave IV (4Q **185**). As is often the case in Wisdom
literature, events of the patriarchal and Mosaic past are used for
didactic purposes. See J. M. Allegro, A. A. Anderson, *DJD* v, pp.
85–7; cf. J. Strugnell, *Revue de Qumrân*, 1970, pp. 269–73.

I ...
And you, sons of men, woe to you!
For he (man) sprouts from his ground like grass,
    and his grace blossoms like a flower.
His [gl]ory blows away and his ... dries up,
    and the wind carries away its flower
...
so that it is found no more ...
They shall seek him but shall not find him,
    and there is no hope (for him);
    and his days are like shadow over the ea[rth].
Now pray hearken to me, my people;
    heed me, o you Simple;
    become wise through the might of God.
Remember His miracles which He did in Egypt,
    and His marvels in the land of Ham.
Let your heart shake because of His fear,
II and do His will ...

... your souls according to His good graces,
and search for yourself a way towards life,
a highway [towards ...]
a remnant for your sons after you.
And why have you given up your soul to vanity,
... judgement?
Hearken to me, o my sons,
and do not rebel against the words of YHWH.
Do not walk ...
[but in the way He established] for Jacob,
and in the path which He decreed for Israel.
Is one day not better ...
... His fear,
and not to be afflicted (?) by dread and the fowler's net.
... to be set apart from His angels,
for there is no darkness, nor gloom ...
And you, what do you understand ...
before Him evil shall go towards every people.
Happy is the man to whom it (Wisdom) has been given thus,
... the evil,
nor let the wicked boast, saying:
It has not been given me, nor ...
... to Israel,
and with a good measure He measures it;
and He will redeem His people,
and He will put to death those who hate His Wisdom.

Seek it and find it, grasp it and possess it!
With it is length of days and fatness of bone,
the joy of the heart and ...
Happy is the man who works it
...
who does not seek it ... of deceit,
nor holds to it with flatteries.
As it has belonged to his fathers,
so will he inherit it,
and hold fast to it with all the strength of his might,

and all his immeasurable ...
and he shall cause his offspring to inherit it.

I know how to labour for good ...

III EXEGETICAL DOCUMENTS

The Ages of the Creation

A badly worn manuscript has been published under this title by
J. M. Allegro from cave IV (4Q 180). Its decipherment and interpretation have been further improved by J. Strugnell and J. T.
Milik. The only section yielding coherent sense deals with the myth
of the fallen angels and the daughters of men which is based on
Genesis vi, 1–4, and fully developed in 1 Enoch. If Milik's reconstruction is correct, the work presents human history as divided
into seventy weeks of years (70 x 7 years), the first ten of which
cover the period from Noah to Abraham. See J. M. Allegro, A. A.
Anderson, *DSD* v, pp. 77–9; cf. J. Strugnell, *Revue de Qumrân*,
1970, pp. 252–4; J. T. Milik, *Journal of Jewish Studies*, 1972, pp.
110–24.

Interpretation concerning the ages made by God, all the
ages for the accomplishment [of all the events, past] and
future. Before ever He created them, He determined the
works of ... age by age. And it was engraved on [heavenly]
tablets ... the ages of their domination. This is the order
of the cre[ation of man from Noah to Abraham, un]til he
begot Isaac: ten [weeks (of years)].

And the interpretation concerns Azazel and the angels
who [came to the daughters of men; and] they bore to them
giants. And concerning Azazel ... and iniquity, and to
cause them all to inherit wickedness ... judgements and
judgement of the congregation ...

The Testament of Amram

An Aramaic document surviving in five fragmentary copies in cave IV contains an admonition by Amram, the father of Moses, to his children. The context is that of the Book of Exodus, but the visions and teachings are the author's free compositions. Amram's age at his death (137 years) is borrowed from Exod. vi, 20, but its dating to the 152nd year of the captivity reflects the tradition according to which the Israelites remained in Egypt, not for 430 years (Exod. xii, 40), nor 400 years (Gen. xv, 13), but 210 years. Cf. J. Heinemann, '210 Years of Egyptian Exile', *Journal of Jewish Studies*, 1971, pp. 19–30.

In the gravely damaged text of the vision, Amram sees the chief Angel of Darkness, Melkiresha', already mentioned in the *Curses of Satan and his lot* (p. 252–3 above). He also addresses the leader of the Army of Light, whose name has disappeared in one of the many lacunae. But it is highly probable that one of his 'three names' is Melkizedek, as will appear presently from the reading of the Melkizedek document from cave XI (pp. 265–8 below). See J. T. Milik '4Q visions de 'Amram et une citation d'Origène', *Revue Biblique*, 1972, pp. 77–97.

Copy of the book of the words of the vision of Amram, son of Kehat, son of Levi, al[l that] he explained to his sons and enjoined on them on the day of [his] death, in his one-hundred-and-thirty-seventh year, which was the year of his death, [in] the one-hundred-and-fifty-second year of Israel's exile in Egypt.

(I saw Watchers) in my vision, a dream vision, and behold two (of them) argued about me and said ... and they were engaged in a great quarrel concerning me. I asked them: 'You, what are you ... thus ... [about me?'] They answered and [said to me: 'We have been made m]asters and rule over all the sons of men.' And they said to me: 'Which of us do you [choose ...]

I raised my eyes and saw one of them. His looks were frightening [like those of a vi]per, and his [ga]rm[en]ts were multi-coloured and he was extremely dark ...

And afterwards I looked and behold . . . by his appearance and his face was like that of an adder, and [he was covered with . . . together, and his eyes . . .

. . . this [Watcher]: 'Who is he?' He said to me: 'This Wa[tcher] . . . [and his three names are . . .] and Melkiresha'.'

And I said: 'My Lord, what . . .' [And he said to me] . . . [and all his paths are dark]ness, and all his work is darkness, and he is . . . in darkness . . . you see. And he rules over all darkness and I [rule over all light] . . .

. . . [the order] of the Most High as far as 'the Lands' (beyond the Ocean). I rule over all Light, and over al[l that is God's], and I rule over the men of His grace and p[eace. And I] rule [over all the Sons of Lig]ht.'

And I asked and said to him: 'What are [your names?] . . . [He answered and sa]id to me: '[My] three names are . . .

I an[nou]nce (this) to you [and al]so I will indeed inform y[ou . . . For all the Sons of Light] will shine, [and all the Sons] of Darkness will be dark. [For all the Sons of Light] . . . and by all their knowledge they will . . . and the Sons of Darkness will be burnt . . . For all folly and wicked[ness are dar]k, and all [pea]ce and truth are brigh[t. For all the Sons of Light g]o towards the light, towards [eternal] jo[y and rej]oicin[g], and all the Sons of Dar[kness go towards death] and perdition . . . The people shall have brightness . . . and they will cause them to live . . .

And now to you, Amram my son, [I] enjo[in] . . . and [to] your [son]s, and to their sons I enjoin . . . , and they gave them to Levi my father, and Levi my father [gave them] to me . . . and my books in testimony that they might be warned by them . . .

The New Jerusalem

Fragments belonging to an Aramaic writing describing the Jerusalem of the eschatological age have been identified in caves I (1Q 32), II (2Q 24), IV, V (5Q 15) and XI. They are inspired by Ezekiel xl-xlviii (cf. also Revelation xxi). Among the edited manuscripts, only the text found in cave V, completed by J. T. Milik with the help of two large unpublished parallel fragments from cave IV, provides an intelligible portion.

The visionary responsible for this work accompanies an angelic 'surveyor' who measures everything in the New Jerusalem, from the size of the blocks of houses, the avenues and the streets, to the detailed dimensions of rooms, stairs and windows. A full picture of the city, including also the measurements of the walls, will be available only after the publication of the document from cave IV.

The dimensions are given in 'reeds', each of which consists of seven 'cubits'. But there seem to be two cubits among ancient Jewish measures, one approximately 20 inches (521 mm), the other 18 inches (446 mm) long.

The translation is based on Milik's edition and interpretation of 5Q 15 in *DJD* III, Oxford, 1962, pp. 184–93. (For smaller fragments, see Milik, *DJD* I, Oxford, 1955, pp. 134–5; M. Baillet, *DJD* III, Oxford, 1962, pp. 84–90; B. Jongeling, 'Publication provisoire d'un fragment provenant de la grotte 11 de Qumrân (11Q Jérnouv ar)', *Journal for the Study of Judaism*, 1970, pp. 58–64).

I And he led me into the city, and he measured each block of houses for its length and width, fifty-one reeds by fifty-one, in a square a[ll round] = 357 cubits to each side. A passage surrounds the block of houses, a street gallery, three reeds, = 21 cubits, (wide).

[He] then [showed me the di]mensions of [all] the blo[cks of houses. Between each block there is a street], six reeds, = 42 cubits, wide. And the width of the avenues running from east to west: two of them are ten reeds, = 70 cubits, wide. And the third, that to the [lef]t (i.e. north) of the Temple, measures eighteen reeds, = 126 cubits) in width. And the wid[th of the streets] running from south [to north: t]wo of [them] have nine reeds and four cubits, = 67 cubits, each street.

[And the] mid[dle street passing through the mid]dle of the city, its [width measures] thirt[een] ree[ds] and one cubit, = 92 cubits. And all [the streets of the city] are paved with white stone . . . marble and jasper.

[And he showed me the dimensions of the ei]ghty [side-doors]. The wid[th of the] side-doors is two reeds, [= 14 cubits, . . . Each door has tw]o wings of stone. The width of the w[ing] is [one] reed, [= 7 cubits.]

And he showed me [the dimensions] of the twelve [entranc]es. The width of their doors are three reeds, [= 21] cubits. [Each door has tw]o [wings]. The width of the wing is one reed and a half, = 10 $\frac{1}{2}$ cubits . . . [And beside each door there are two tow]ers, one to [the r]ight and one to the l[ef]t. Its width[is of the same dimension as] its length, [five reeds by five, = 35 cubits. The stairs beside] the inside door, on the [righ]t side of the towers, [rise] to the top of the to[wers. Their width is five cubits. The towers and the stairs are five reeds by five and] five cubits, = 40 [cubits], on each side of the door.

[And he showed me the dimensions of the doors of the blocks of houses, Their width] is two reeds, = 14 cub[its. And the wi]d[th] . . . [And he measured] the wid[th of each th]reshold: two reeds, = 14 cubits, [and the lintel: one cubit. And he measured above each] threshold i[ts win]gs. And he measured beyond the threshold. Its length is [thirteen] cubits [and its width ten cubits.]

[And he] le[d m]e [be]yond the threshold. [And behold] another threshold, and a door next to the inner wall [on the right side, of the same dimensions as the outer door. Its width] is four [cu]bits, [its] height seven [cubits], and it has two wings. And in front of this door there is [an entrance threshold. Its width is one reed] II 7 [cubits]. And the l[eng]th of the entrance is two reeds, = 14 cubits, and its height is two reeds, = 14 cubits. [And the door] fa[cing the other do]or opening into the block of houses has the same dimensions as the outer door. On the left of this entrance, he showed [me] a round [stair-case]. Its length is of the same dimension as its width: two reeds by two, =14 cubits. The do[ors (of the stair-case) facing] the other doors are of the same dimensions. And a pillar is inside the stair-case around which the stairs ri[se]; its width and d[epth are six cubits by six], square. And the stairs which rise beside it, their width is four cubits, and they rise in a spiral [to] a height of [two] r[eeds] to [the roof].

And he led me [into] the block of houses, and he showed me the houses there. From one door to the oth[er, there are fifteen: eigh]t on one side as far as the corner, and sev]en from the corner to the other door. The length of the house[s is three reed]s, =2[1 cubits, and their width], two [reed]s, =14 cubits. Likewise, for all the chambers; [and their height is t]wo [reeds], =1[4] cu[bit]s, [and their doors are in the middle.] (Their) width is t[w]o reeds, =1[4] cubits. [And he measured the width (of the rooms) in the middle of the house, and inside the upper floor: four [cubits]. Length and height: one reed, =7 cubits.

[And he showed me the dimensions of the dining-[halls]. Each has [a length] of ninete[en] cubits [and a width] of twelve [cubits]. Each contains twenty-two couche[s and ele]ven windows of lattice-work (?) above [the couches]. And next to the hall is an outer conduit. [And he measured] the . . . of the window: its height, two cubits; [its width: . . . cubits;] and its depth is that of the width of the wall. [The height of the inner (aspect of the window) is . . . cubits, and that of the outer (aspect), . . . cubits.]

[And he measured the l]im[it]s of the . . . [Their length] is nineteen [cubits] and [their] width, [twelve cubits] . . .

An Account of David's Poems

Column xxvii of the Psalms Scroll found in cave xi contains a midrashic supplement on the poetic activities of David. Instead of being credited, as in the case of traditional Judaism and Christian-

ity, with one hundred and fifty Psalms, the Qumran writer ascribes to him 4,050 compositions divided into 3,600 Psalms, 364 Songs for the Perpetual Sacrifice, 52 Songs for the Sabbath Offerings, 30 Songs for Festivals, and 4 Songs for exorcism. See J. A. Sanders, *DJD* iv, Oxford, 1965, pp. 91–3.

The figure of 4,050 should be viewed against the similarly prolific literary achievement of Solomon, to whom the Hebrew text of 1 Kings v, 12 assigns 3,000 proverbs and 1,005 songs, and the corresponding Greek Septuagint text, 3,000 proverbs and 5,000 songs. Josephus credits Solomon with 1,005 *books* of odes and songs, and 3,000 *books* of parables and similitudes (*Jewish Antiquities* viii, 44)!

Rabbinic literature identifies Psalm xci as a 'Song for the stricken (by evil spirits)' (Palestinian Talmud: *Shabbath* 8b; *Erubin* 26c; Babylonian Talmud: *Shebuoth* 15b; on exorcism, see G. Vermes, *Jesus the Jew*, London, 1973, pp. 63–9).

The year of 52 weeks, i.e. 364 days, is typical of the Qumran calendar (cf. above, p. 43).

XXVII David son of Jesse was wise and brilliant like the light of the sun; (he was) a scribe, intelligent and perfect in all his ways before God and men.

YHWH gave him an intelligent and brilliant spirit, and he wrote 3,600 psalms and 364 songs to sing before the altar for the daily perpetual sacrifice, for all the days of the year; and 52 songs for the Sabbath offerings; and 30 songs for the New Moons, for Feast days and for the Day of Atonement.

In all, the songs which he uttered were 446, and 4 songs to make music on behalf of those stricken (by evil spirits).

In all, they were 4,050.

All these he uttered through prophecy which was given him from before the Most High.

The Heavenly Prince Melkizedek

A striking document, composed of thirteen fragments from cave XI, and centred on the mysterious figure of Melkizedek was first published by A. S. van der Woude in 1965. It takes the form of an eschatological midrash in which the proclamation of liberty to the

captives at the end of days (Isa. lxi, 1) is understood as being part of the general restoration of property during the year of Jubilee (Lev. xxv, 13), seen in the Bible (Deut. xv, 2) as a remission of debts.

The heavenly deliverer is Melkizedek. Identical with the archangel Michael, he is the head of the 'sons of Heaven' or 'gods of Justice' and is referred to as *elohim* and *el*. These Hebrew words normally mean 'God', but in certain specific contexts Jewish tradition also explains *elohim* as primarily designating a 'judge'. Here, Melkizedek is portrayed as presiding over the final Judgement and condemnation of his demonic counterpart, Belial/Satan, the Prince of Darkness, elsewhere also called Melkiresha' (cf. above pp. 253, 260). The great act of deliverance is expected to occur on the Day of Atonement at the end of the tenth Jubilee cycle.

This manuscript sheds valuable light not only on the Melkizedek figure of the Epistle to the Hebrews vii, but also on the development of the messianic concept in the New Testament and early Christianity. (On messianism see G. Vermes, *Jesus the Jew*, London, 1973, pp. 129–59, 250–56).

For the text, see A. S. van der Woude, 'Melchisedek als himmlische Erlösergestalt . . .', *Oudtestamentische Studien*, Leiden, 1965, pp. 354–73; M. de Jonge, A. S. van der Woude, '11Q Melchizedek and the New Testament', *New Testament Studies*, 1966, pp. 301–26; J. T. Milik, *Journal of Jewish Studies*, 1972, pp. 96–109.

. . . And concerning that which He said, *In* [*this*] *year of Jubilee* [*each of you shall return to his property* (Lev. xxv, 13); and likewise, *And this is the manner of release:*] *every creditor shall release that which he has lent* [*to his neighbour. He shall not exact it of his neighbour and his brother*], *for God's release* [*has been proclaimed*] (Deut. xv, 2). [And it will be proclaimed at] the end of days concerning the captives as [He said, *To proclaim liberty to the captives* (Isa. lxi, 1). Its interpretation is that He] will assign them to the Sons of Heaven and to the inheritance of Melkizedek; f[or He will cast] their [lot] amid the po[rtions of Melkize]dek, who will return them there and will proclaim to them liberty, forgiving them [the wrongdoings] of all their iniquities.

And this thing will [occur] in the first week of the Jubilee

that follows the nine Jubilees. And the Day of Atonement is the e[nd of the] tenth [Ju]bilee, when all the Sons of [Light] and the men of the lot of Mel[ki]zedek will be atoned for. [And] a statute concerns them [to prov]ide them with their rewards. For this is the moment of the Year of Grace for Melkizedek. [And h]e will, by his strength, judge the holy ones of God, executing judgement as it is written concerning him in the Songs of David, who said, ELOHIM *has taken his place in the divine council; in the midst of the gods he holds judgement* (Psalms lxxxii, 1). And it was concerning him that he said, (Let the assembly of the peoples) *return to the height above them;* EL *(god) will judge the peoples* (Psalms vii, 7–8). As for that which he s[aid, *How long will you] judge unjustly and show partiality to the wicked? Selah* (Psalms lxxxii, 2), its interpretation concerns Satan and the spirits of his lot [who] rebelled by turning away from the precepts of God to . . . And Melkizedek will avenge the vengeance of the judgements of God . . . and he will drag [them from the hand of] Satan and from the hand of all the sp[irits of] his [lot]. And all the 'gods [of Justice'] will come to his aid [to] attend to the de[struction] of Satan. And *the height* is . . . all the sons of God . . . this . . . This is the day of [Peace/Salvation] concerning which [God] spoke [through Isa]iah the prophet, who said, [*How] beautiful upon the mountains are the feet of the messenger who proclaims peace, who brings good news, who proclaims salvation, who says to Zion: Your* ELOHIM *[reigns]* (Isa. lii, 7). Its interpretation: *the mountains* are the prophets . . . and *the messenger* is the Anointed one of the spirit, concerning whom Dan[iel] said, [*Until an anointed one, a prince* (Dan. ix, 25)] . . . [And he *who brings*] good [*news*], who proclaims [*salvation*]: it is concerning him that it is written . . . [*To comfort all who mourn, to grant to those who mourn in Zion*] (Isa. lxi, 2–3). *To comfort* [*those who mourn*: its interpretation], to make them understand all the ages of t[ime]. . . In truth . . . will turn away from Satan . . . by the judgement[s] of God, as it is written concerning him, [*who says to Zi*]*on: your* ELOHIM *reigns. Zion is* . . ., those who uphold the Covenant, who turn from walking [in] the way of the people. And *your* ELOHIM is [Melkizedek, who will save them from] the hand of Satan.

As for that which He said, *Then you shall send abroad* [*the loud*] *trump*[*et*] *in the* [*seventh*] *m*[*on*]*th* (Lev. xxv, 9). . .

IV HOROSCOPES

Two documents from cave IV, one in Hebrew, the other in Aramaic, contain fragments of horoscopes.

The Hebrew text, published by J. M. Allegro, is written in a childish cypher. The text runs from left to right instead of the normal right to left and uses, in addition to the current Hebrew 'square' alphabet, letters borrowed from the archaic Hebrew (or Phoenician) and from the Greek scripts. The spiritual qualities of three individuals described there are reflected in their share of Light and Darkness. The first man is largely good: six parts of Light against three parts of Darkness. The second is very wicked: eight parts of Darkness to a single part of Light. The last is almost perfect: eight portions of Light and only one of Darkness.

As far as physical characteristics are concerned, shortness, fatness and irregularity of the features are associated with wickedness, and their opposites reflect virtue.

In the astrological terminology of the document, the 'second Column' doubtless means the 'second House'; and a birthday 'in the foot of the Bull' should probably be interpreted as the presence, at that moment, of the sun in the lower part of the constellation Taurus.

The Aramaic horoscope, first edited by J. Starcky, appears to be that of the final Prince of the Congregation, or Royal Messiah, if we are permitted to judge from the concluding part of the text. His education is to be compared to the schedule outlined in the Messianic Rule (cf. p. 119 above). If the 'Book of Meditation', mentioned there as the young man's text-book, is identified with the Bible (cf. pp. 19–20 above), then the 'three books' referred to here may also indicate the three sections of the Hebrew Scriptures, 'the Law, the Prophets and the other Writings' (Ecclesiasticus, Prologue) or 'the Law, the Prophets and the Psalms' (Luke xxiv, 44).

Whether the sectaries forecast the future by means of astrology, or merely used horoscopes as literary devices, it is impossible to decide at present, though I am inclined towards the latter alternative. That such texts are found among the Scrolls should not, however, surprise anyone. For if many Jews frowned on astrology, others, such as the Hellenistic Jewish writer Eupolemus, credited its invention to Abraham! (Cf. G. Vermes, *Scripture and Tradition in Judaism*, Leiden, 1973, pp. 80–82.)

For the texts see J. M. Allegro, A. A. Anderson, *DJD* v, pp. 88–91; J. Strugnell, *Revue de Qumrân*, 1970, pp. 274–6; J. Starcky, 'Un texte messianique araméen de la grotte 4 de Qumrân', *Mémorial du cinquantenaire de l'École des langues orientales anciennes de l'Institut Catholique de Paris*, Paris, 1964, pp. 51–66.

Horoscopes 4Q 186(1)

II ... and his thighs are long and lean, and his toes are thin and long. He is of the second Column. His spirit consists of six (parts) in the House of Light and three in the Pit of Darkness. And this is his birthday on which he (is to be/ was?) born: in the foot of the Bull. He will be meek. And his animal is the bull.

III ... and his head ... [and his cheeks are] fat. His teeth are of uneven length (?). His fingers are thick, and his thighs are thick and very hairy, each one. His toes are thick and short. His spirit consists of eight (parts) in the House of Darkness and one from the House of Light. ..

Horoscopes 4Q 186(2)

I ... order. His eyes are black and glowing. His beard is ... and it is ... His voice is gentle. His teeth are fine and well aligned. He is neither tall, nor short. And he ... And his fingers are thin and long. And his thighs are smooth. And the soles of his feet ... [And his toes] are well aligned. His spirit consists of eight (parts) [in the House of Light, of] the second Column, and one [in the House of Darkness.

And this is] his birthday on which he (is to be/was) born:
. . . . And his animal is. . .

Horoscope of the Messiah (?)

I . . . of his hand: two . . . a birthmark. And the hair will be red. And there will be lentils on . . . and small birthmarks on his thigh. [And after t]wo years he will know (how to distinguish) one thing from another. In his youth, he shall be like . . . [like a m]an who knows nothing until the time when he knows the three Books.

And then he will acquire wisdom and learn und[erstanding] . . . vision to come to him on his knees. And with his father and his ancestors . . . life and old age. Counsel and prudence will be with him, and he will know the secrets of man. His wisdom will reach all the peoples, and he will know the secrets of all the living. And all their designs against him will come to nothing, and (his) rule over all the living will be great. His designs [will succeed] for he is the Elect of God. His birth and the breath of his spirit . . . and his designs shall be for ever . . .

APPENDICES

The Copper Scroll

Strictly speaking, The Copper Scroll does not fall within the scope of the present book since it is a non-religious document, but it has stimulated so much curiosity and speculation that the reader may appreciate a brief summary of its discovery and contents, and of the argument surrounding it.

It was found by archaeologists in cave III during the excavations of 1952, but the metal had become so badly oxydized during the course of the centuries that the scroll could not be unfolded. It was therefore sent to Professor H. Wright Baker of the Manchester College of Science and Technology who, in 1956, carefully divided it into logitudinal strips and, in the same year, returned it to Jordan.

The first translation of the work, by J. T. Milik, appeared in *Revue Biblique* in 1959. It was followed, in 1960, by J. M. Allegro's book, *The Treasure of the Copper Scroll*, which, in addition to a translation, provided a copy of the text drawn by an artist. It was not until 1962 that the official edition was published. For this – Volume III of *Discoveries in the Judaean Desert of Jordan*, complete with a photographic reproduction of the scroll – Milik was again responsible.

The inscription lists over sixty hiding-places where gold, silver, aromatics, scrolls, etc., are said to have been deposited. Allegro reckons that the treasure must have amounted to over three thousand talents of silver, nearly one thousand three hundred talents of gold, sixty-five bars of gold, six hundred and eight pitchers containing silver, and six hundred and nineteen gold and silver vessels. In other words, using the post-biblical value of the talent as a yard-stick, the total weight of precious metal must have added up to sixty-five tons of silver and twenty-six tons of gold.

Who could have possessed such a fortune? Was there ever any truth in it?

J. T. Milik thinks not. He believes that the exaggerated sums indicate that the scroll is a work of fiction and that its chief interest

271

to scholars lies in the fields of linguistics and topography. He dates it from about A.D. 100, thus ruling out any connection with the rest of the Qumran writings since the latter were placed in the caves not later than A.D. 68.

Other scholars hold that the treasure was a real one. A. Dupont-Sommer maintains that it represented the fortune of the Essene sect, while K. G. Kuhn, Chaim Rabin, and J. M. Allegro believe that it belonged to the Temple of Jerusalem, Allegro adding to this hypothesis the theory that the Zealots were responsible for the concealment of the gold and silver and for the writing of the scroll.

Milik's argument would certainly seem to account for the vast quantities of treasure mentioned. It does not, however, explain two of the document's most striking characteristics, namely, the dry realism of its style, very different from that of ancient legends, and the fact that it is recorded on copper instead of on the less expensive leather or papyrus. For if it is, in fact, a sort of fairy-story, the present text can only represent the outline of such a tale, and who in their senses would have engraved their literary notes on valuable metal?

It goes without saying that the contention that the treasure was a real one is supported by the very arguments which undermine Milik's. From the business-like approach, and the enduring material on which the catalogue is inscribed, it might sensibly be supposed that the writer was not indulging some frivolous dream. Again, in view of the fact that the Copper Scroll was found among writings known to come from Qumran, Dupont-Sommer would appear justified in allocating the fortune to the Essenes. It requires, by comparison, a strong feat of the imagination to accept that all this wealth belonged originally to the treasure chambers of the Temple, and that it was placed in hiding, in a hostile environment, in A.D. 68: before, that is to say, there was any immediate danger to the capital city of Jerusalem. Allegro bypasses this objection by presuming that, as Qumran was by then in the hands of the Zealots, it was no longer unfriendly to the Jerusalem authorities. But it has not yet been explained why the sack of the Temple and city should have been foreseen, and provided for, so early.

In favour of Kuhn, Rabin, and Allegro, it is nevertheless possible to envisage that the Temple possessed such riches as these, whereas, despite Dupont-Sommer's undoubtedly true remarks concerning the apparent compatibility of religious poverty and fat revenues, it is still hard to accept that the Essenes, a relatively small community, should have amassed such disproportionate wealth.

This is all that can safely be said of the Copper Scroll at the present time. Access to the original document will allow scholars to improve their reading of the extremely difficult text – the published reproductions are of little use in this respect – but even so, it will probably be some time before a convincing answer is given to the many puzzles confronting us.

Qumran and Masada

Between 1963 and 1965 the ruins of Masada, the last Zealot stronghold conquered by the Romans in A.D. 74, were excavated under the direction of the Israeli archaeologist, Professor Yigael Yadin. Among the manuscripts discovered was a fragment of the *Angelic Liturgy*, a sectarian document belonging to the Dead Sea Scrolls literature (see above, pp. 210 ff.). The presence of this Qumran text in a Zealot settlement may be explained by means of the following hypotheses:

1) The sect of the Scrolls and the Zealot party was one and the same.

2) The site abandoned by the Qumran community was occupied for a time by Zealots who laid their hands on one of the manuscript caches and transferred its contents to Masada.

3) A group of Qumran sectaries joined the Zealots in the rebellion against Rome and brought with them some of their writings.

The first theory appears unlikely on general grounds (see p. 55). Yadin pronounces in favour of the third. I, on the other hand, am inclined to think that 2) and 3) are equally possible.

See Y. Yadin, *Masada, Herod's Fortress and the Zealots' Last Stand* (London, 1966). On the newly established date of the fall of Masada (A.D. 74 instead of 73), see E. Schürer, G. Vermes, F. Millar, *The History of the Jewish People in the Age of Jesus Christ*, vol. 1 (Edinburgh, 1973), p. 512.

SELECTED BIBLIOGRAPHY

The following list contains only books published in English and suitable for the general reader. Those interested in more technical information may consult B. Jongeling, *A Classified Bibliography of the Finds in the Desert of Judah, 1958–1969*, Leiden, 1971; J. A. Sanders, 'Palestinian Manuscripts 1947–1972', *Journal of Jewish Studies*, 1973, pp. 74–83; E. Schürer, G. Vermes, F. Millar, *The History of the Jewish People in the Age of Jesus Christ*, vol. I, Edinburgh 1973, pp. 118–22, or the bibliographical section of *Revue de Qumrân*.

General Studies

CROSS, F. M., *The Ancient Library of Qumran and Modern Biblical Study* (London, 1958).

MILIK, J. T., *Ten Years of Discovery in the Wilderness of Judaea* (London, 1959).

DRIVER, G. R., *The Judaean Scrolls* (Oxford, 1965).

FREEDMAN, D. N., GREENFIELD, J. C. (eds.), *New Directions in Biblical Archaeology* (New York, 1971), pp. 70–166.

VAUX, R. DE, *The Archaeology of the Dead Sea Scrolls* (London, 1973).

Translations with Introductions

GASTER, T. H., *The Scriptures of the Dead Sea Sect* (London, 1957).

DUPONT-SOMMER, A., *The Essene Writings from Qumran* (Oxford, 1961).

The Scrolls and the New Testament

STENDAHL, K. (ed.), *The Scrolls and the New Testament* (London, 1958).

BLACK, M., *The Scrolls and Christian Origins* (London, 1961).

MURPHY-O'CONNOR, J. (ed.), *Paul and Qumran* (London, 1968).

BLACK, M. (ed.), *The Scrolls and Christianity* (London, 1969).

CHARLESWORTH, J. H. (ed.), *John and Qumran* (London, 1972).

INDEX

MORE ABOUT PENGUINS
AND PELICANS

Penguinews, which appears every month, contains details of all the new books issued by Penguins as they are published. From time to time it is supplemented by *Penguins in Print*, which is a complete list of all titles available. (There are some five thousand of these.)

A specimen copy of *Penguinews* will be sent to you free on request. For a year's issues (including the complete lists) please send 50p if you live in the British Isles, or 75p if you live elsewhere. Just write to Dept EP, Penguin Books Ltd, Harmondsworth, Middlesex, enclosing a cheque or postal order, and your name will be added to the mailing list.

In the U.S.A.: For a complete list of books available from Penguin in the United States write to Dept CS, Penguin Books Inc., 7110 Ambassador Road, Baltimore, Maryland 21207.

In Canada: For a complete list of books available from Penguin in Canada write to Penguin Books Canada Ltd, 41 Steelcase Road West, Markham, Ontario.

FORGOTTEN SCRIPTS
The Story of their Decipherment

Cyrus H. Gordon

'A remarkably clear exposition of the history of decipherment and an account of the people involved' – David Holloway in the *Daily Telegraph*

Professor Cyrus Gordon has himself made considerable contributions to the decipherment of ancient scripts. Here he combines professional sympathy with a readable style to describe the tortuous efforts of his predecessors in an exacting field. His account covers not only the prodigious genius of Champollion, who deciphered the Egyptian hieroglyphs of the Rosetta Stone; Grotefend's partial solution of Old Persian cuneiform and Henry Rawlinson's adventurous translation of the vast inscription on the rock-face at Behistun; and Ventris's decipherment of the Cretan Linear B; but also the inspired insights and obstinate errors of many other scholars struggling with texts in Sumerian, Hittite, Ugaritic and other ancient languages.

The frustrations of tackling an unknown language in an unknown script, the formidable requirements in knowledge, the importance of informed guesswork and intellectual flexibility are made very clear in this history of a pursuit which, in less than two centuries, has pushed the frontier of history back by two millennia.

THE DEAD SEA SCROLLS

John Allegro

This is a revised edition of the best popular account of the Dead Sea Scrolls.

In the early summer of 1947 an Arab shepherd stumbled on a cave near the Dead Sea and brought to light seven ancient scrolls. They proved to be part of the library of a Jewish monastic community which was in existence before and during the time of Christ. With the later discovery of the remains of hundreds more scrolls we have today an undreamt-of insight into Jewish sectarianism of this all-important period. It is already clear that many of the characteristic ideas of Jewish Christianity were cradled in just such a religious environment.

John Allegro has long been connected with this exciting new field of research, both as an expert linguist and as trustee and secretary of the Dead Sea Scrolls Fund. In this new edition he has reappraised the discoveries, with their particular import-ance for New Testament studies, in the light of the very latest finds, and has discussed the possibility of future finds. Hitherto unpublished texts concerning the Essenes have been added to the book, which now includes a completely new set of plates.